SWEET TOOTH

THE RETURN

SWEET TOOTH

THE RETURN

JEFF LEMIRE
CREATOR, WRITER, ARTIST

JOSÉ VILLARRUBIA
COLORIST

STEVE WANDS
LETTERER

JEFF LEMIRE WITH **JOSÉ VILLARRUBIA**
COVERS

AMEDEO TURTURRO Editor – Original Series and Collected Edition
STEVE COOK Design Director – Books
AMIE BROCKWAY-METCALF Publication Design
SUZANNAH ROWNTREE Publication Production

MARIE JAVINS Editor-in-Chief, DC Comics

DANIEL CHERRY III Senior VP – General Manager
JIM LEE Publisher & Chief Creative Officer
JOEN CHOE VP – Global Brand & Creative Services
DON FALLETTI VP – Manufacturing Operations & Workflow Management
LAWRENCE GANEM VP – Talent Services
ALISON GILL Senior VP – Manufacturing & Operations
NICK J. NAPOLITANO VP – Manufacturing Administration & Design
NANCY SPEARS VP – Revenue

SWEET TOOTH: THE RETURN

DC Comics, 2900 West Alameda Ave., Burbank, CA 91505
Printed by Solisco Printers, Scott, QC, Canada. 7/9/21.
First Printing.
ISBN: 978-1-77951-032-7

Library of Congress Cataloging-in-Publication Data is available.

PEFC Certified

This product is from
sustainably managed
forests, recycled and
controlled sources

PEFC/26-31-02   www.pefc.org

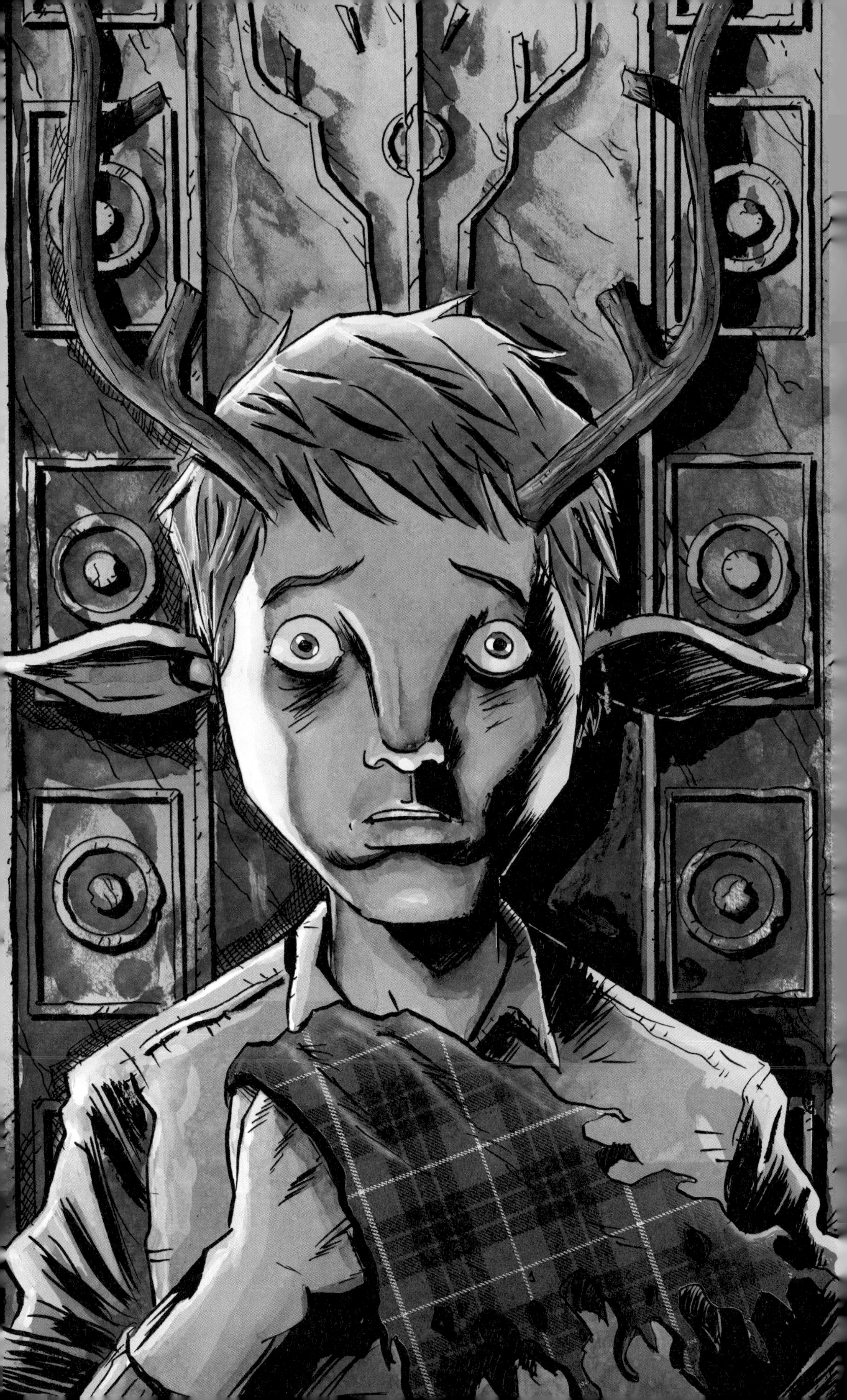

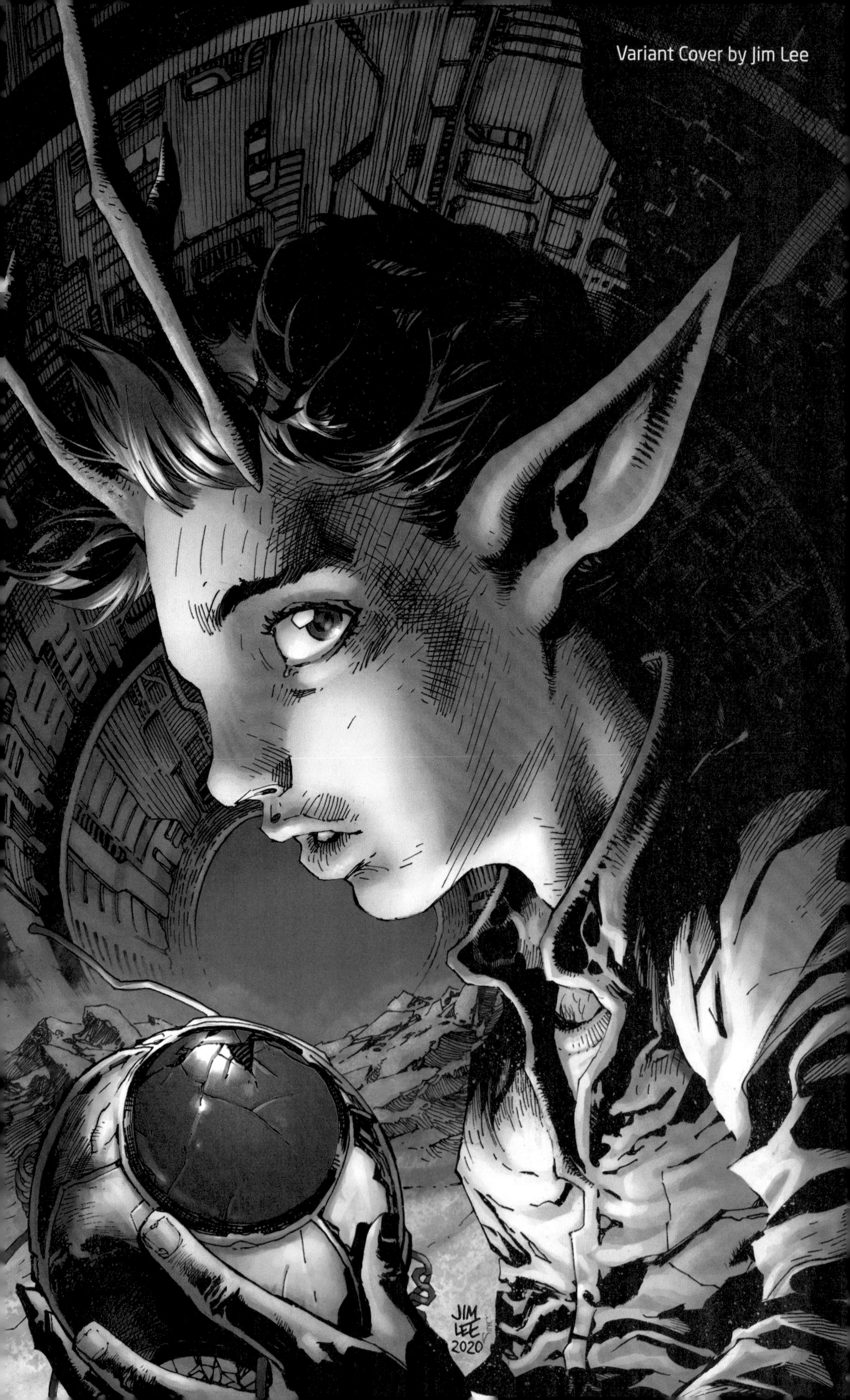
JIM
LEE
2020
Variant Cover by Jim Lee

300 YEARS LATER...

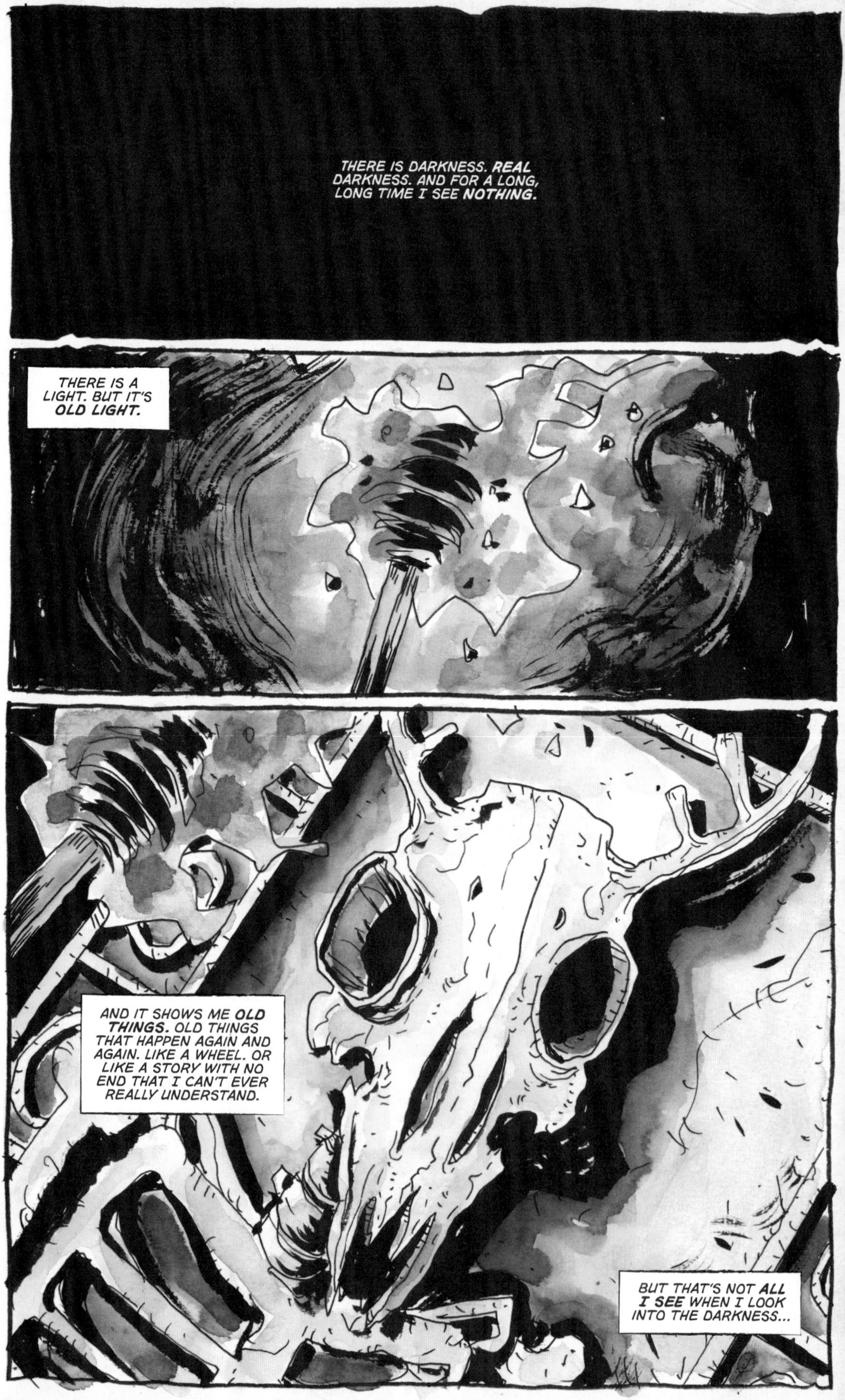
THERE IS DARKNESS. REAL DARKNESS. AND FOR A LONG, LONG TIME I SEE NOTHING.
THERE IS A LIGHT. BUT IT'S OLD LIGHT.
AND IT SHOWS ME OLD THINGS. OLD THINGS THAT HAPPEN AGAIN AND AGAIN. LIKE A WHEEL. OR LIKE A STORY WITH NO END THAT I CAN'T EVER REALLY UNDERSTAND.
BUT THAT'S NOT ALL I SEE WHEN I LOOK INTO THE DARKNESS...

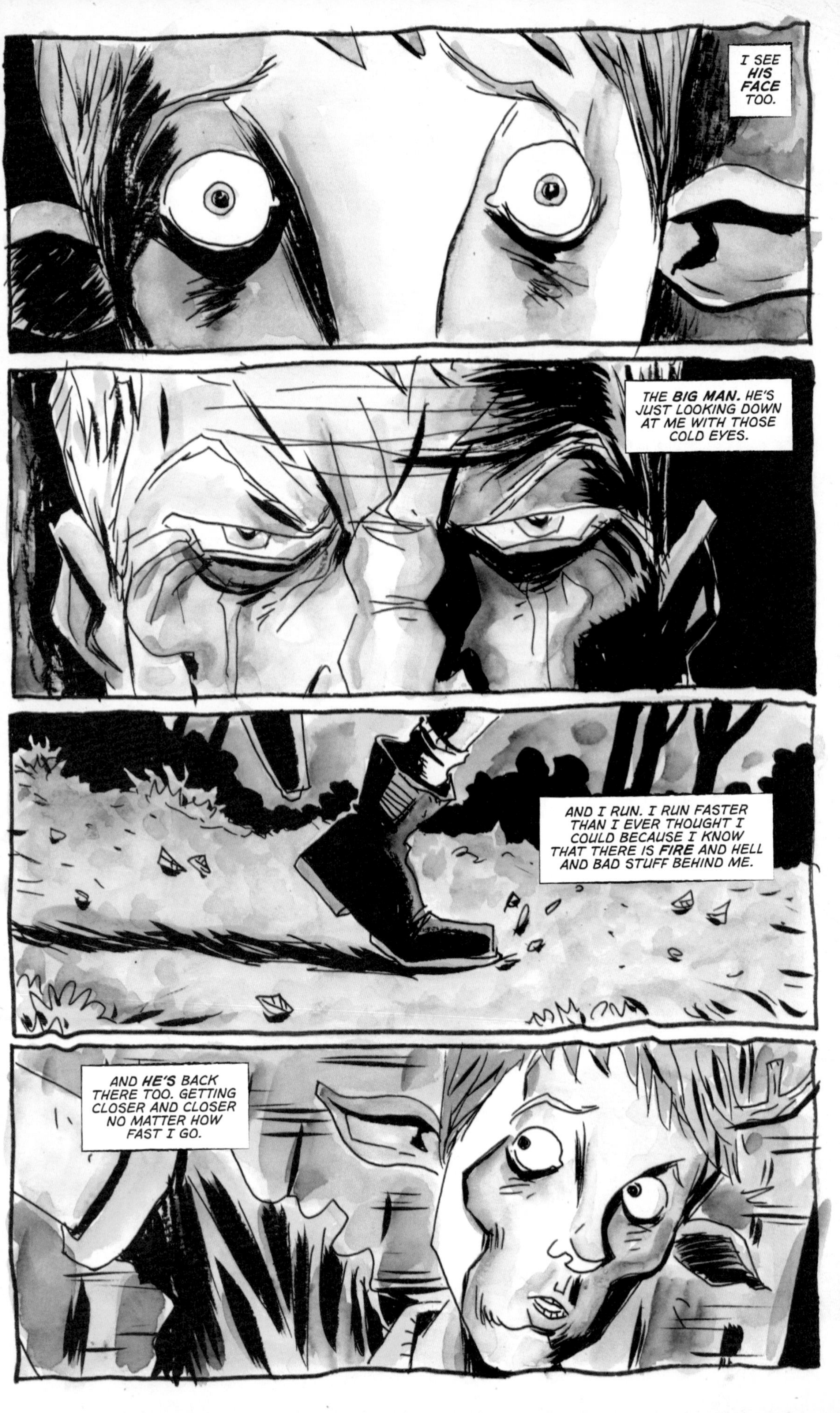
I SEE HIS FACE TOO.
THE BIG MAN. HE'S JUST LOOKING DOWN AT ME WITH THOSE COLD EYES.
AND I RUN. I RUN FASTER THAN I EVER THOUGHT I COULD BECAUSE I KNOW THAT THERE IS FIRE AND HELL AND BAD STUFF BEHIND ME.
AND HE'S BACK THERE TOO. GETTING CLOSER AND CLOSER NO MATTER HOW FAST I GO.

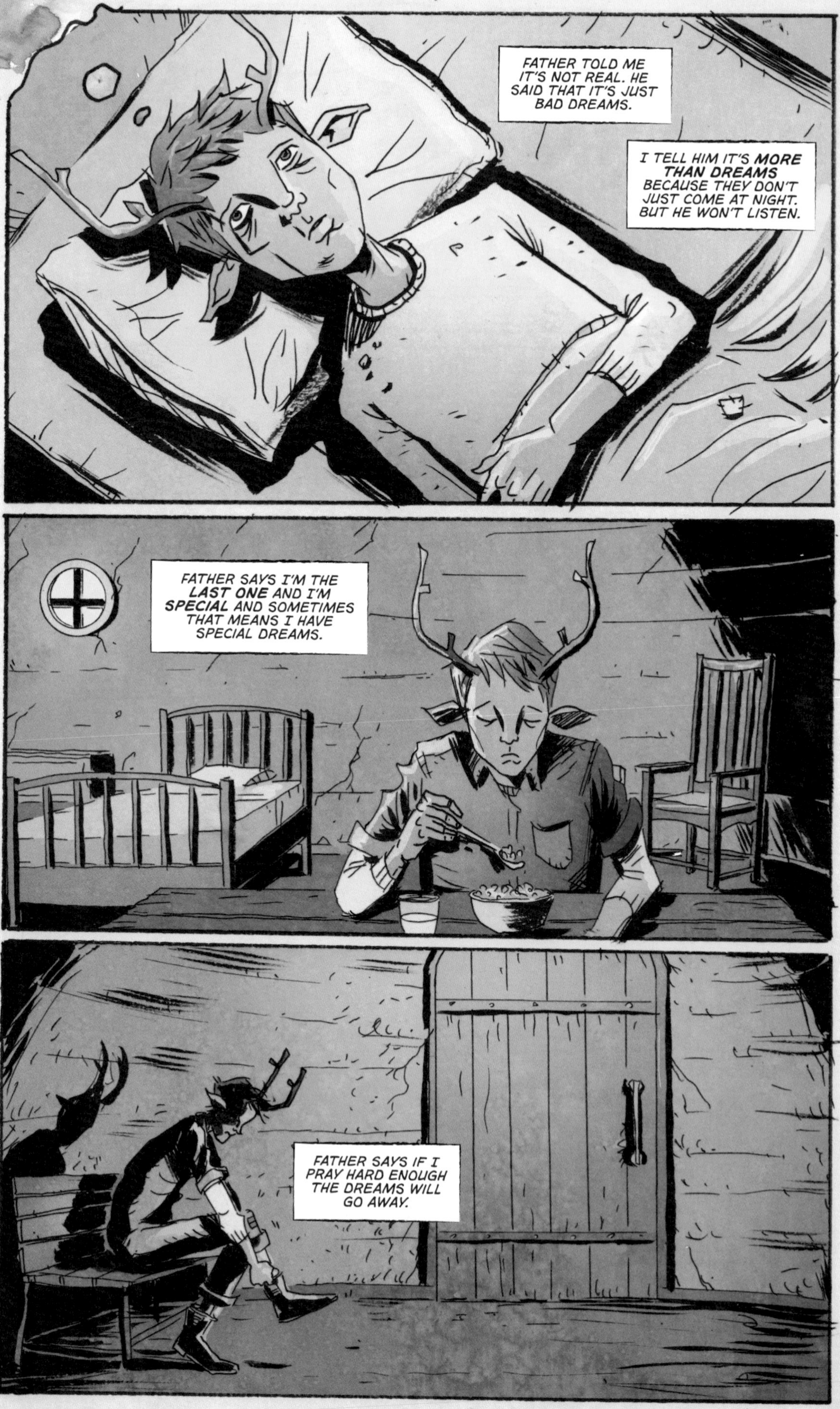
FATHER TOLD ME IT'S NOT REAL. HE SAID THAT IT'S JUST BAD DREAMS.
I TELL HIM IT'S **MORE THAN DREAMS** BECAUSE THEY DON'T JUST COME AT NIGHT. BUT HE WON'T LISTEN.
FATHER SAYS I'M THE **LAST ONE** AND I'M **SPECIAL** AND SOMETIMES THAT MEANS I HAVE SPECIAL DREAMS.
FATHER SAYS IF I PRAY HARD ENOUGH THE DREAMS WILL GO AWAY.

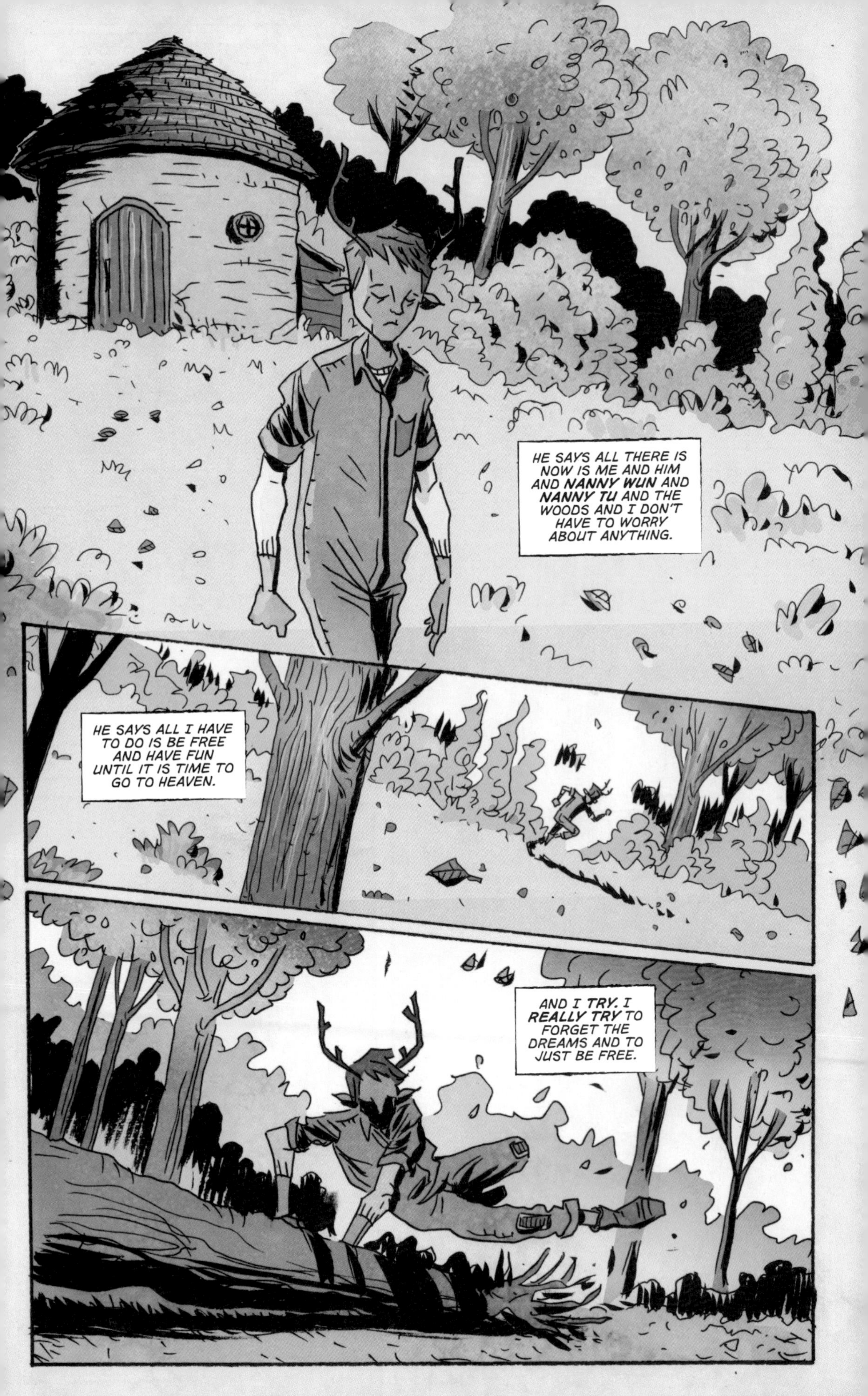
HE SAYS ALL THERE IS NOW IS ME AND HIM AND **NANNY WUN** AND **NANNY TU** AND THE WOODS AND I DON'T HAVE TO WORRY ABOUT ANYTHING.
HE SAYS ALL I HAVE TO DO IS BE FREE AND HAVE FUN UNTIL IT IS TIME TO GO TO HEAVEN.
AND I **TRY.** I **REALLY TRY** TO FORGET THE DREAMS AND TO JUST BE FREE.

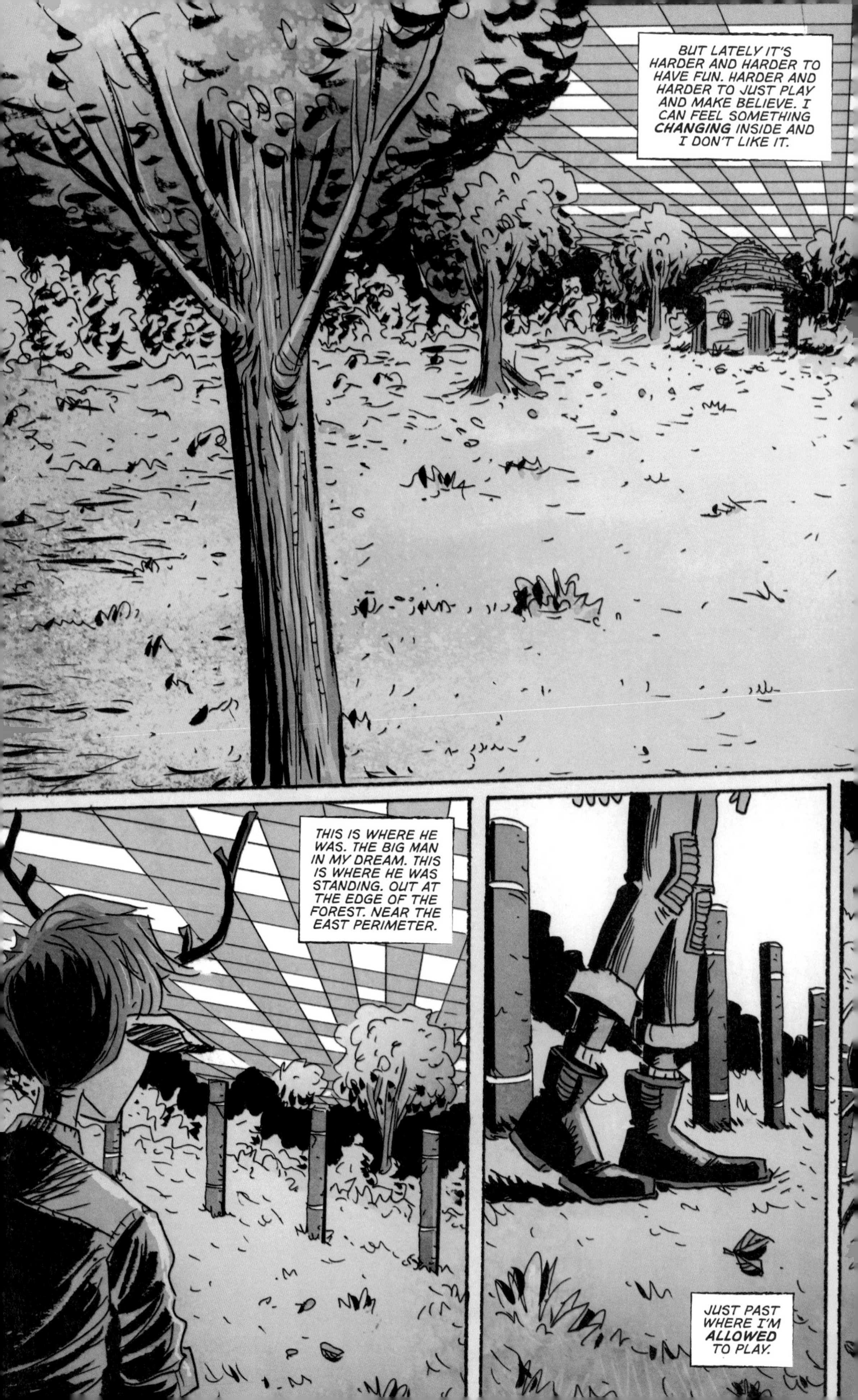
BUT LATELY IT'S HARDER AND HARDER TO HAVE FUN. HARDER AND HARDER TO JUST PLAY AND MAKE BELIEVE. I CAN FEEL SOMETHING **CHANGING** INSIDE AND I DON'T LIKE IT.
THIS IS WHERE HE WAS. THE BIG MAN IN MY DREAM. THIS IS WHERE HE WAS STANDING. OUT AT THE EDGE OF THE FOREST. NEAR THE EAST PERIMETER.
JUST PAST WHERE I'M **ALLOWED** TO PLAY.

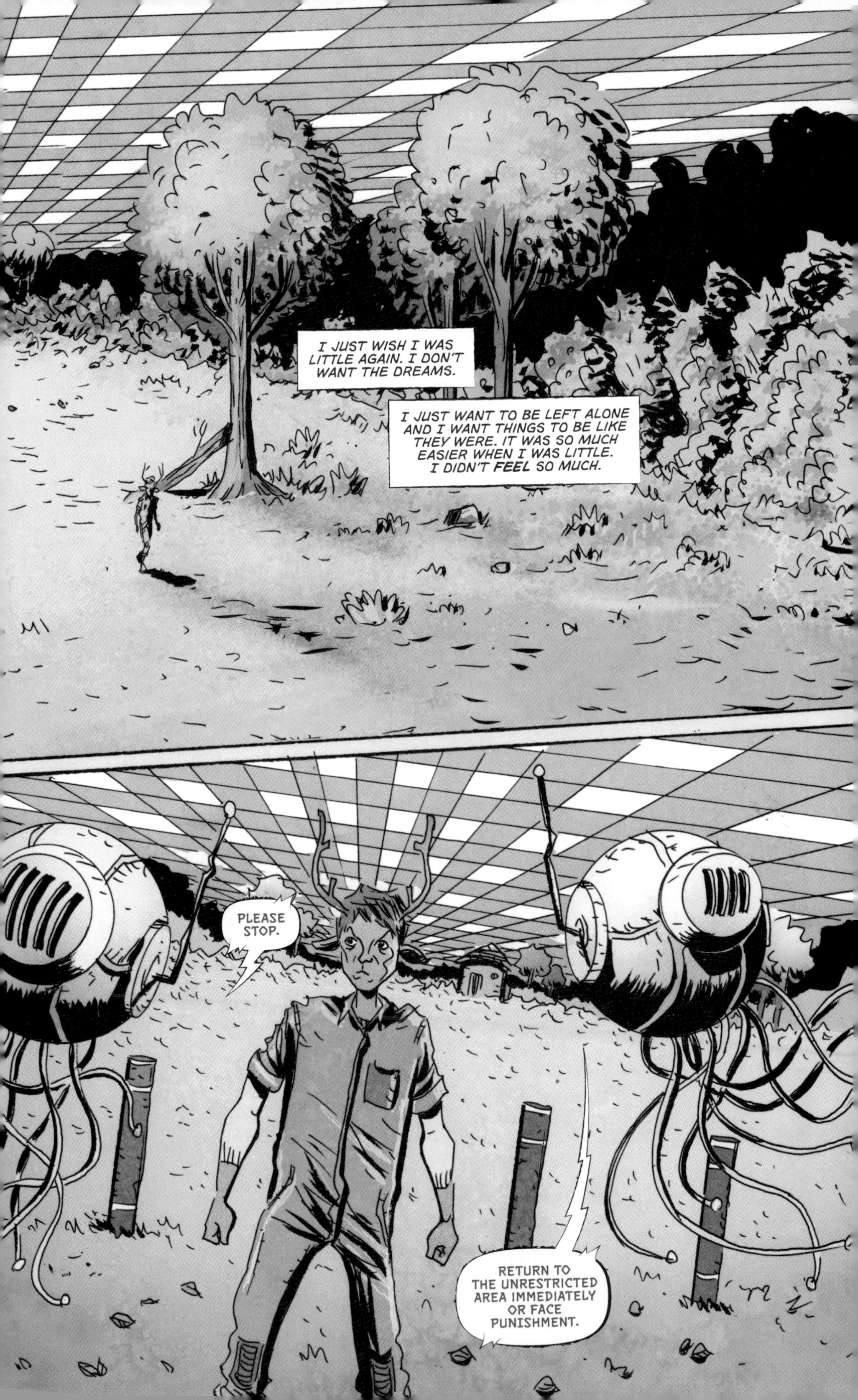
I JUST WISH I WAS LITTLE AGAIN. I DON'T WANT THE DREAMS.
I JUST WANT TO BE LEFT ALONE AND I WANT THINGS TO BE LIKE THEY WERE. IT WAS SO MUCH EASIER WHEN I WAS LITTLE. I DIDN'T **FEEL** SO MUCH.
PLEASE STOP.
RETURN TO THE UNRESTRICTED AREA IMMEDIATELY OR FACE PUNISHMENT.

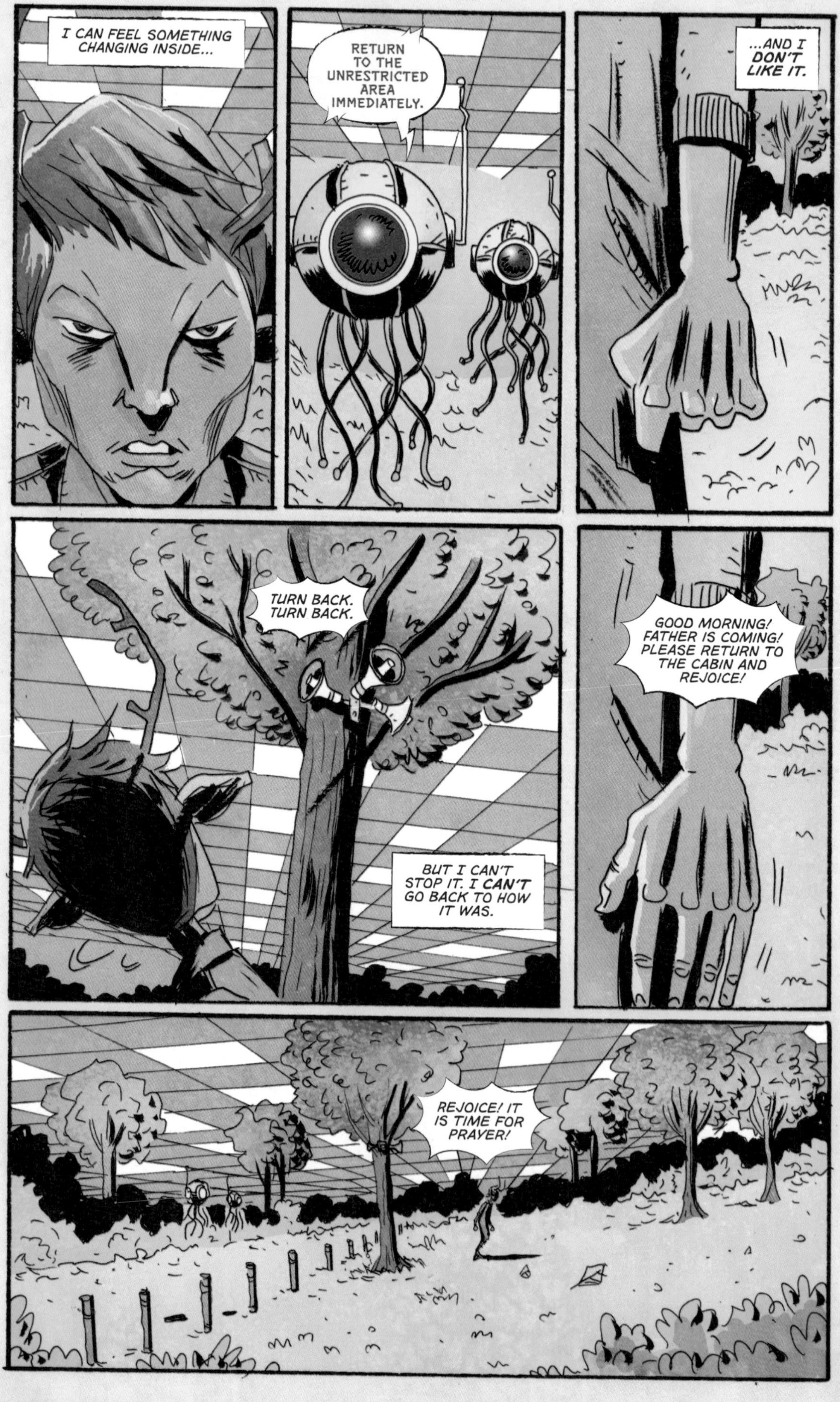
I CAN FEEL SOMETHING CHANGING INSIDE...
RETURN TO THE UNRESTRICTED AREA IMMEDIATELY.
...AND I DON'T LIKE IT.
TURN BACK. TURN BACK.
BUT I CAN'T STOP IT. I CAN'T GO BACK TO HOW IT WAS.
GOOD MORNING! FATHER IS COMING! PLEASE RETURN TO THE CABIN AND REJOICE!
REJOICE! IT IS TIME FOR PRAYER!

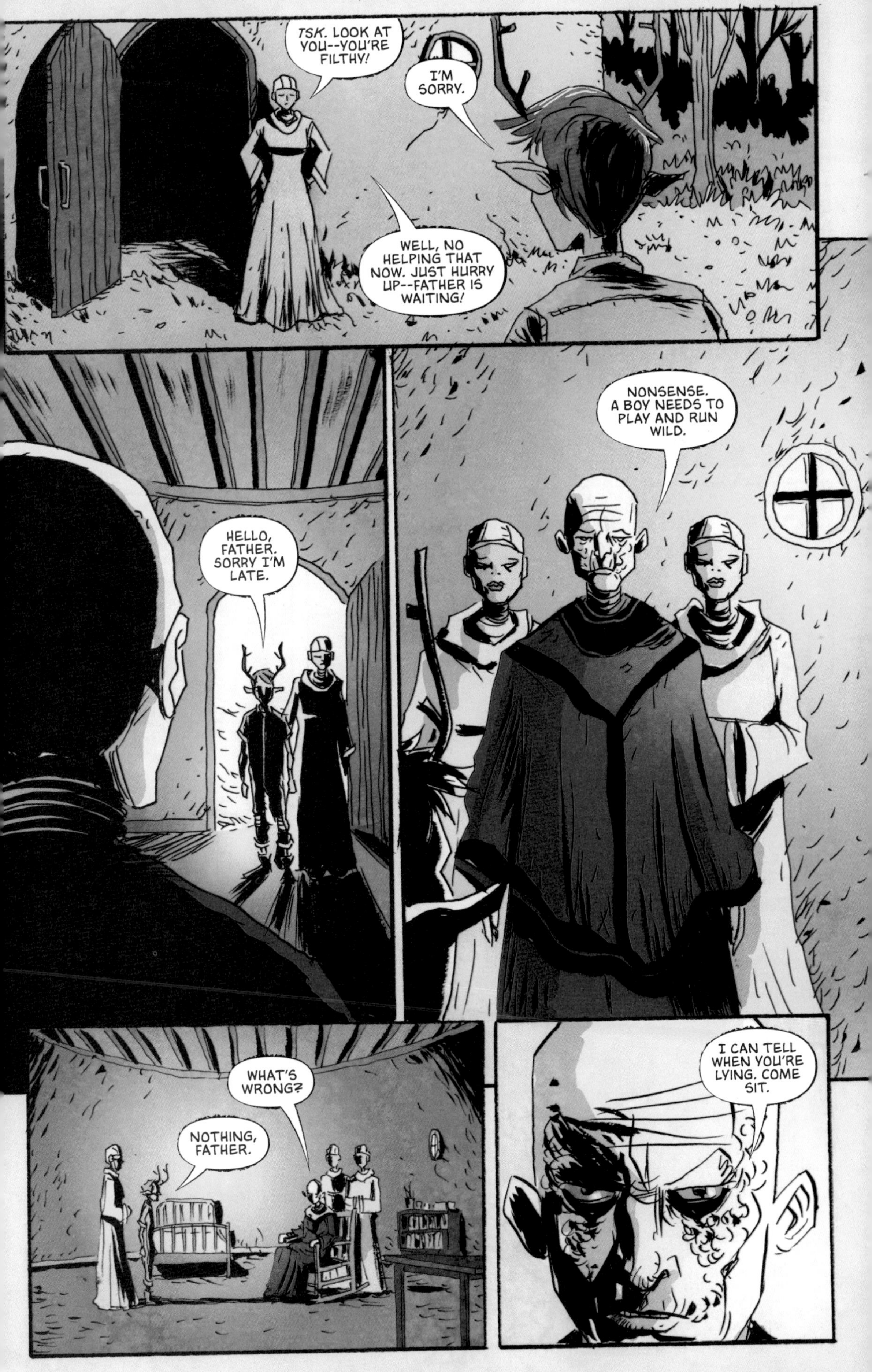
TSK. LOOK AT YOU--YOU'RE FILTHY!
I'M SORRY.
WELL, NO HELPING THAT NOW. JUST HURRY UP--FATHER IS WAITING!
HELLO, FATHER. SORRY I'M LATE.
NONSENSE. A BOY NEEDS TO PLAY AND RUN WILD.
WHAT'S WRONG?
NOTHING, FATHER.
I CAN TELL WHEN YOU'RE LYING. COME SIT.

THIS IS NOT ABOUT THOSE DREAMS AGAIN IS IT?

NO. IT AIN'T JUST THAT.

"AIN'T"? WHAT HAVE I TOLD YOU ABOUT TALKING *LIKE THAT*?

SORRY. I MEAN, IT'S *NOT* JUST THE DREAMS. I JUST--I DON'T UNDERSTAND WHY I CAN'T GO WHERE *YOU GO* WHEN YOU LEAVE THE WOODS.

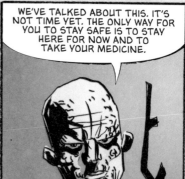

WE'VE TALKED ABOUT THIS. IT'S NOT TIME YET. THE ONLY WAY FOR YOU TO STAY SAFE IS TO STAY HERE FOR NOW AND TO TAKE YOUR MEDICINE.

YOU KNOW THAT IF YOU DON'T, *THE SICKNESS* WILL TAKE YOU LIKE IT TOOK *ALL THE OTHER HYBRIDS.*

I CAN'T PROTECT YOU FROM THAT. NOT EVEN GOD CAN.

BUT I GET LONELY HERE.

YOU HAVE ME. YOU HAVE THE NANNY WUN AND NANNY TU. YOU KNOW YOU'RE *NOT* ALONE.

BUT I *WILL* GET TO LEAVE, RIGHT? THAT'S NOT JUST A STORY YOU TELL ME? I MEAN, EVENTUALLY I WILL GET TO GO UP TO HEAVEN RIGHT?

OF COURSE, CHILD. WHEN GOD TELLS US IT IS FINALLY SAFE, YOU WILL BE FREE, AND WE WILL GO UP TOGETHER AND IT WILL BE GLORIOUS, AND WE WILL ALL BATHE IN *HIS LIGHT* AT LAST.

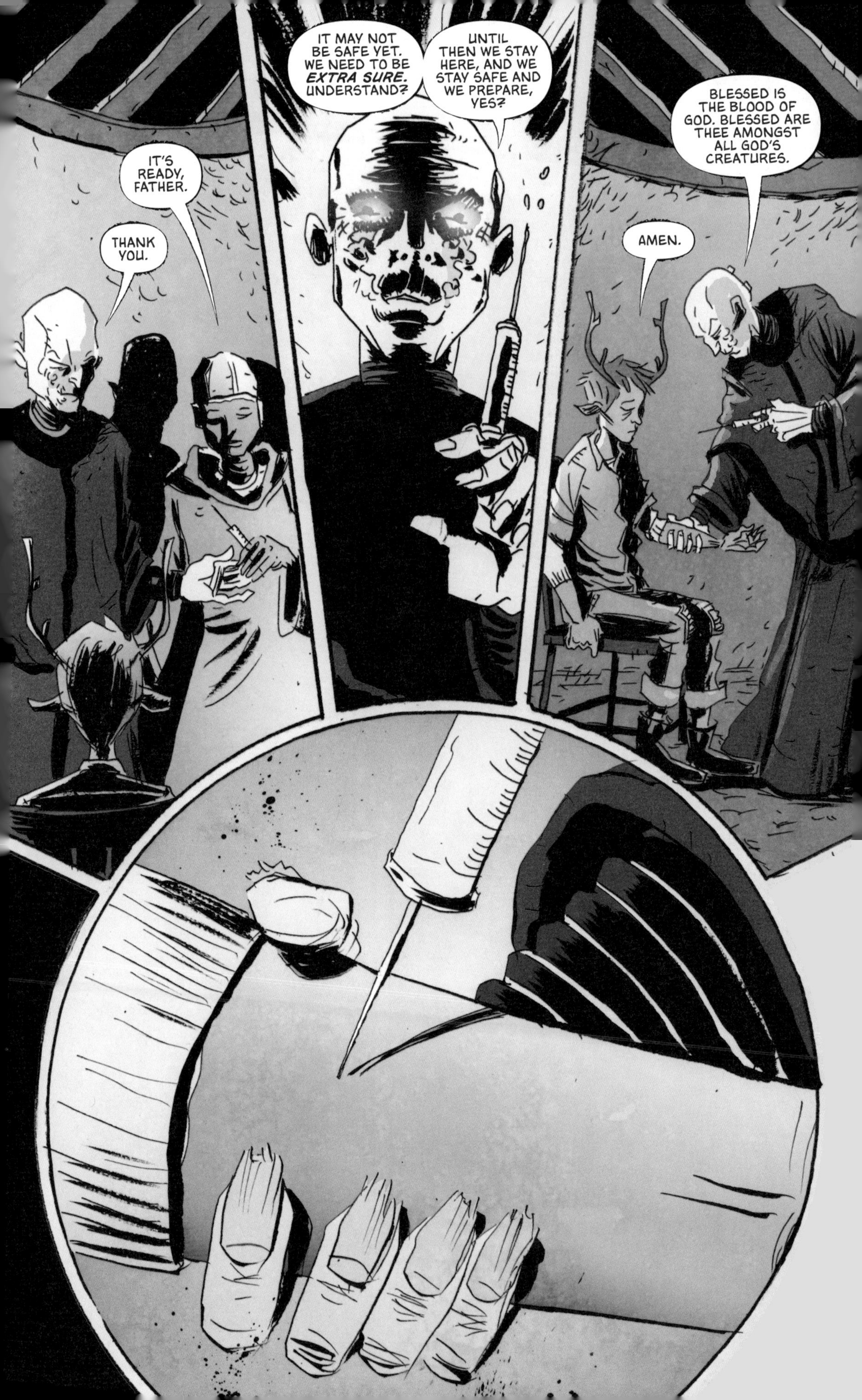
IT'S READY, FATHER.
THANK YOU.
IT MAY NOT BE SAFE YET. WE NEED TO BE *EXTRA SURE.* UNDERSTAND?
UNTIL THEN WE STAY HERE, AND WE STAY SAFE AND WE PREPARE, YES?
BLESSED IS THE BLOOD OF GOD. BLESSED ARE THEE AMONGST ALL GOD'S CREATURES.
AMEN.

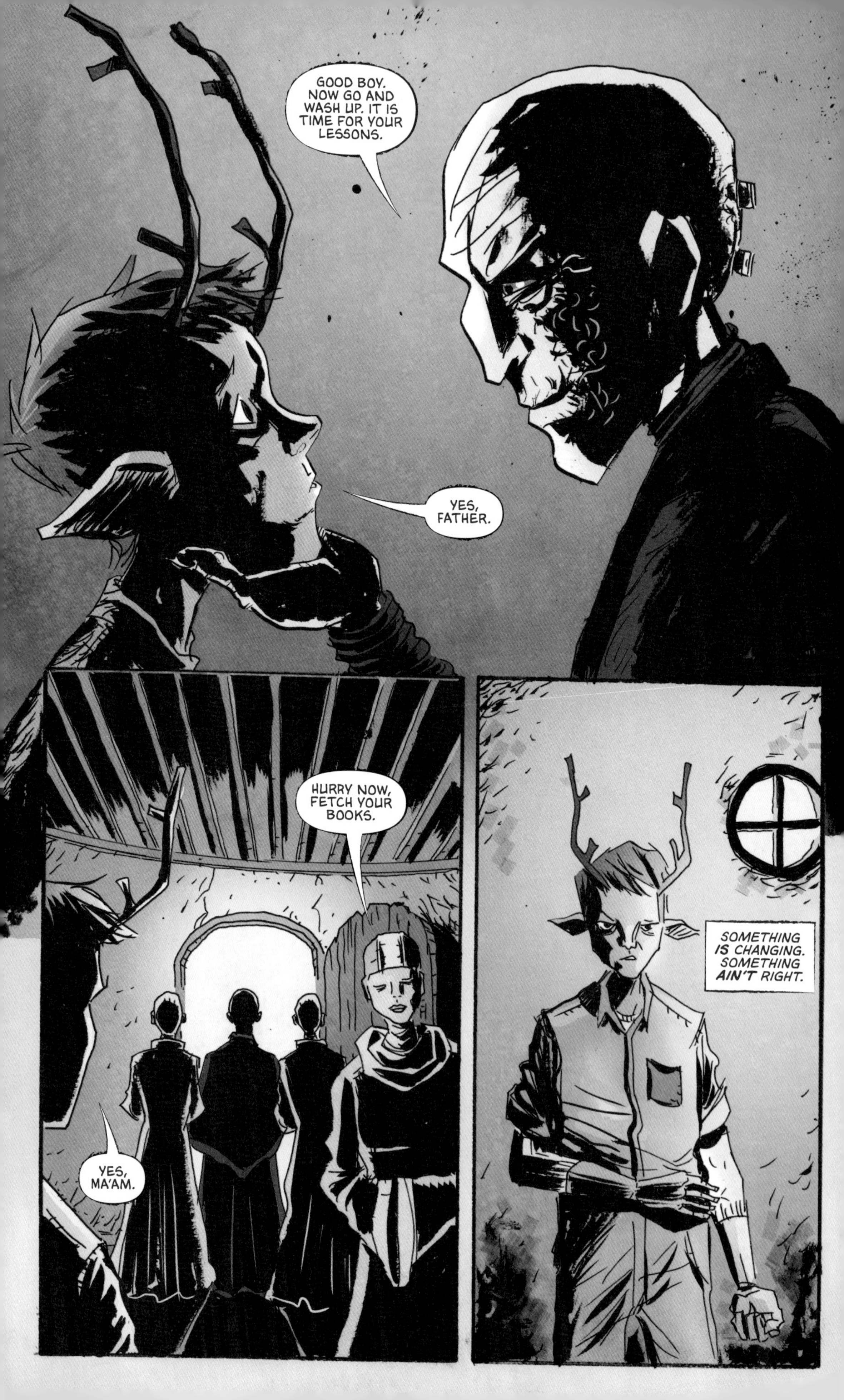
GOOD BOY. NOW GO AND WASH UP. IT IS TIME FOR YOUR LESSONS.
YES, FATHER.
HURRY NOW, FETCH YOUR BOOKS.
YES, MA'AM.
SOMETHING **IS** CHANGING. SOMETHING **AIN'T** RIGHT.

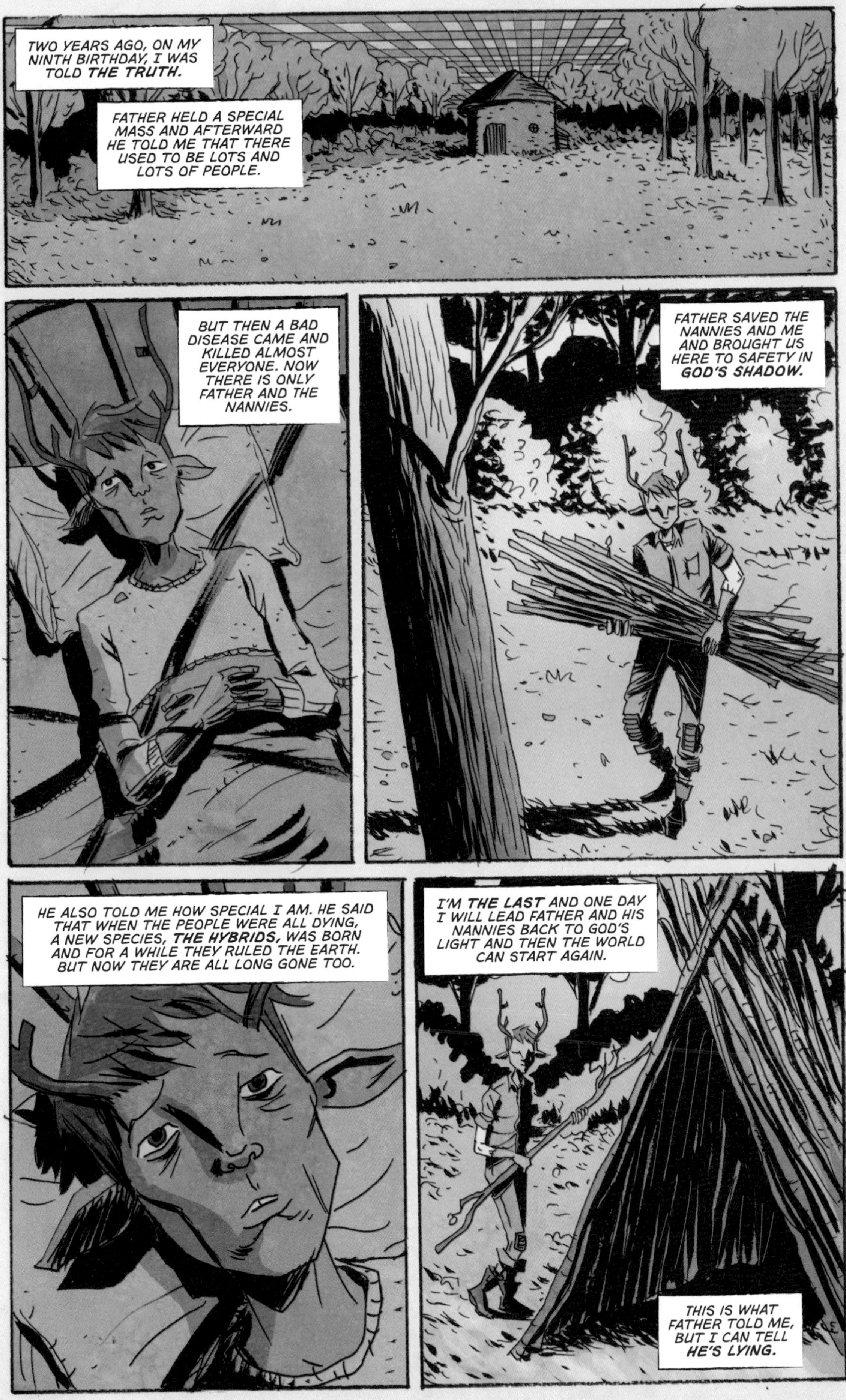
TWO YEARS AGO, ON MY NINTH BIRTHDAY, I WAS TOLD THE TRUTH.
FATHER HELD A SPECIAL MASS AND AFTERWARD HE TOLD ME THAT THERE USED TO BE LOTS AND LOTS OF PEOPLE.
BUT THEN A BAD DISEASE CAME AND KILLED ALMOST EVERYONE. NOW THERE IS ONLY FATHER AND THE NANNIES.
FATHER SAVED THE NANNIES AND ME AND BROUGHT US HERE TO SAFETY IN GOD'S SHADOW.
HE ALSO TOLD ME HOW SPECIAL I AM. HE SAID THAT WHEN THE PEOPLE WERE ALL DYING, A NEW SPECIES, THE HYBRIDS, WAS BORN AND FOR A WHILE THEY RULED THE EARTH. BUT NOW THEY ARE ALL LONG GONE TOO.
I'M THE LAST AND ONE DAY I WILL LEAD FATHER AND HIS NANNIES BACK TO GOD'S LIGHT AND THEN THE WORLD CAN START AGAIN.
THIS IS WHAT FATHER TOLD ME, BUT I CAN TELL HE'S LYING.

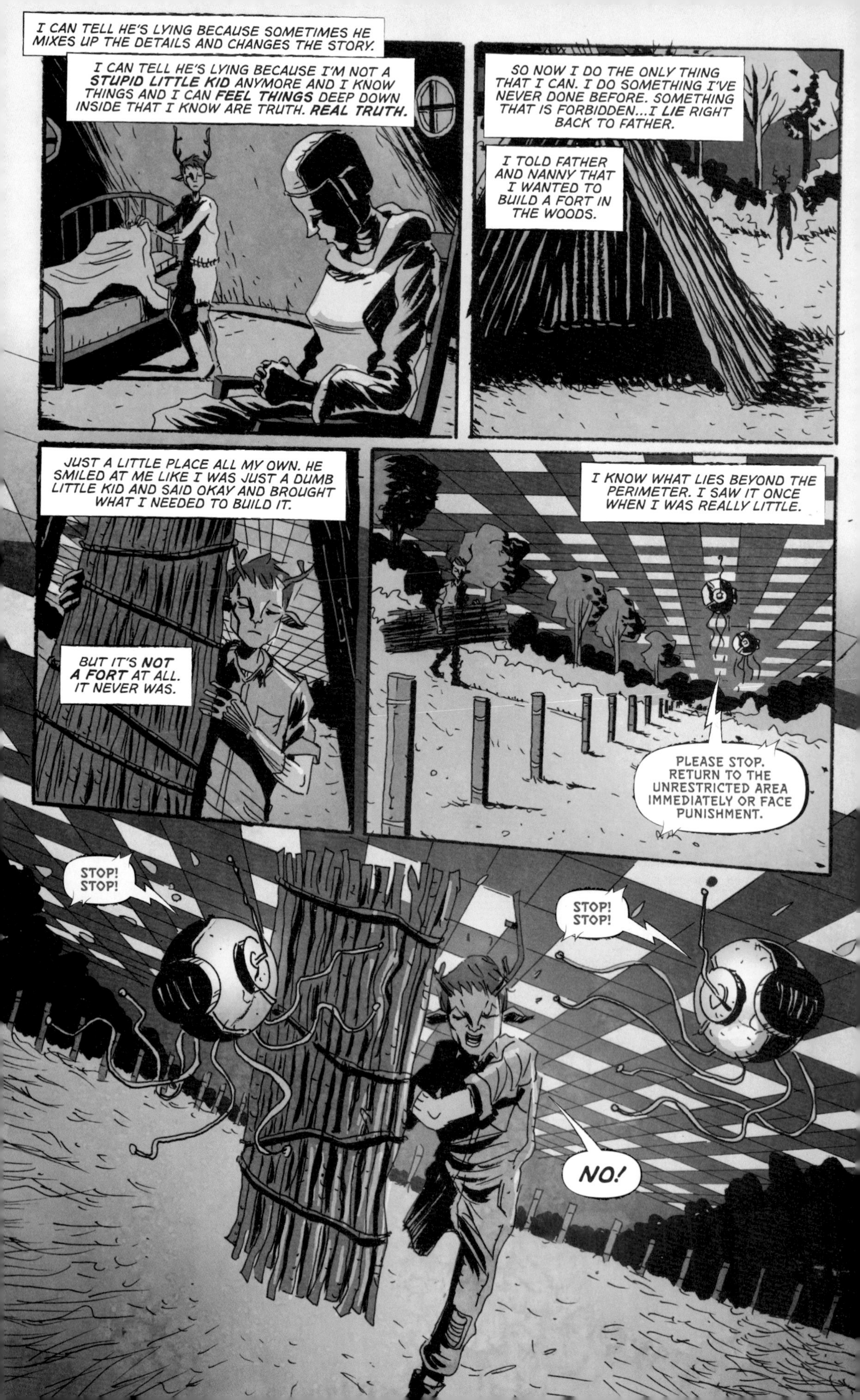
I CAN TELL HE'S LYING BECAUSE SOMETIMES HE MIXES UP THE DETAILS AND CHANGES THE STORY.
I CAN TELL HE'S LYING BECAUSE I'M NOT A STUPID LITTLE KID ANYMORE AND I KNOW THINGS AND I CAN FEEL THINGS DEEP DOWN INSIDE THAT I KNOW ARE TRUTH. REAL TRUTH.
SO NOW I DO THE ONLY THING THAT I CAN. I DO SOMETHING I'VE NEVER DONE BEFORE. SOMETHING THAT IS FORBIDDEN...I LIE RIGHT BACK TO FATHER.
I TOLD FATHER AND NANNY THAT I WANTED TO BUILD A FORT IN THE WOODS.
JUST A LITTLE PLACE ALL MY OWN. HE SMILED AT ME LIKE I WAS JUST A DUMB LITTLE KID AND SAID OKAY AND BROUGHT WHAT I NEEDED TO BUILD IT.
BUT IT'S NOT A FORT AT ALL. IT NEVER WAS.
I KNOW WHAT LIES BEYOND THE PERIMETER. I SAW IT ONCE WHEN I WAS REALLY LITTLE.
PLEASE STOP. RETURN TO THE UNRESTRICTED AREA IMMEDIATELY OR FACE PUNISHMENT.
STOP! STOP!
STOP! STOP!
NO!

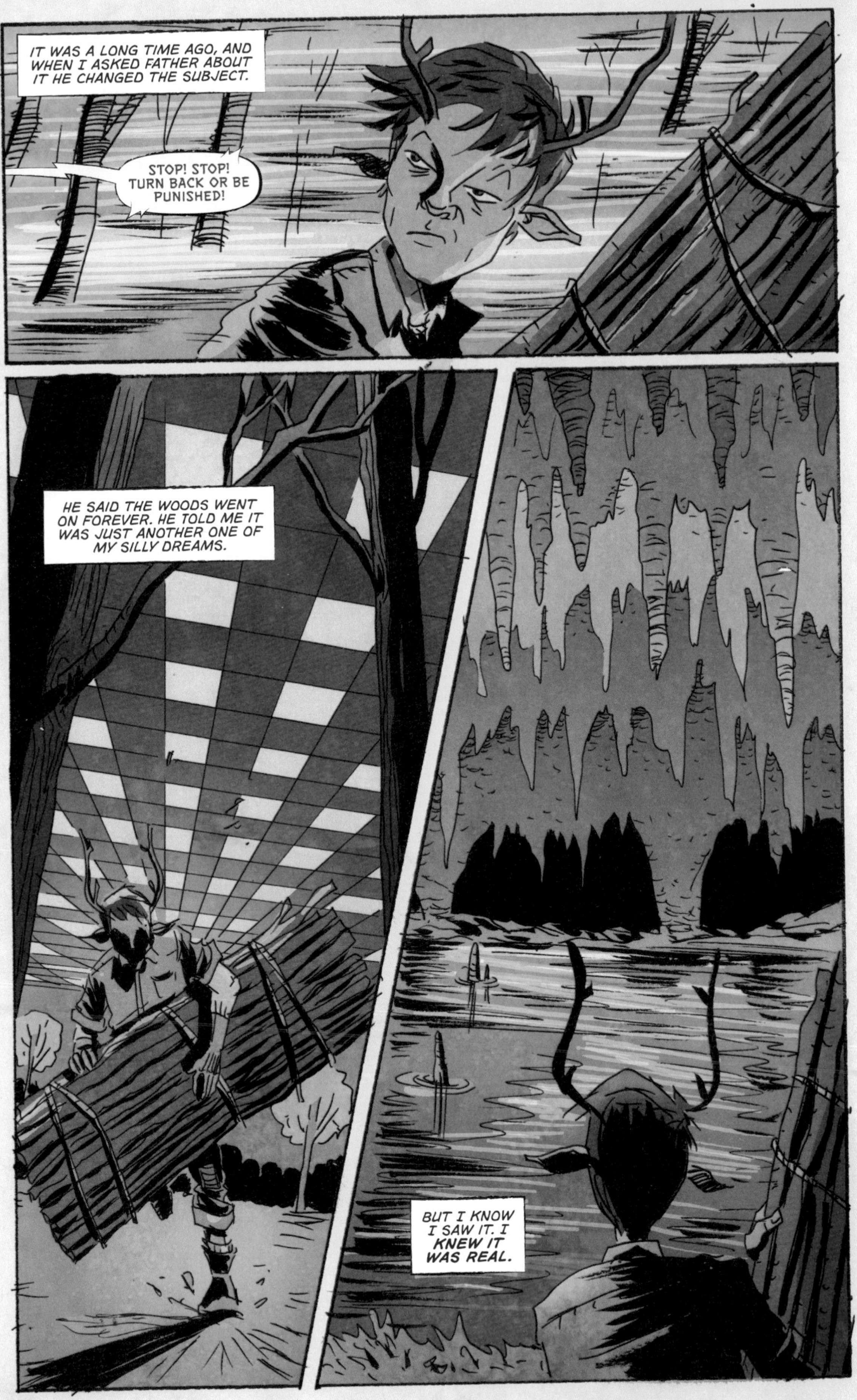
IT WAS A LONG TIME AGO, AND WHEN I ASKED FATHER ABOUT IT HE CHANGED THE SUBJECT.
STOP! STOP! TURN BACK OR BE PUNISHED!
HE SAID THE WOODS WENT ON FOREVER. HE TOLD ME IT WAS JUST ANOTHER ONE OF MY SILLY DREAMS.
BUT I KNOW I SAW IT. I KNEW IT WAS REAL.

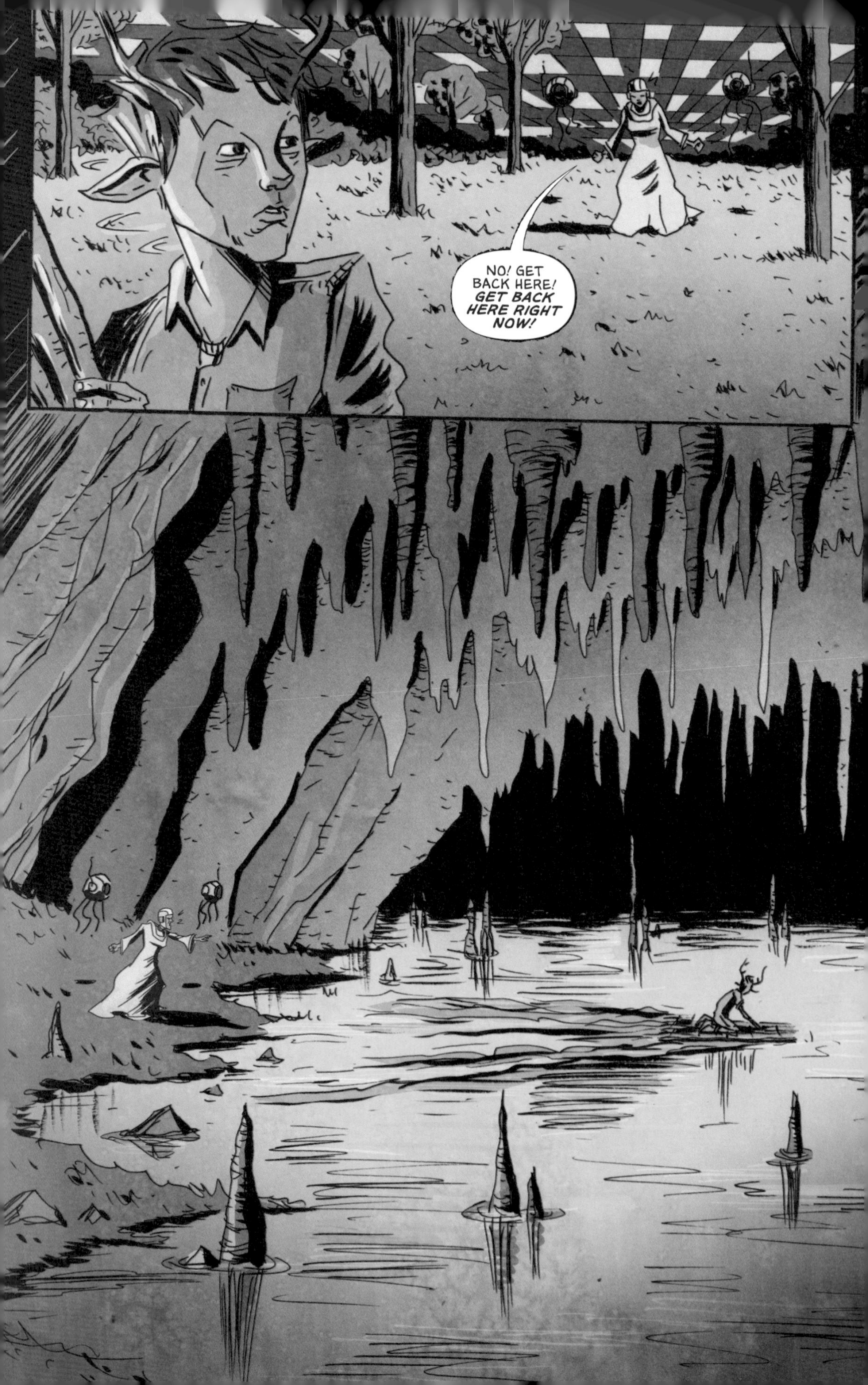
NO! GET BACK HERE! *GET BACK HERE RIGHT NOW!*

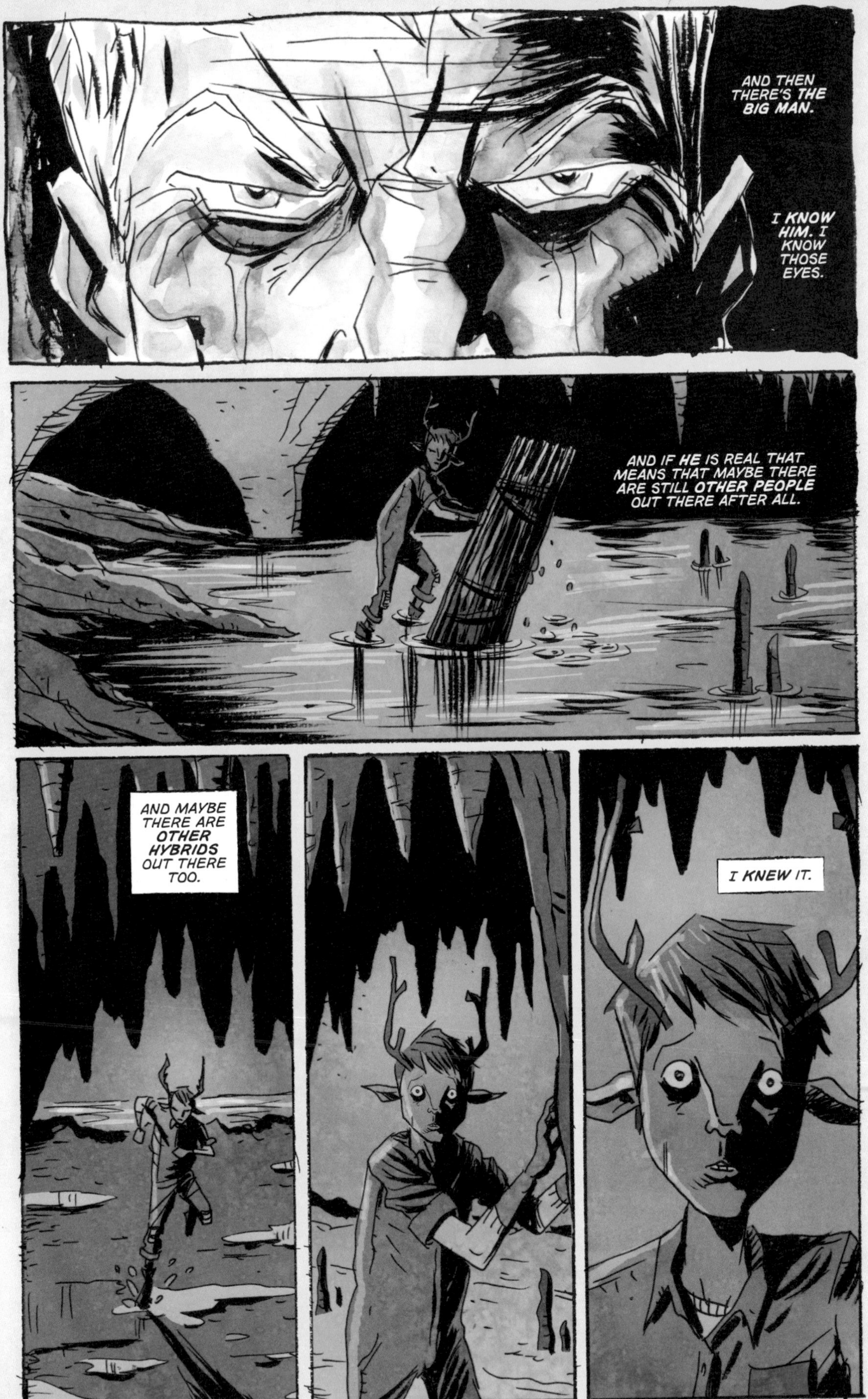
AND THEN THERE'S THE BIG MAN.
I KNOW HIM. I KNOW THOSE EYES.
AND IF HE IS REAL THAT MEANS THAT MAYBE THERE ARE STILL OTHER PEOPLE OUT THERE AFTER ALL.
AND MAYBE THERE ARE OTHER HYBRIDS OUT THERE TOO.
I KNEW IT.

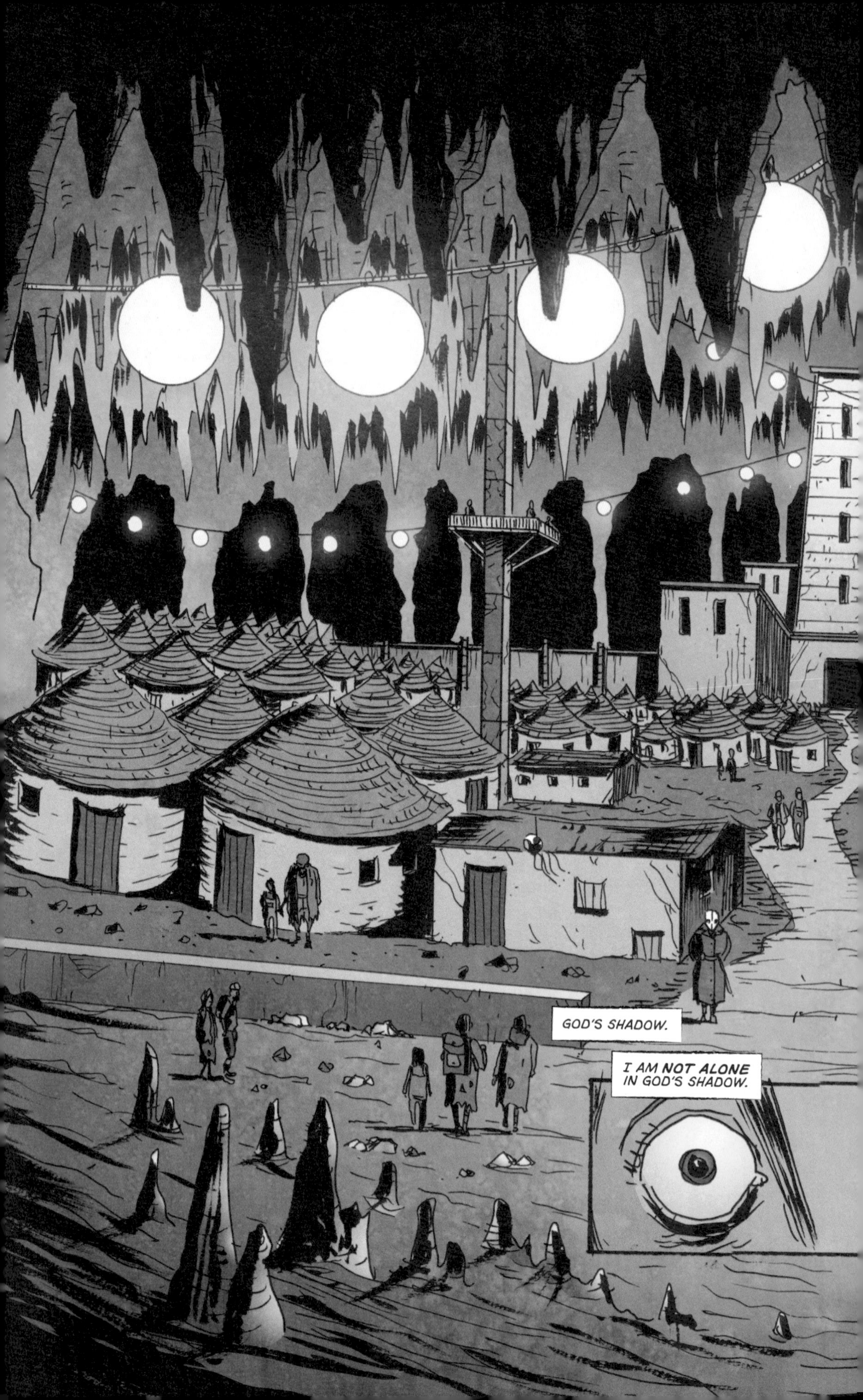
GOD'S SHADOW.
I AM NOT ALONE IN GOD'S SHADOW.

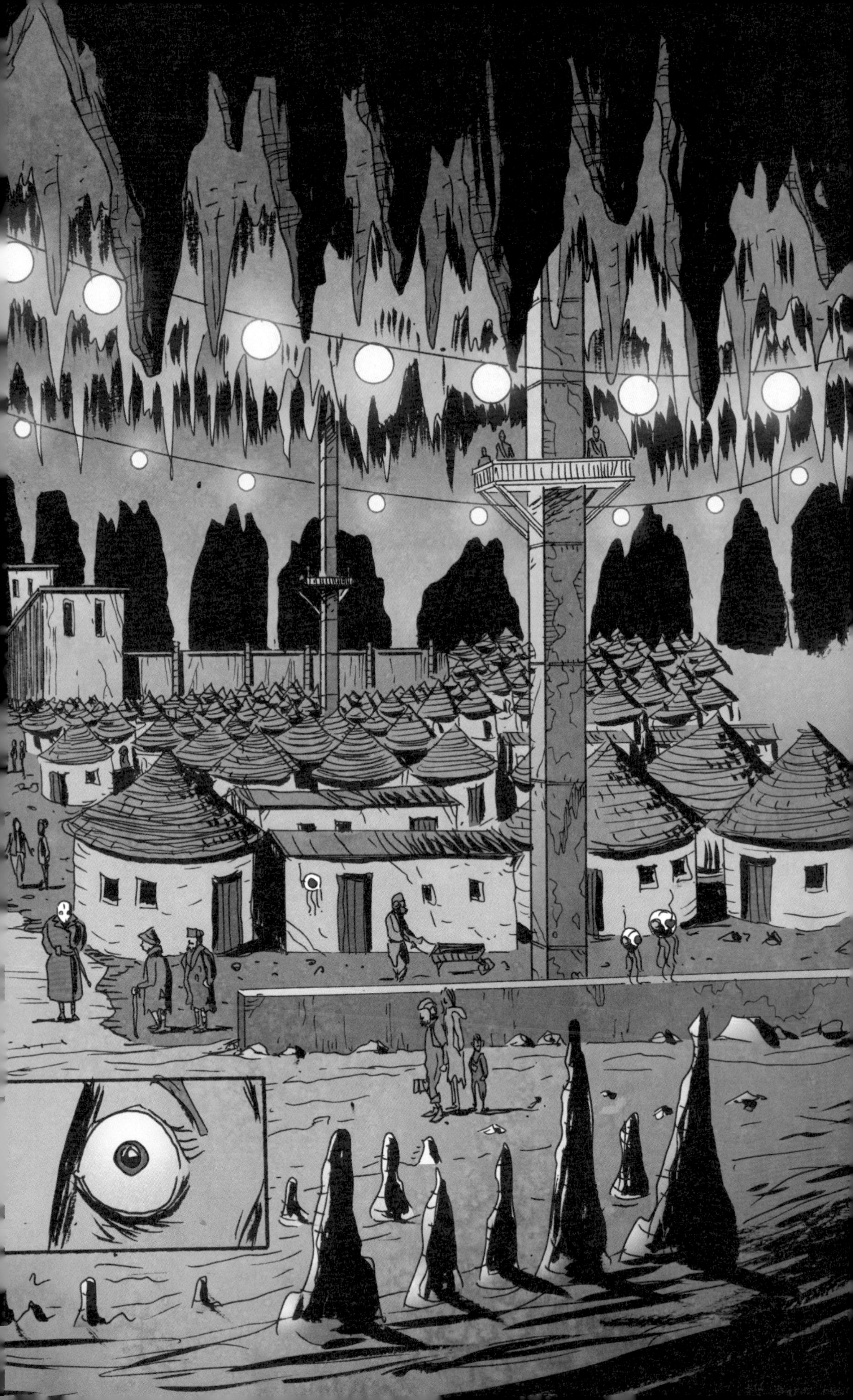

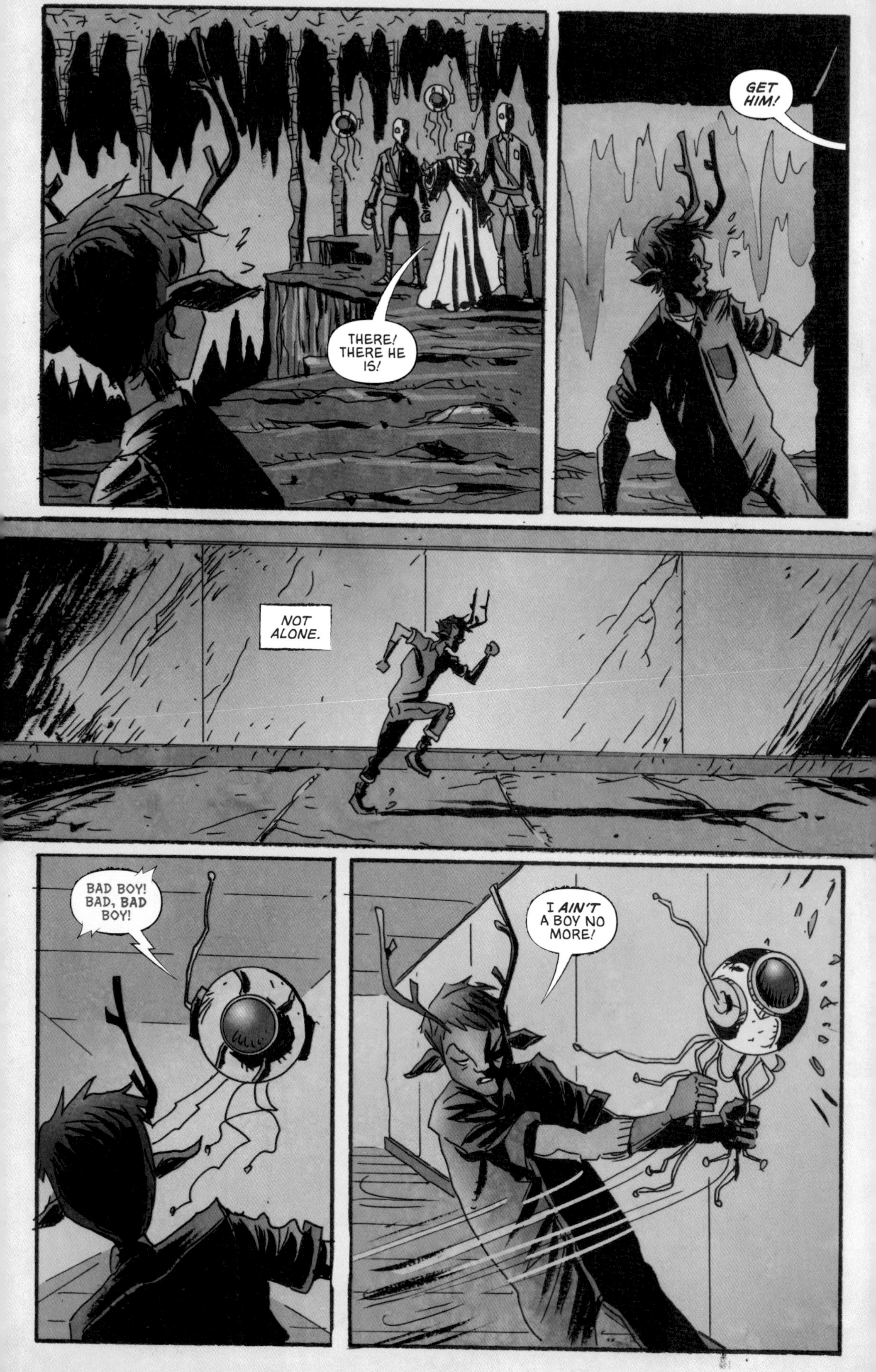
THERE! THERE HE IS!
GET HIM!
NOT ALONE.
BAD BOY! BAD, BAD BOY!
I AIN'T A BOY NO MORE!

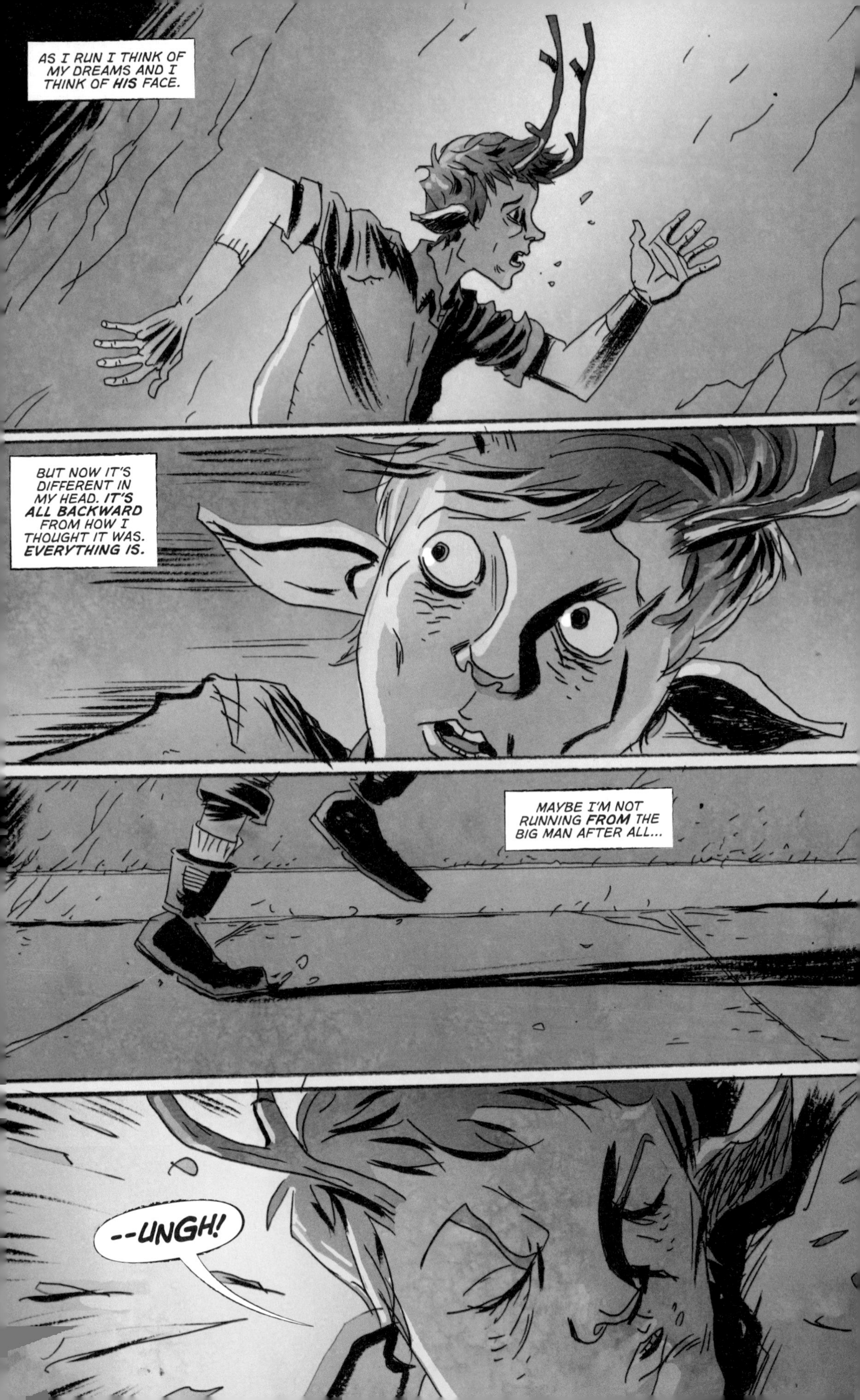
AS I RUN I THINK OF MY DREAMS AND I THINK OF HIS FACE.
BUT NOW IT'S DIFFERENT IN MY HEAD. IT'S ALL BACKWARD FROM HOW I THOUGHT IT WAS. EVERYTHING IS.
MAYBE I'M NOT RUNNING FROM THE BIG MAN AFTER ALL...
--UNGH!

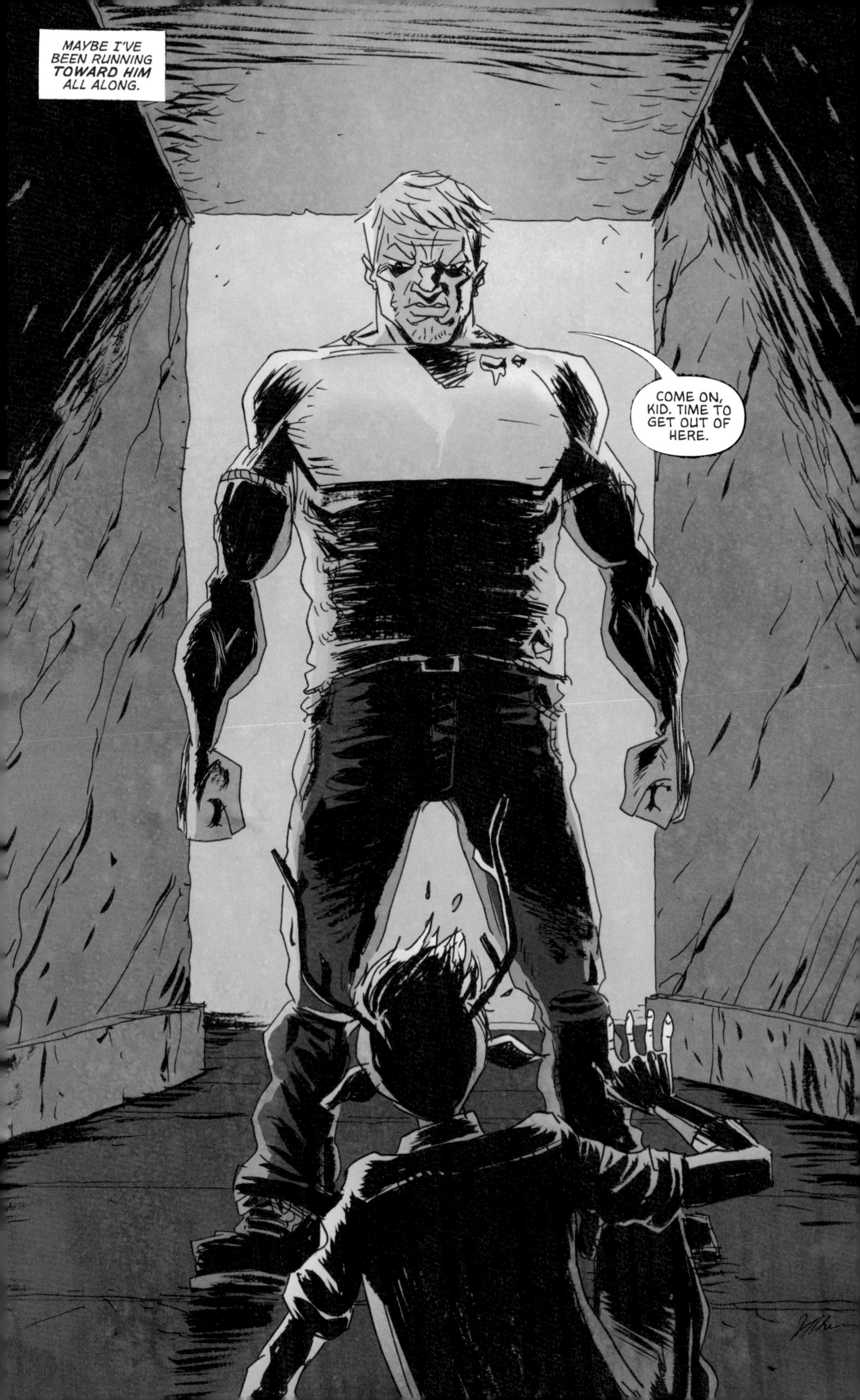
MAYBE I'VE BEEN RUNNING TOWARD HIM ALL ALONG.
COME ON, KID. TIME TO GET OUT OF HERE.

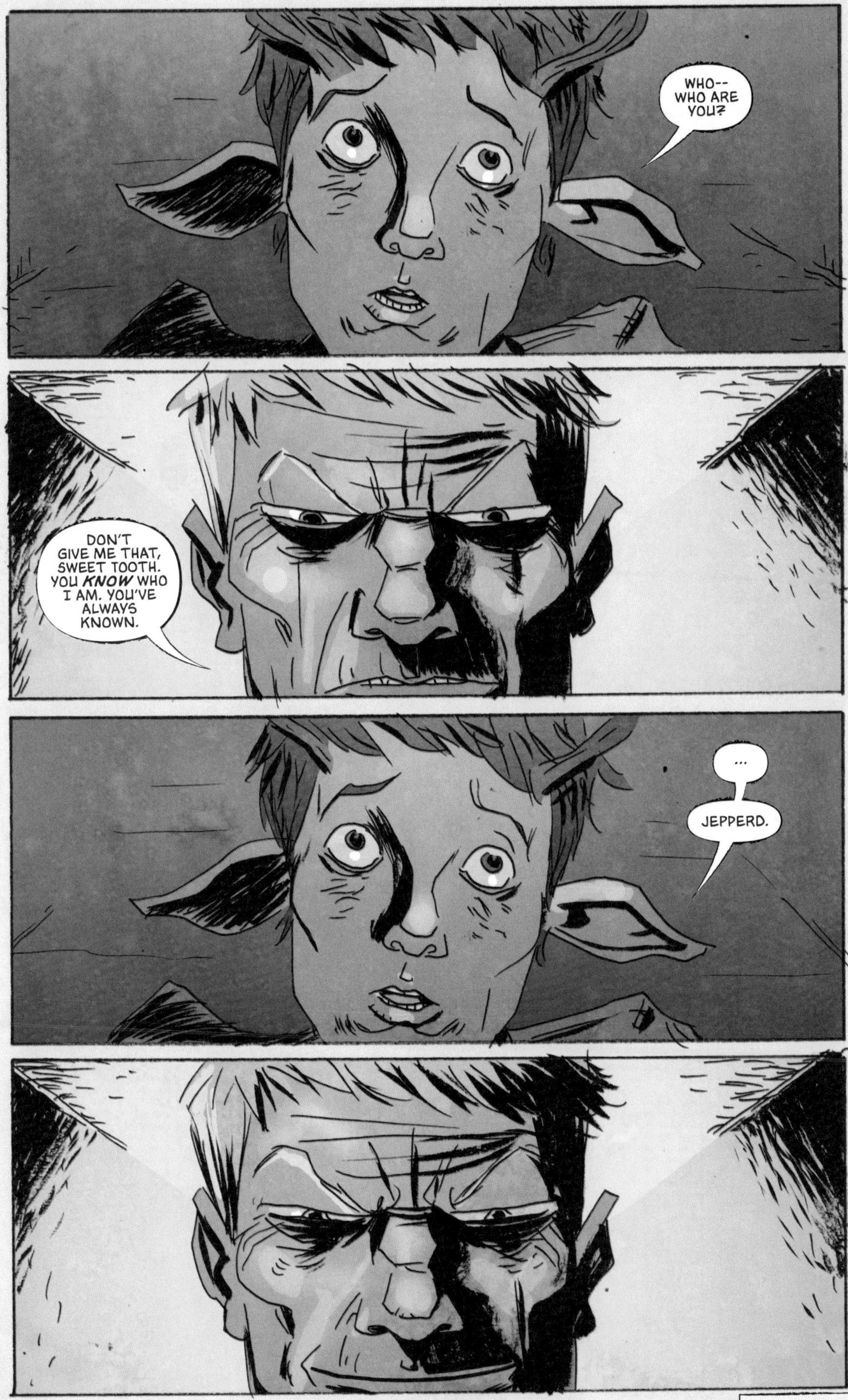
WHO--
WHO ARE YOU?
DON'T GIVE ME THAT, SWEET TOOTH. YOU *KNOW* WHO I AM. YOU'VE ALWAYS KNOWN.
...
JEPPERD.

TO BE CONTINUED

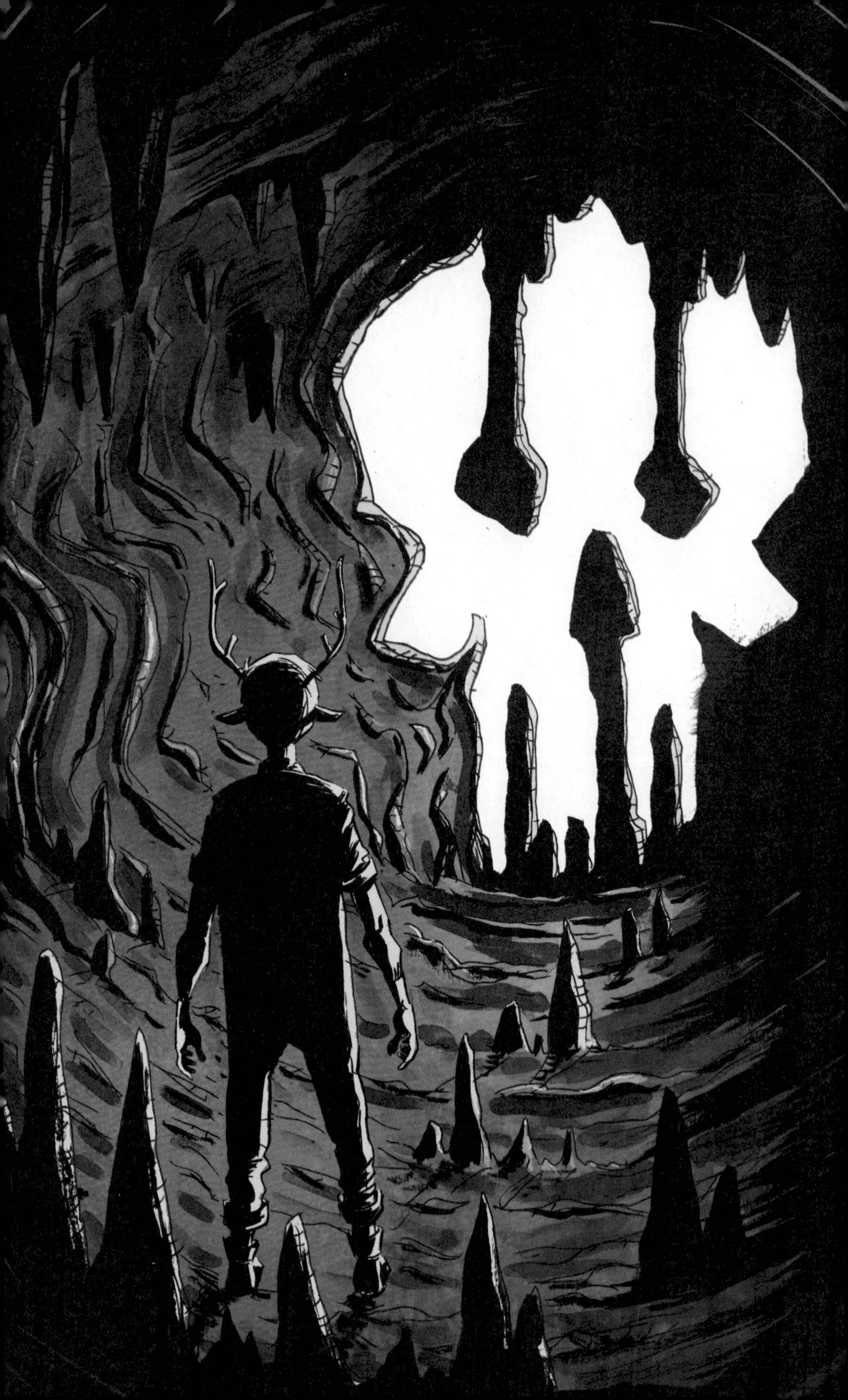

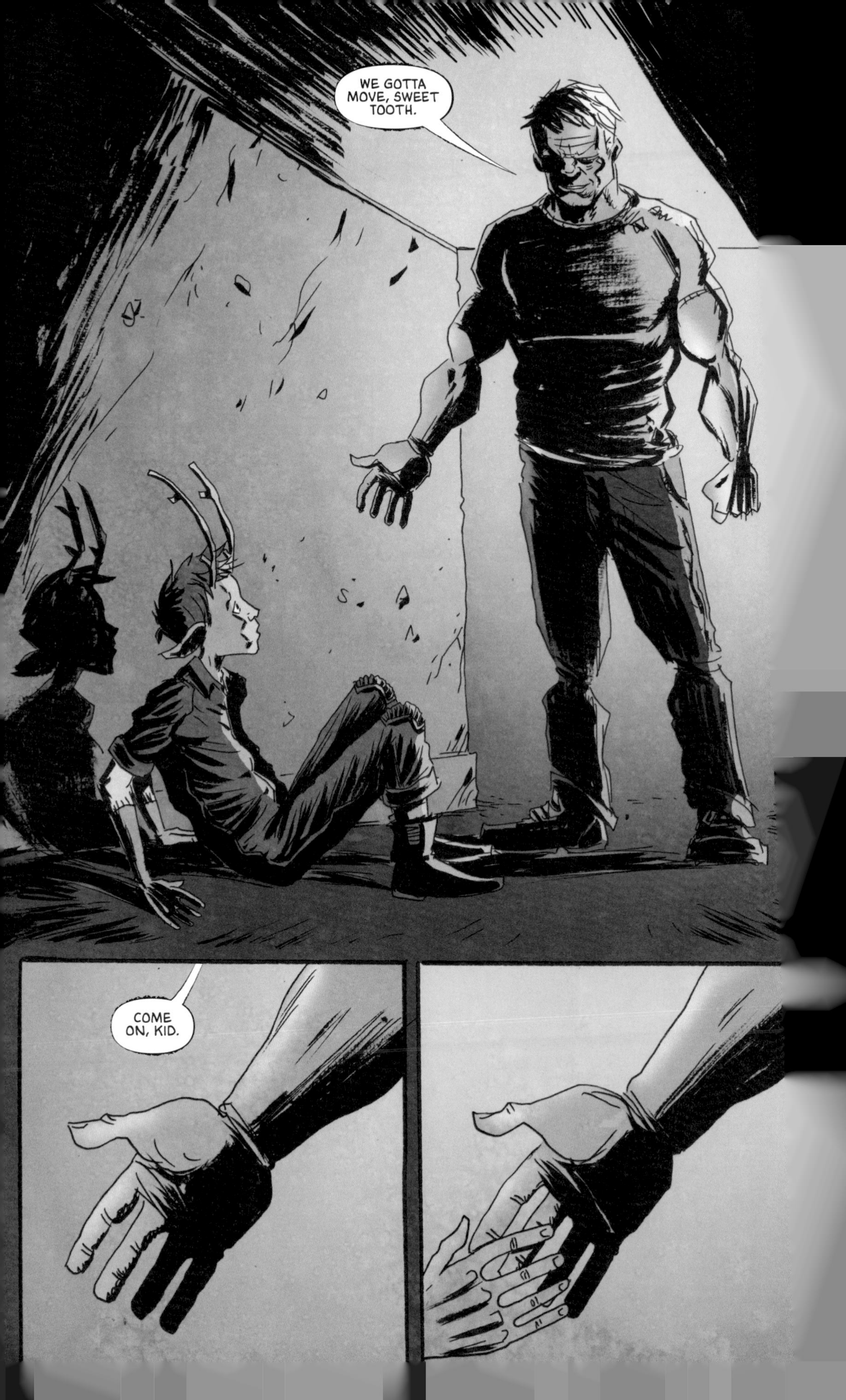
WE GOTTA MOVE, SWEET TOOTH.
COME ON, KID.

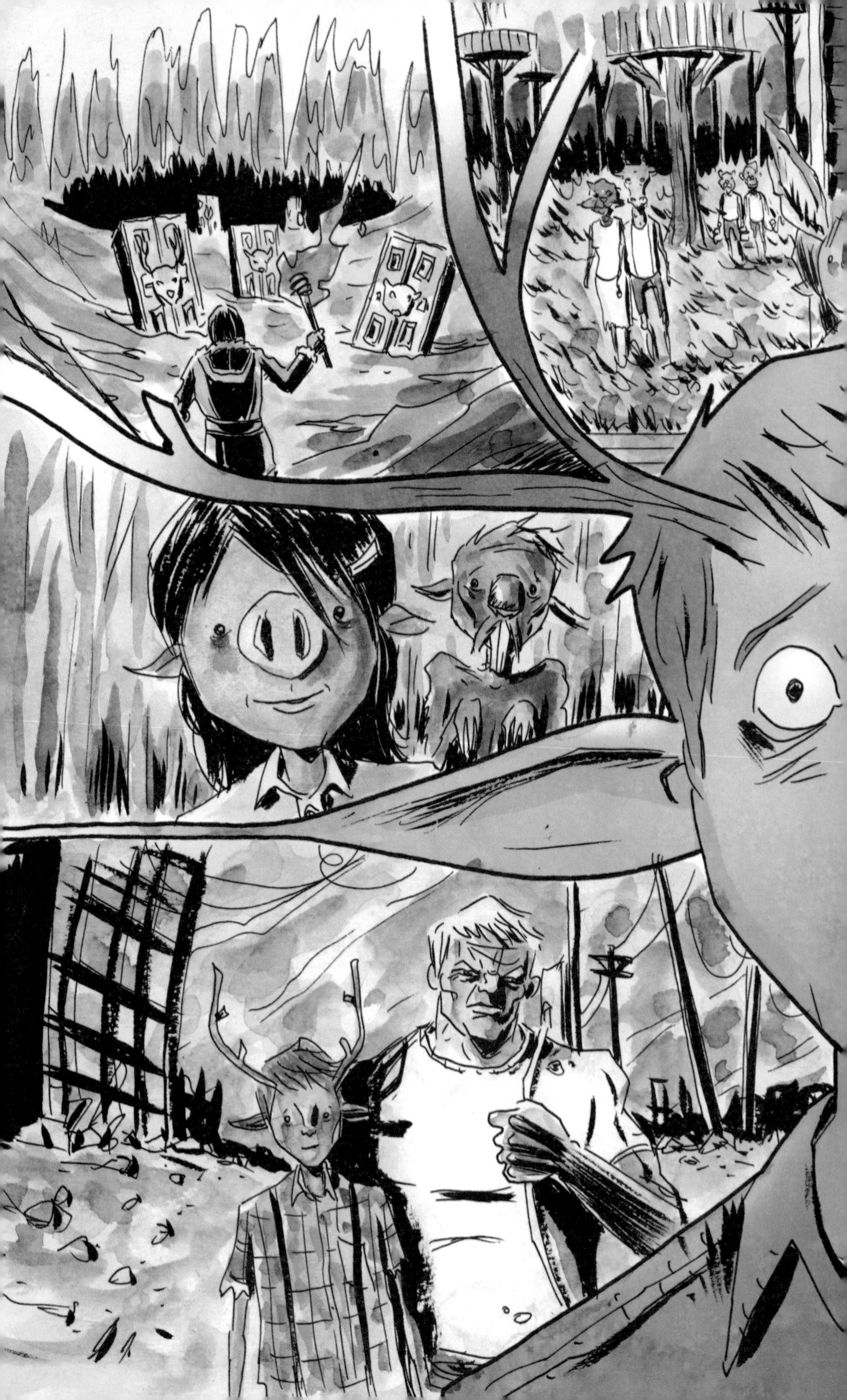

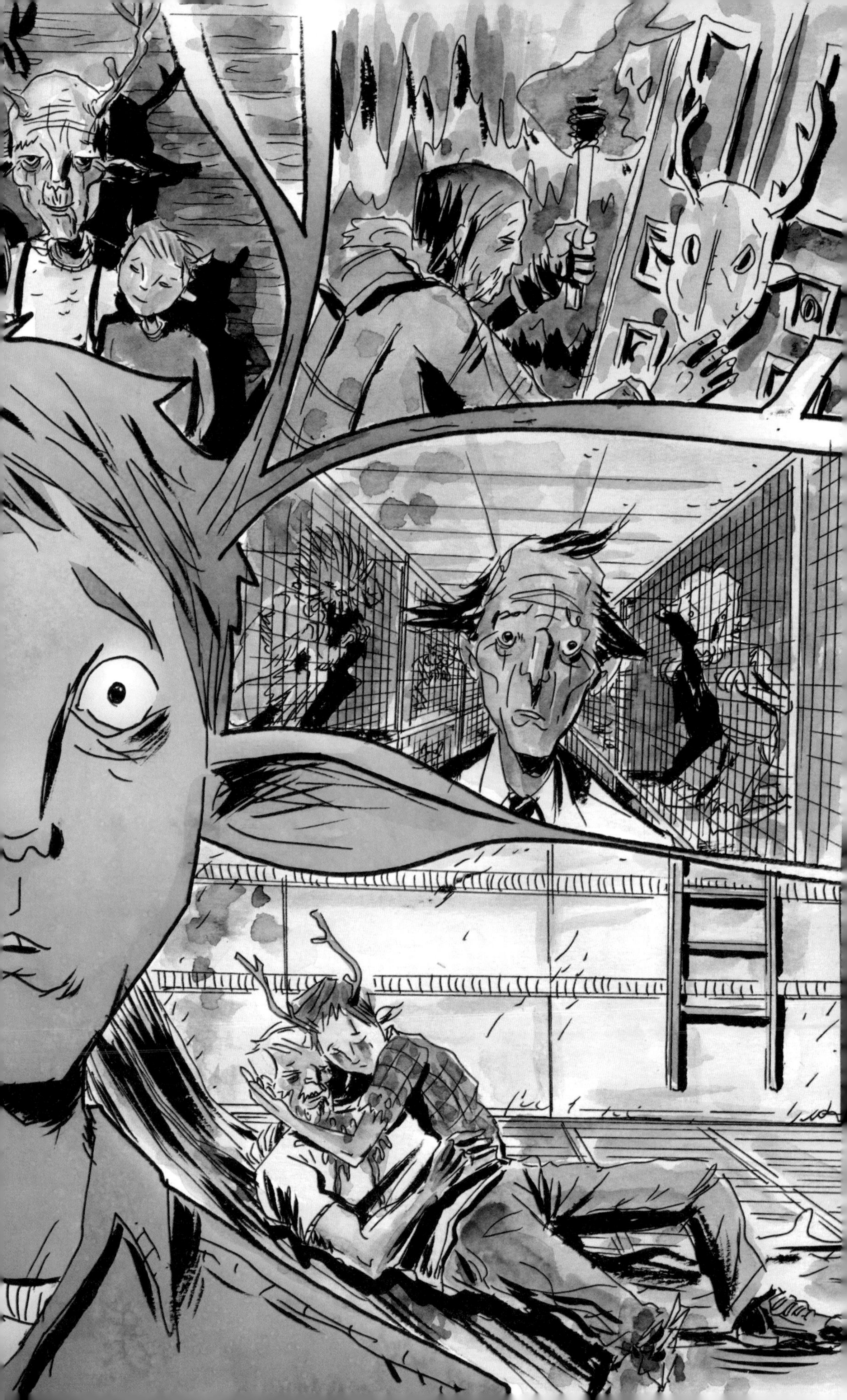

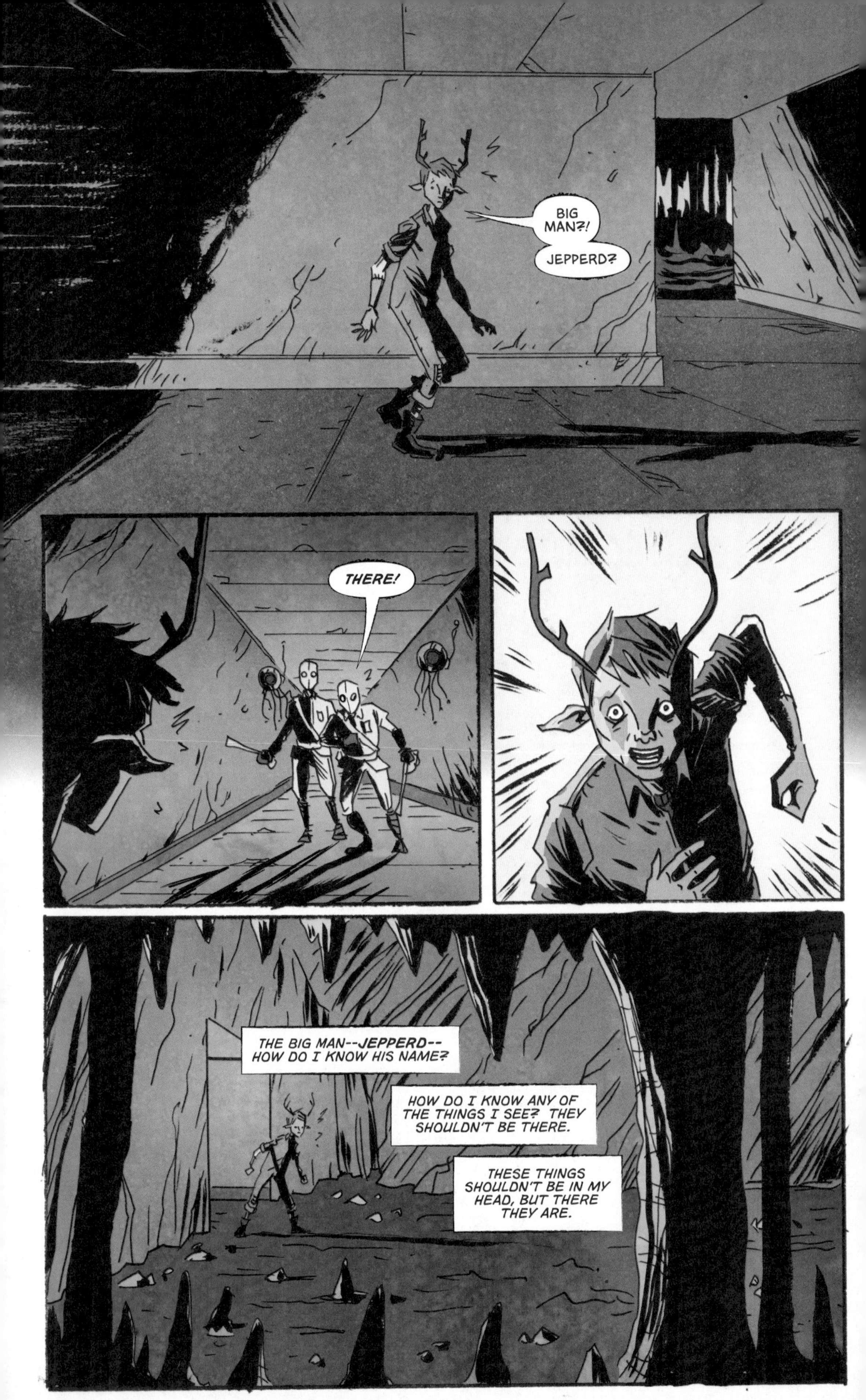
BIG MAN?!
JEPPERD?
THERE!
THE BIG MAN--JEPPERD-- HOW DO I KNOW HIS NAME?
HOW DO I KNOW ANY OF THE THINGS I SEE? THEY SHOULDN'T BE THERE.
THESE THINGS SHOULDN'T BE IN MY HEAD, BUT THERE THEY ARE.

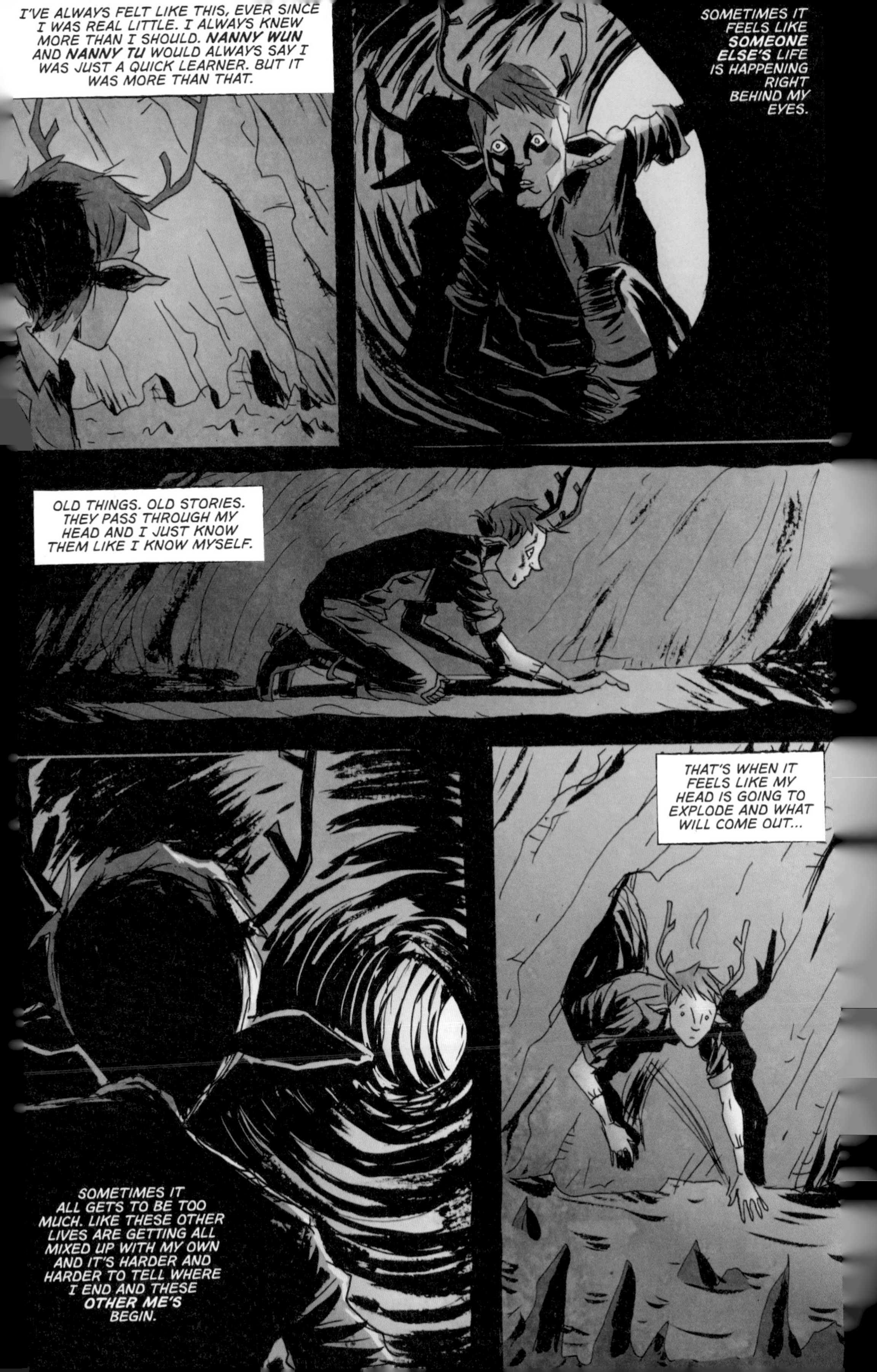
I'VE ALWAYS FELT LIKE THIS, EVER SINCE I WAS REAL LITTLE. I ALWAYS KNEW MORE THAN I SHOULD. NANNY WUN AND NANNY TU WOULD ALWAYS SAY I WAS JUST A QUICK LEARNER. BUT IT WAS MORE THAN THAT.
SOMETIMES IT FEELS LIKE SOMEONE ELSE'S LIFE IS HAPPENING RIGHT BEHIND MY EYES.
OLD THINGS. OLD STORIES. THEY PASS THROUGH MY HEAD AND I JUST KNOW THEM LIKE I KNOW MYSELF.
SOMETIMES IT ALL GETS TO BE TOO MUCH. LIKE THESE OTHER LIVES ARE GETTING ALL MIXED UP WITH MY OWN AND IT'S HARDER AND HARDER TO TELL WHERE I END AND THESE OTHER ME'S BEGIN.
THAT'S WHEN IT FEELS LIKE MY HEAD IS GOING TO EXPLODE AND WHAT WILL COME OUT...

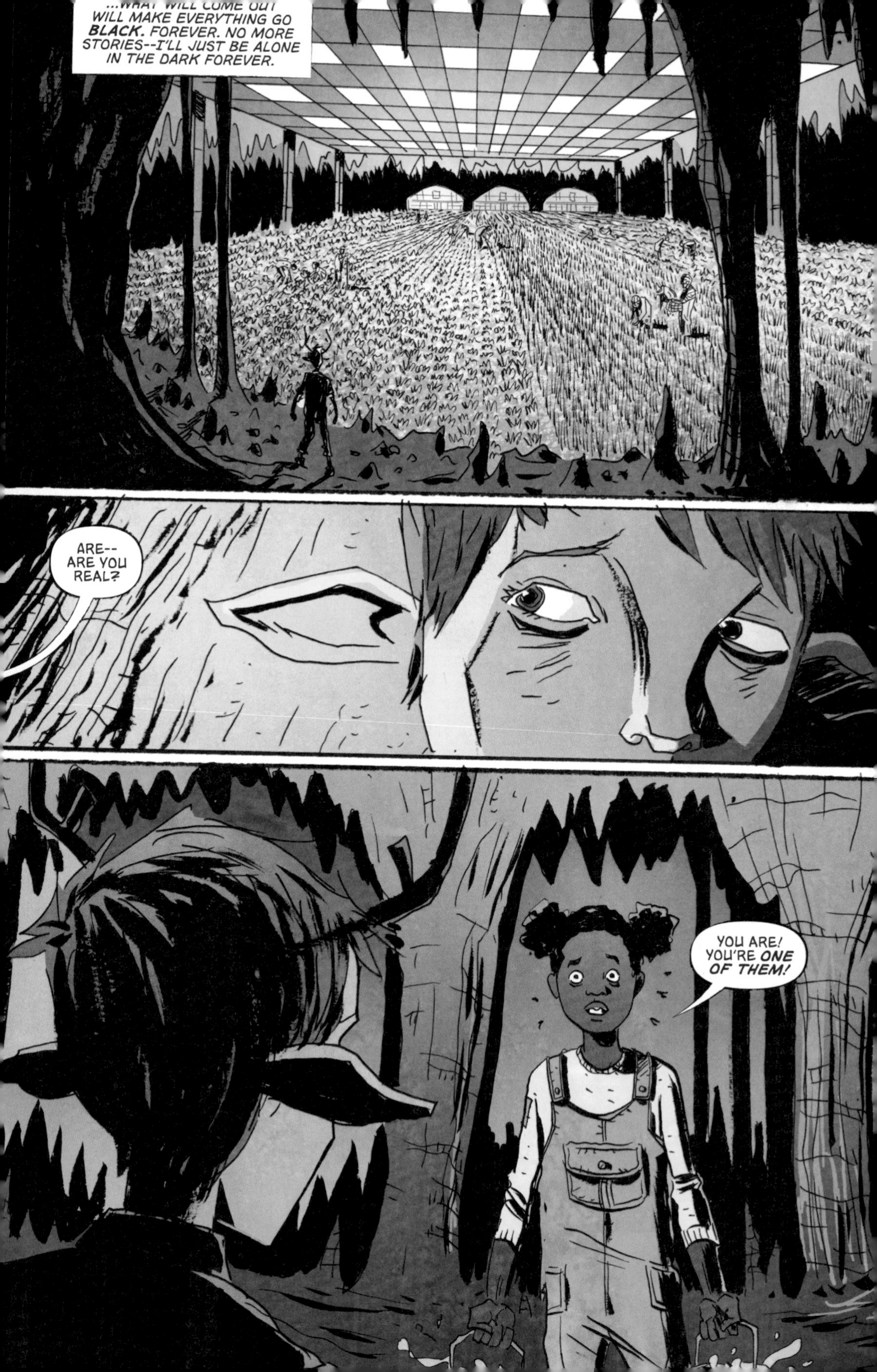
...WHAT WILL COME OUT WILL MAKE EVERYTHING GO **BLACK.** FOREVER. NO MORE STORIES--I'LL JUST BE ALONE IN THE DARK FOREVER.
ARE-- ARE YOU REAL?
YOU ARE! YOU'RE *ONE OF THEM!*

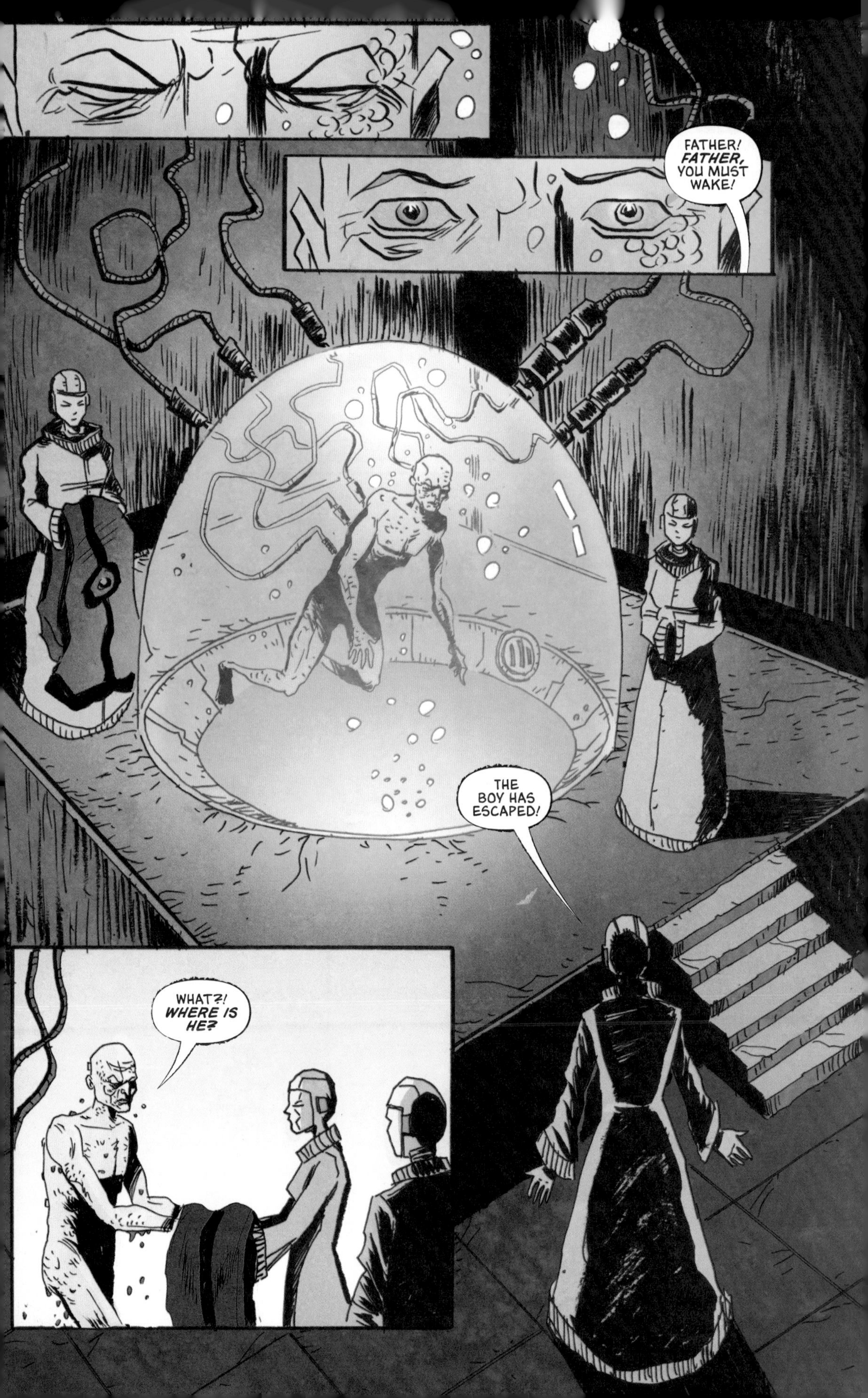
FATHER! FATHER, YOU MUST WAKE!
THE BOY HAS ESCAPED!
WHAT?! WHERE IS HE?

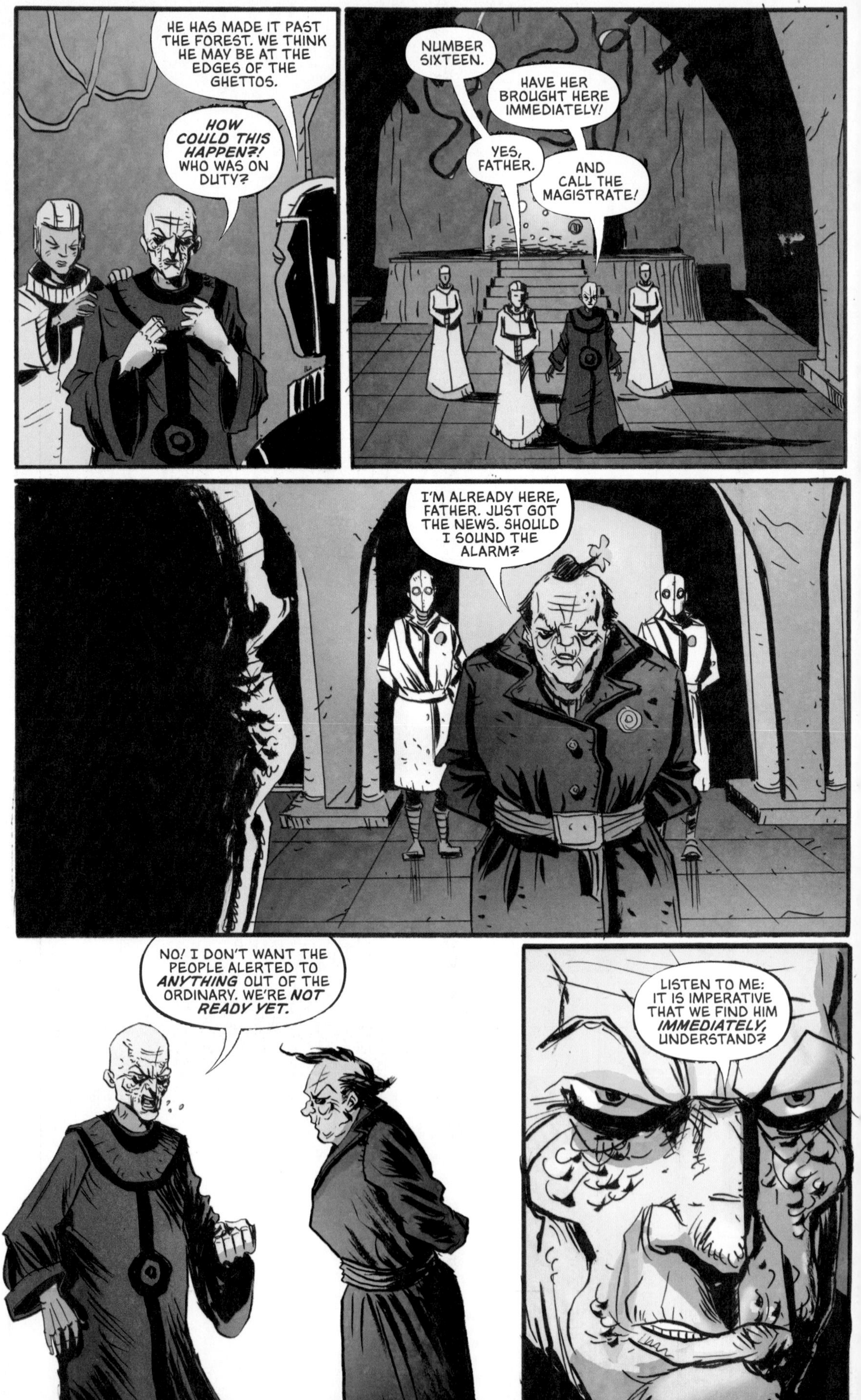
HE HAS MADE IT PAST THE FOREST. WE THINK HE MAY BE AT THE EDGES OF THE GHETTOS.
HOW COULD THIS HAPPEN?! WHO WAS ON DUTY?
NUMBER SIXTEEN.
HAVE HER BROUGHT HERE IMMEDIATELY!
YES, FATHER.
AND CALL THE MAGISTRATE!
I'M ALREADY HERE, FATHER. JUST GOT THE NEWS. SHOULD I SOUND THE ALARM?
NO! I DON'T WANT THE PEOPLE ALERTED TO ANYTHING OUT OF THE ORDINARY. WE'RE NOT READY YET.
LISTEN TO ME: IT IS IMPERATIVE THAT WE FIND HIM IMMEDIATELY, UNDERSTAND?

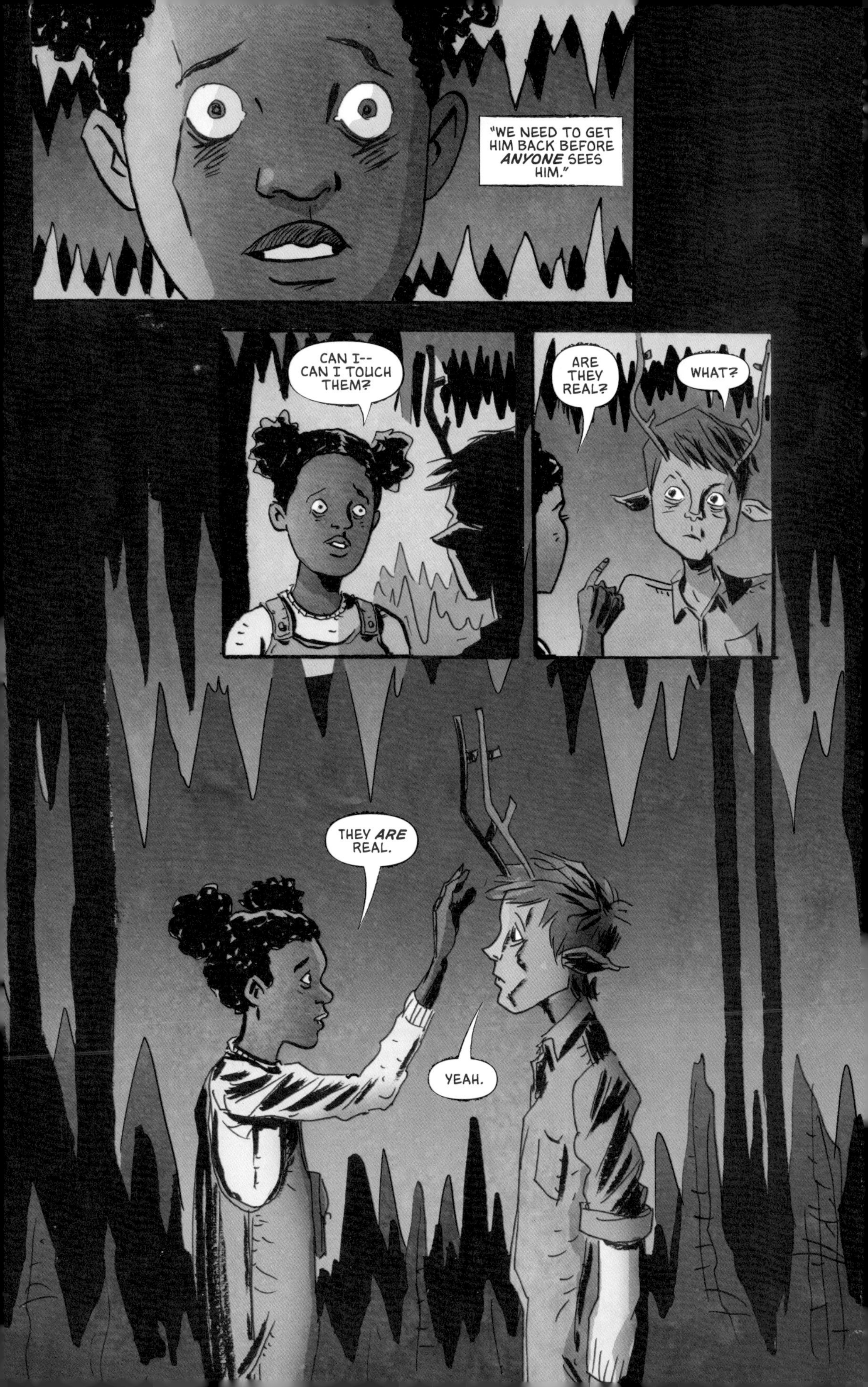
"WE NEED TO GET HIM BACK BEFORE *ANYONE* SEES HIM."
CAN I-- CAN I TOUCH THEM?
ARE THEY REAL?
WHAT?
THEY *ARE* REAL.
YEAH.

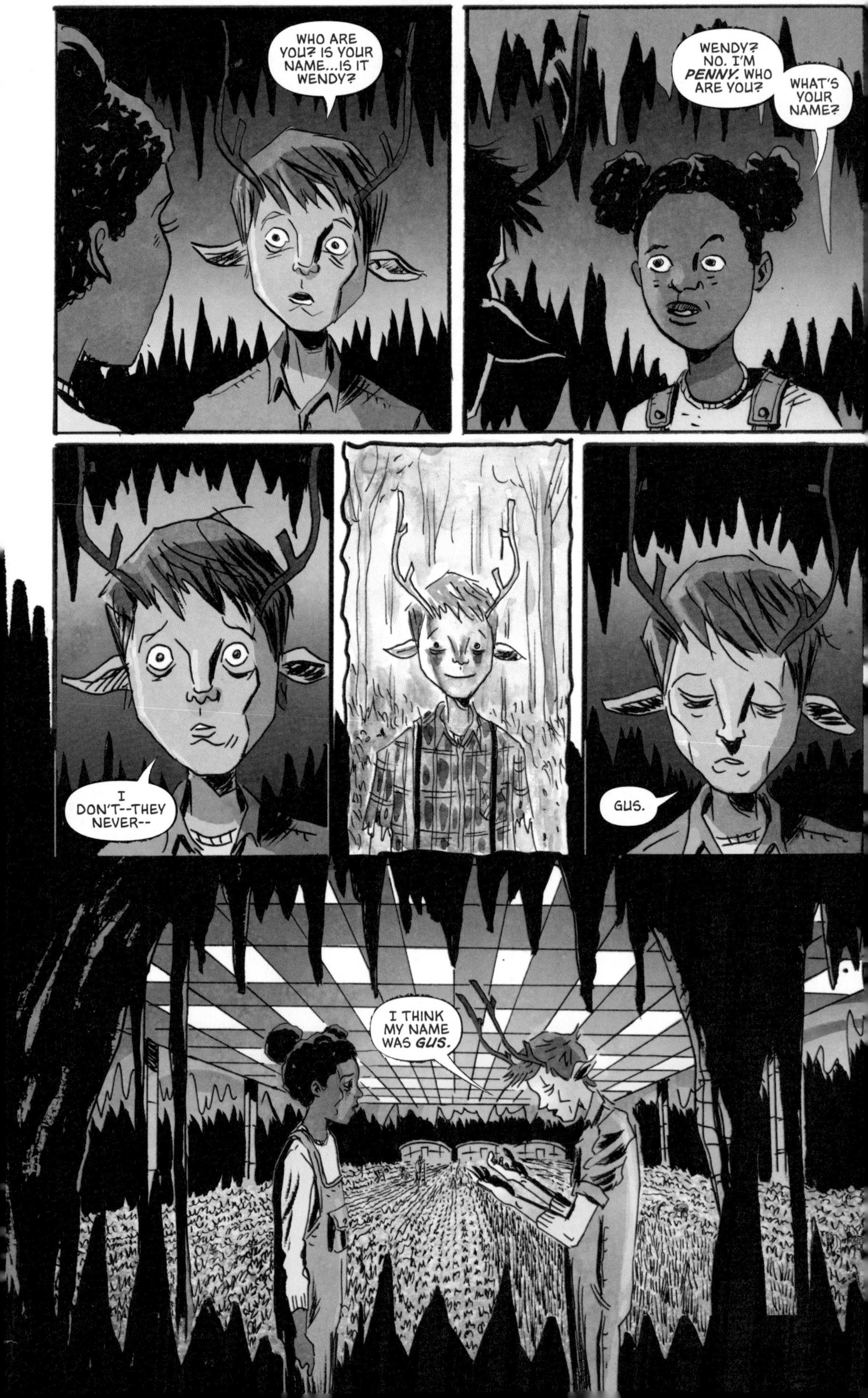
WHO ARE YOU? IS YOUR NAME...IS IT WENDY?
WENDY? NO. I'M PENNY. WHO ARE YOU?
WHAT'S YOUR NAME?
I DON'T--THEY NEVER--
GUS.
I THINK MY NAME WAS GUS.

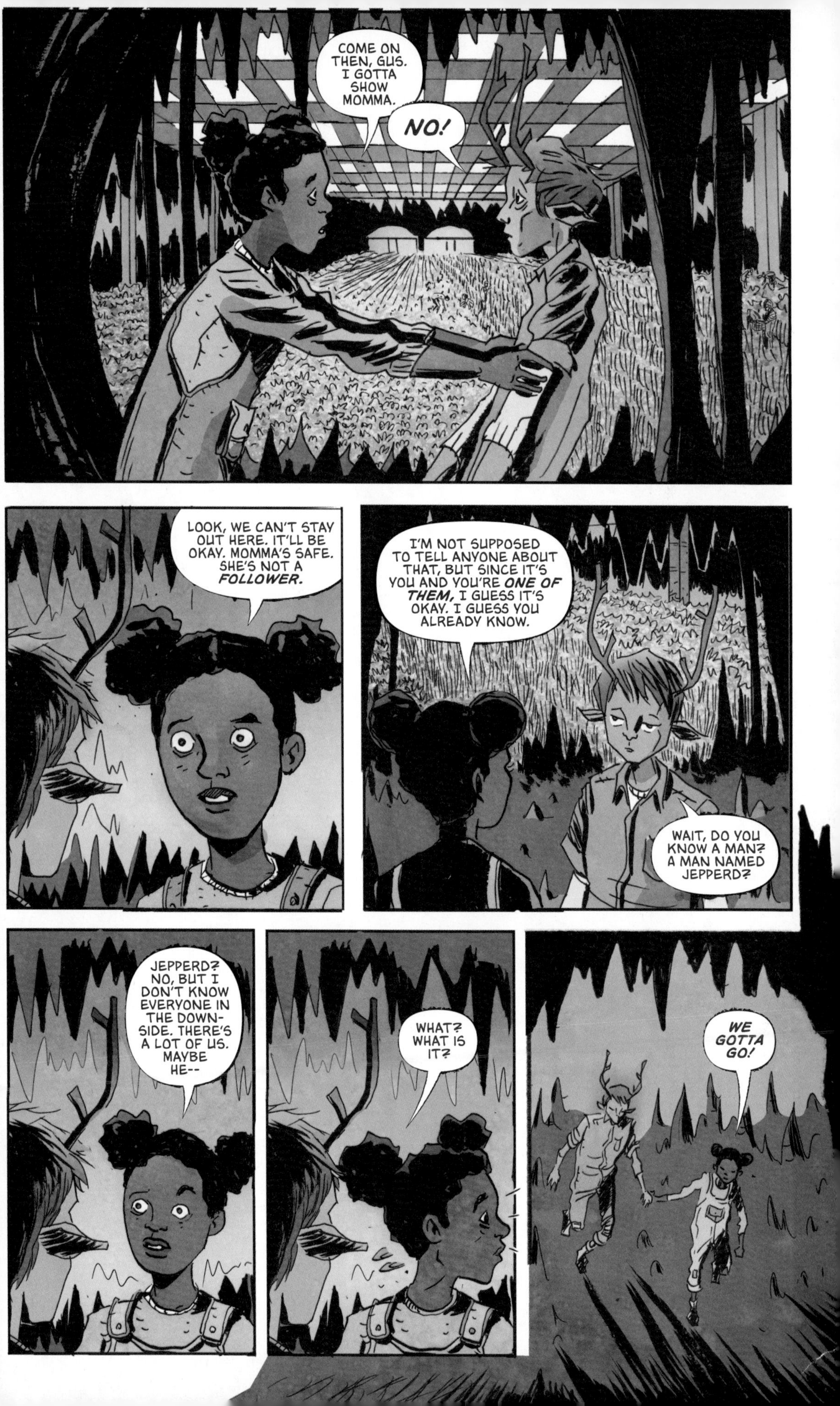
COME ON THEN, GUS. I GOTTA SHOW MOMMA.
NO!
LOOK, WE CAN'T STAY OUT HERE. IT'LL BE OKAY. MOMMA'S SAFE. SHE'S NOT A FOLLOWER.
I'M NOT SUPPOSED TO TELL ANYONE ABOUT THAT, BUT SINCE IT'S YOU AND YOU'RE ONE OF THEM, I GUESS IT'S OKAY. I GUESS YOU ALREADY KNOW.
WAIT, DO YOU KNOW A MAN? A MAN NAMED JEPPERD?
JEPPERD? NO, BUT I DON'T KNOW EVERYONE IN THE DOWN-SIDE. THERE'S A LOT OF US. MAYBE HE--
WHAT? WHAT IS IT?
WE GOTTA GO!

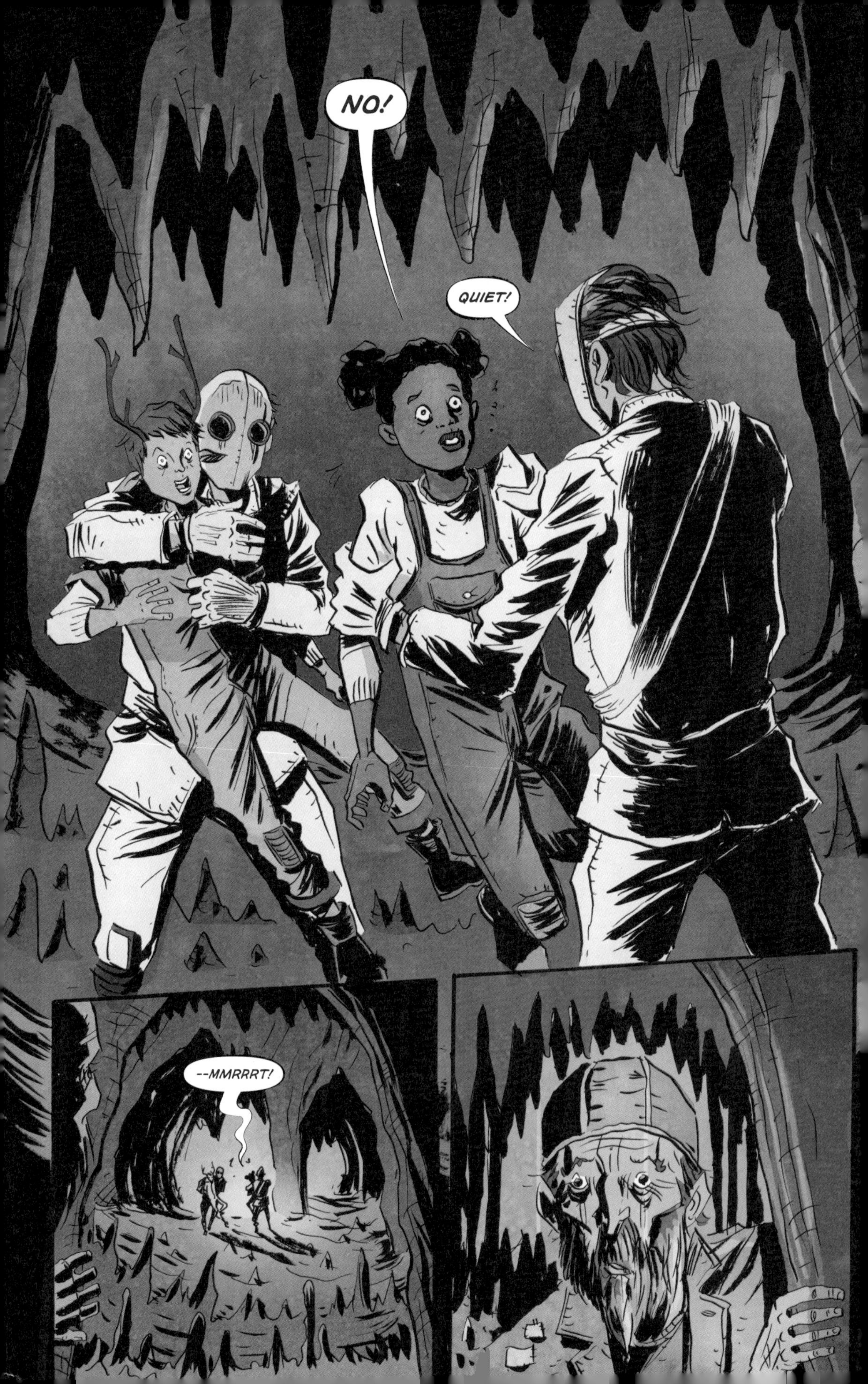
NO!
QUIET!
--MMRRRT!

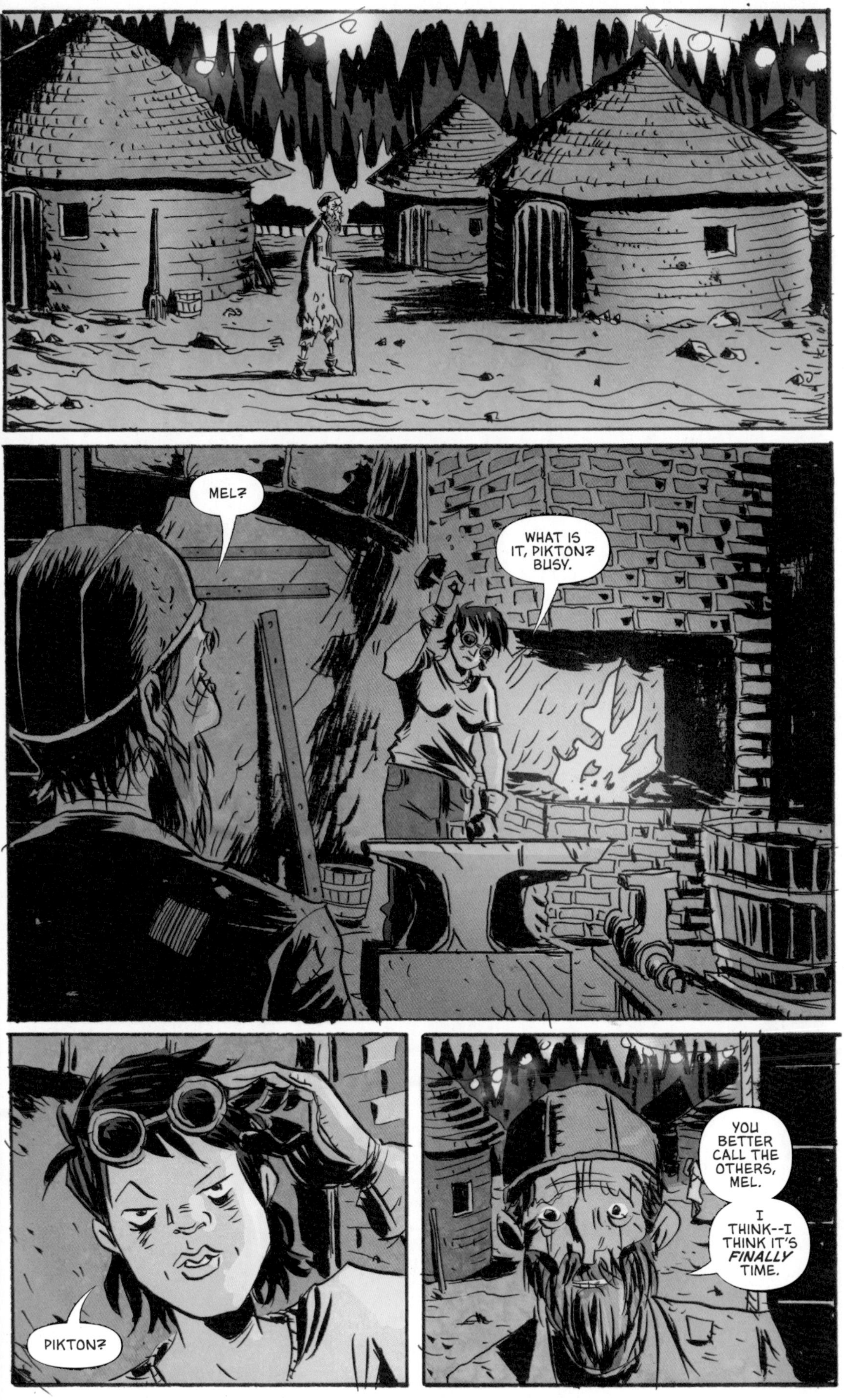
MEL?
WHAT IS IT, PIKTON? BUSY.
PIKTON?
YOU BETTER CALL THE OTHERS, MEL.
I THINK--I THINK IT'S *FINALLY* TIME.

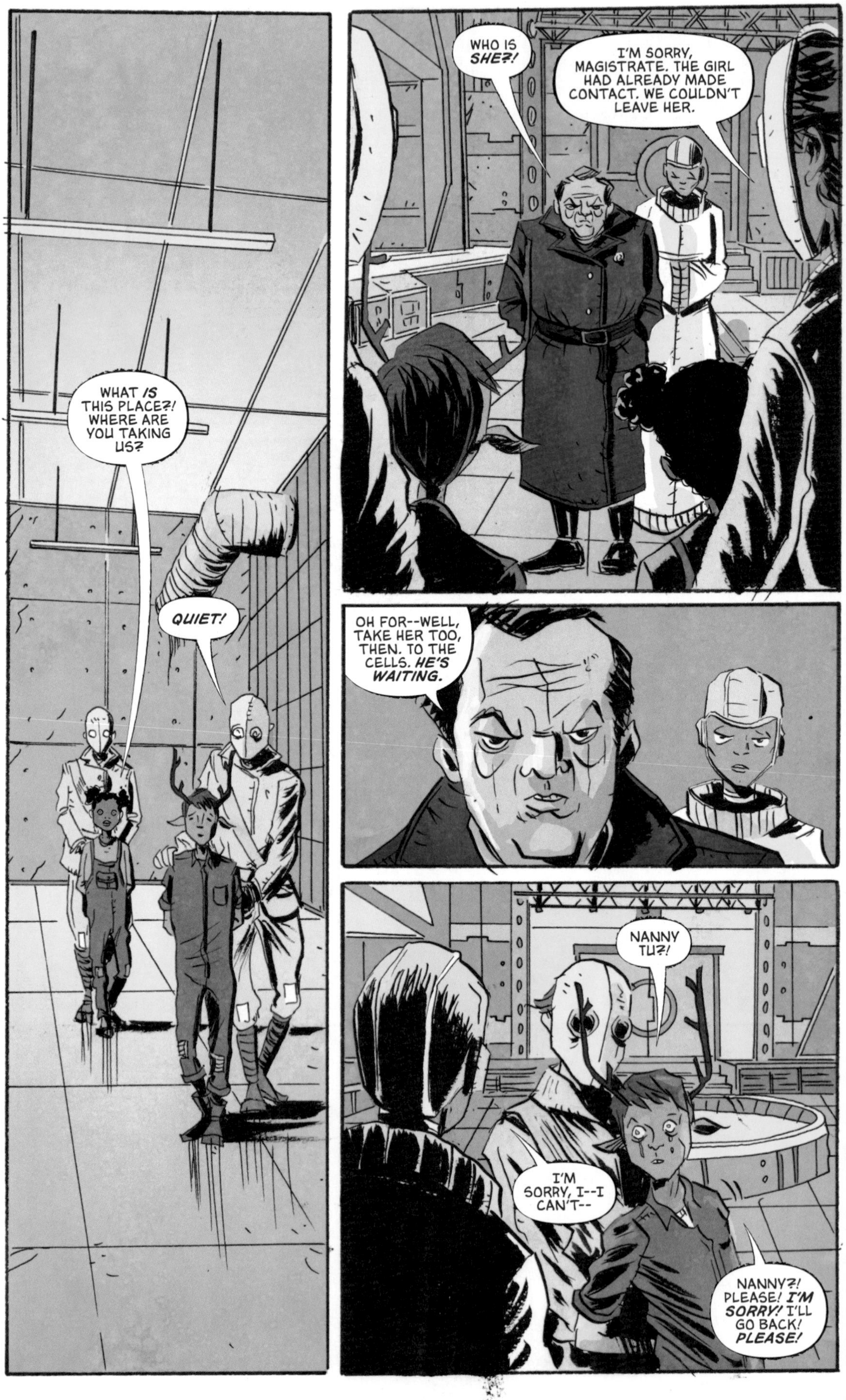
WHAT IS THIS PLACE?! WHERE ARE YOU TAKING US?
QUIET!
WHO IS SHE?!
I'M SORRY, MAGISTRATE. THE GIRL HAD ALREADY MADE CONTACT. WE COULDN'T LEAVE HER.
OH FOR--WELL, TAKE HER TOO, THEN. TO THE CELLS. HE'S WAITING.
NANNY TU?!
I'M SORRY, I--I CAN'T--
NANNY?! PLEASE! I'M SORRY! I'LL GO BACK! PLEASE!

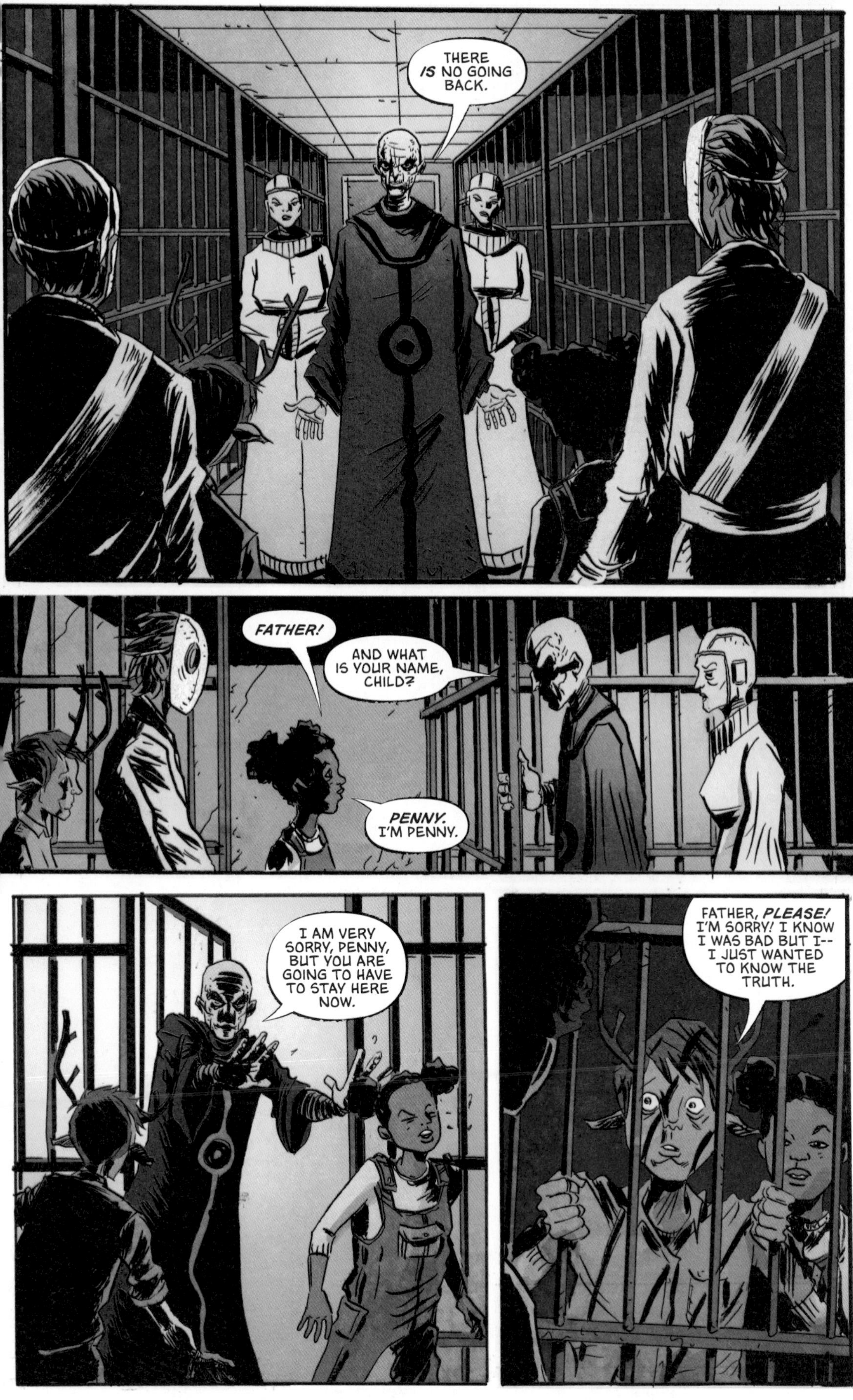
THERE *IS* NO GOING BACK.
FATHER!
AND WHAT IS YOUR NAME, CHILD?
PENNY. I'M PENNY.
I AM VERY SORRY, PENNY, BUT YOU ARE GOING TO HAVE TO STAY HERE NOW.
FATHER, *PLEASE!* I'M SORRY! I KNOW I WAS BAD BUT I-- I JUST WANTED TO KNOW THE TRUTH.

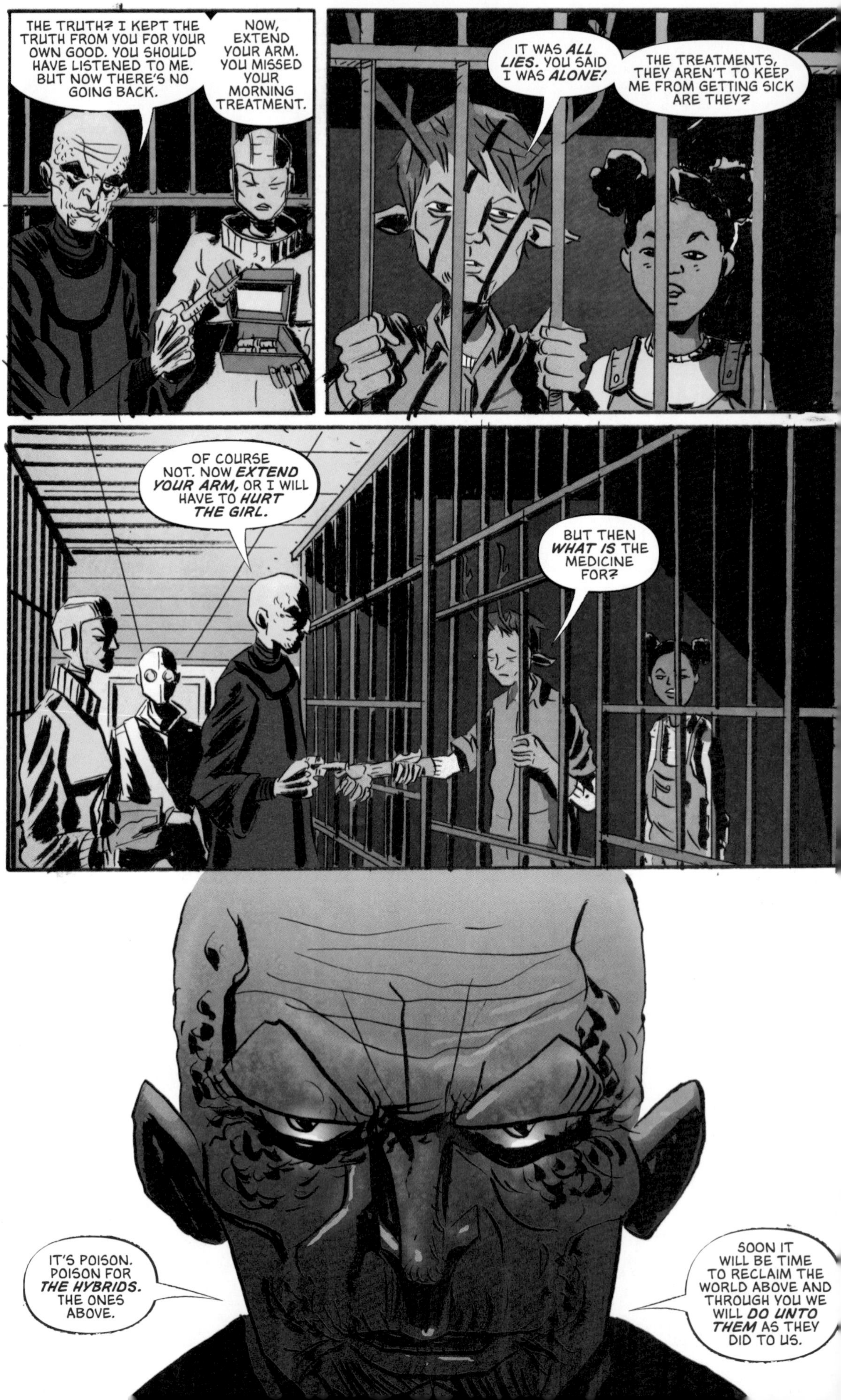
THE TRUTH? I KEPT THE TRUTH FROM YOU FOR YOUR OWN GOOD. YOU SHOULD HAVE LISTENED TO ME. BUT NOW THERE'S NO GOING BACK.
NOW, EXTEND YOUR ARM. YOU MISSED YOUR MORNING TREATMENT.
IT WAS ALL LIES. YOU SAID I WAS ALONE!
THE TREATMENTS, THEY AREN'T TO KEEP ME FROM GETTING SICK ARE THEY?
OF COURSE NOT. NOW EXTEND YOUR ARM, OR I WILL HAVE TO HURT THE GIRL.
BUT THEN WHAT IS THE MEDICINE FOR?
IT'S POISON. POISON FOR THE HYBRIDS. THE ONES ABOVE.
SOON IT WILL BE TIME TO RECLAIM THE WORLD ABOVE AND THROUGH YOU WE WILL DO UNTO THEM AS THEY DID TO US.

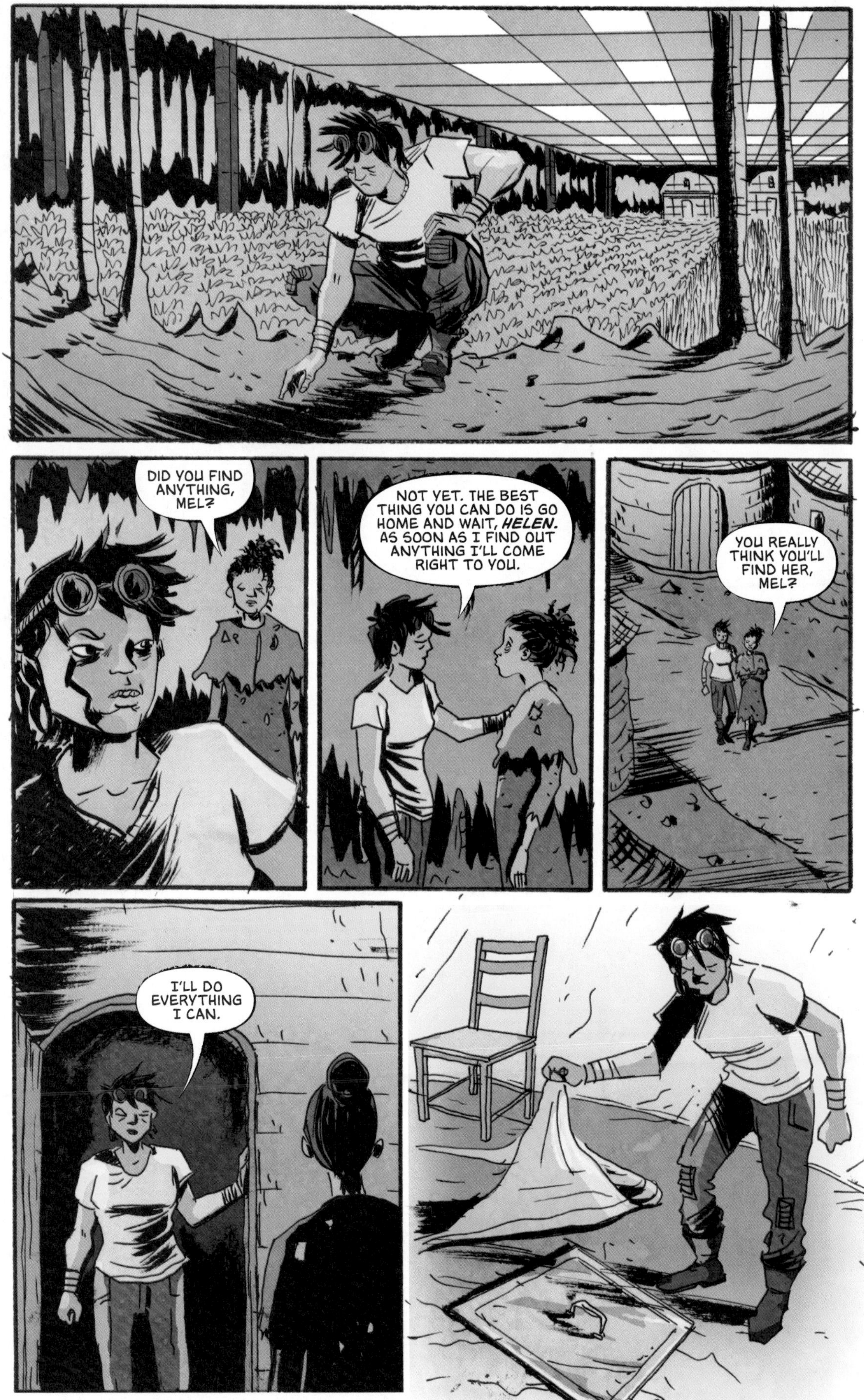
DID YOU FIND ANYTHING, MEL?
NOT YET. THE BEST THING YOU CAN DO IS GO HOME AND WAIT, HELEN. AS SOON AS I FIND OUT ANYTHING I'LL COME RIGHT TO YOU.
YOU REALLY THINK YOU'LL FIND HER, MEL?
I'LL DO EVERYTHING I CAN.

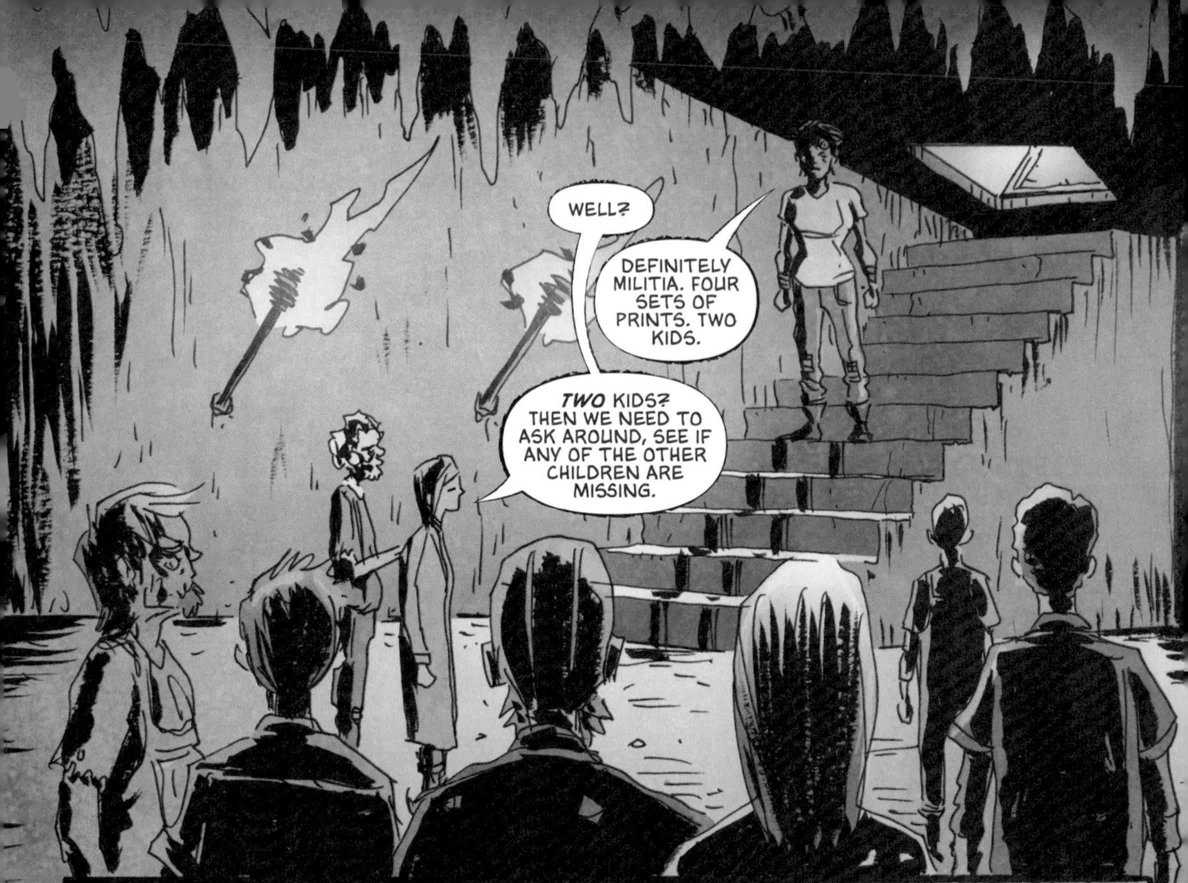
WELL?
DEFINITELY MILITIA. FOUR SETS OF PRINTS. TWO KIDS.
TWO KIDS? THEN WE NEED TO ASK AROUND, SEE IF ANY OF THE OTHER CHILDREN ARE MISSING.

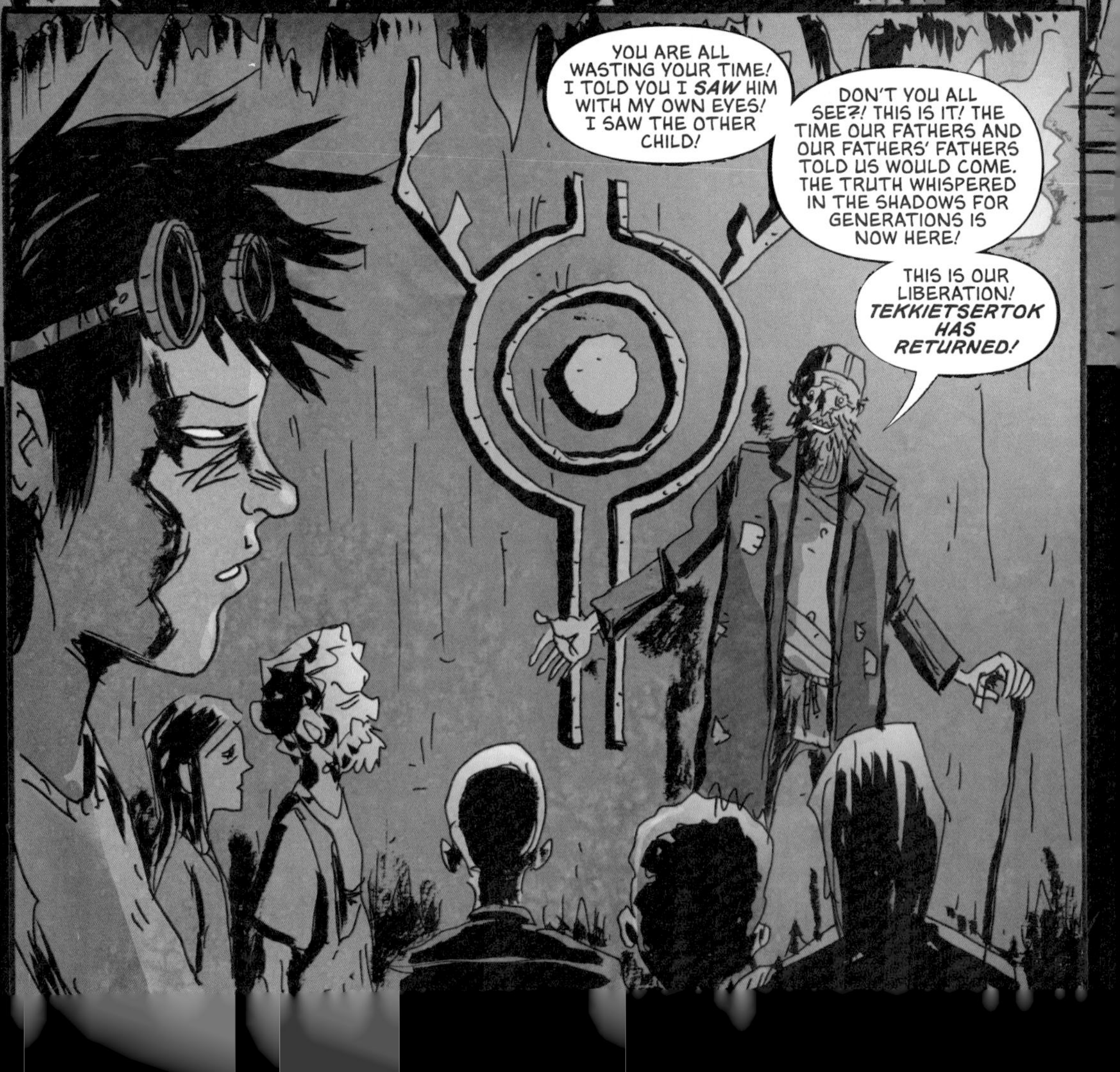
YOU ARE ALL WASTING YOUR TIME! I TOLD YOU I *SAW* HIM WITH MY OWN EYES! I SAW THE OTHER CHILD!
DON'T YOU ALL SEE?! THIS IS IT! THE TIME OUR FATHERS AND OUR FATHERS' FATHERS TOLD US WOULD COME. THE TRUTH WHISPERED IN THE SHADOWS FOR GENERATIONS IS NOW HERE!
THIS IS OUR LIBERATION! ***TEKKIETSERTOK HAS RETURNED!***

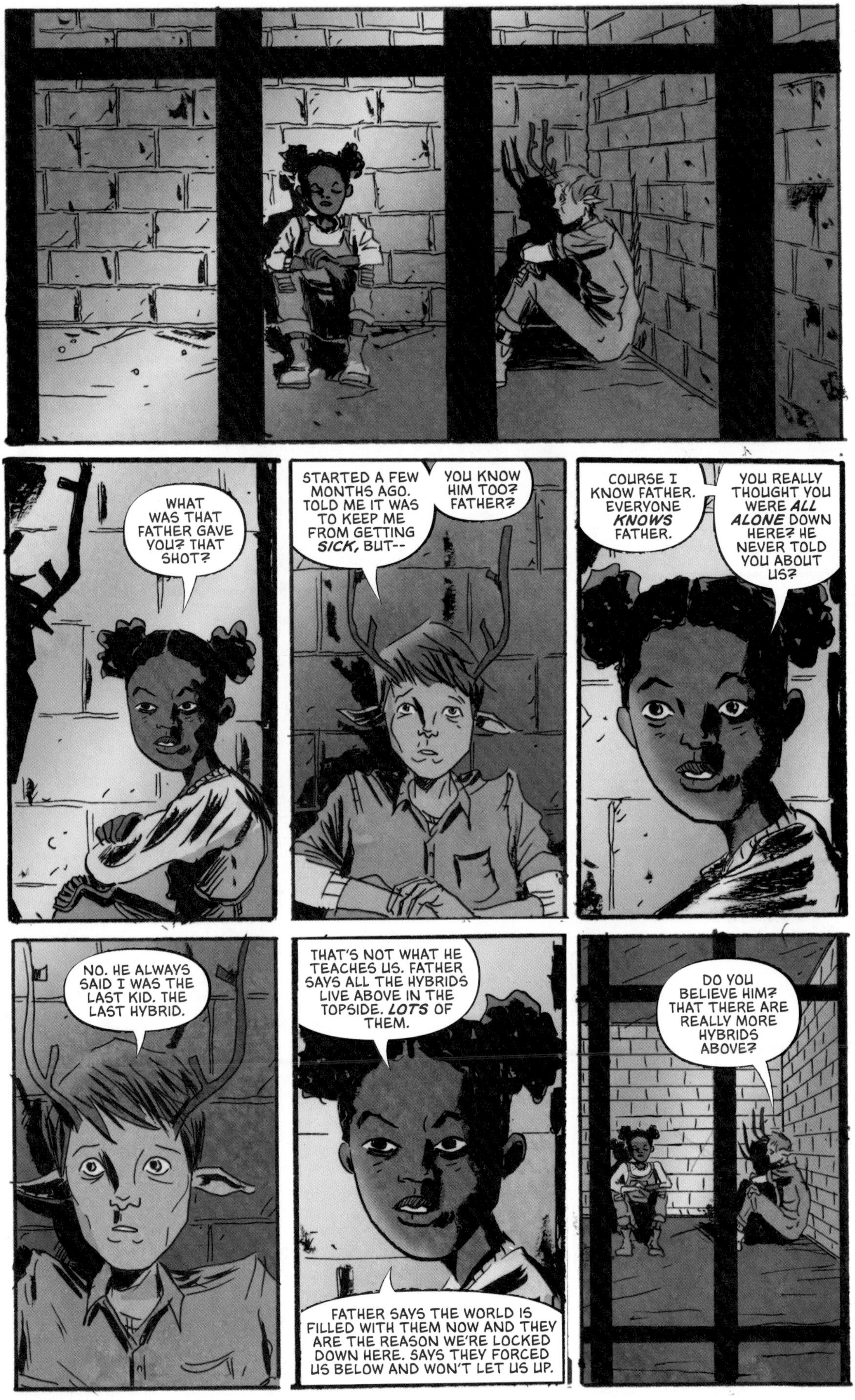
WHAT WAS THAT FATHER GAVE YOU? THAT SHOT?
STARTED A FEW MONTHS AGO. TOLD ME IT WAS TO KEEP ME FROM GETTING SICK, BUT--
YOU KNOW HIM TOO? FATHER?
COURSE I KNOW FATHER. EVERYONE KNOWS FATHER.
YOU REALLY THOUGHT YOU WERE ALL ALONE DOWN HERE? HE NEVER TOLD YOU ABOUT US?
NO. HE ALWAYS SAID I WAS THE LAST KID. THE LAST HYBRID.
THAT'S NOT WHAT HE TEACHES US. FATHER SAYS ALL THE HYBRIDS LIVE ABOVE IN THE TOPSIDE. LOTS OF THEM.
FATHER SAYS THE WORLD IS FILLED WITH THEM NOW AND THEY ARE THE REASON WE'RE LOCKED DOWN HERE. SAYS THEY FORCED US BELOW AND WON'T LET US UP.
DO YOU BELIEVE HIM? THAT THERE ARE REALLY MORE HYBRIDS ABOVE?

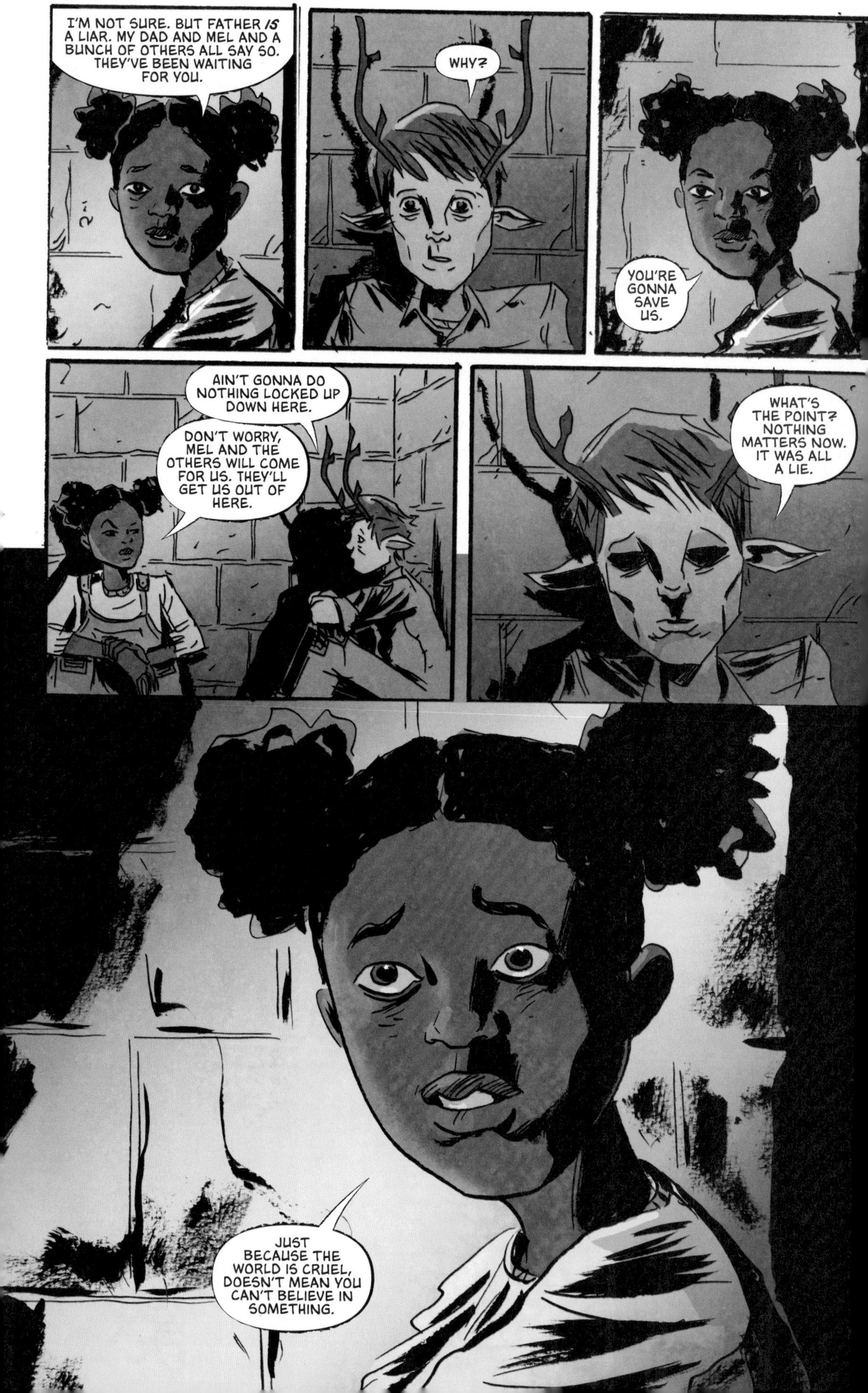
I'M NOT SURE. BUT FATHER *IS* A LIAR. MY DAD AND MEL AND A BUNCH OF OTHERS ALL SAY SO. THEY'VE BEEN WAITING FOR YOU.
WHY?
YOU'RE GONNA SAVE US.
AIN'T GONNA DO NOTHING LOCKED UP DOWN HERE.
DON'T WORRY, MEL AND THE OTHERS WILL COME FOR US. THEY'LL GET US OUT OF HERE.
WHAT'S THE POINT? NOTHING MATTERS NOW. IT WAS ALL A LIE.
JUST BECAUSE THE WORLD IS CRUEL, DOESN'T MEAN YOU CAN'T BELIEVE IN SOMETHING.

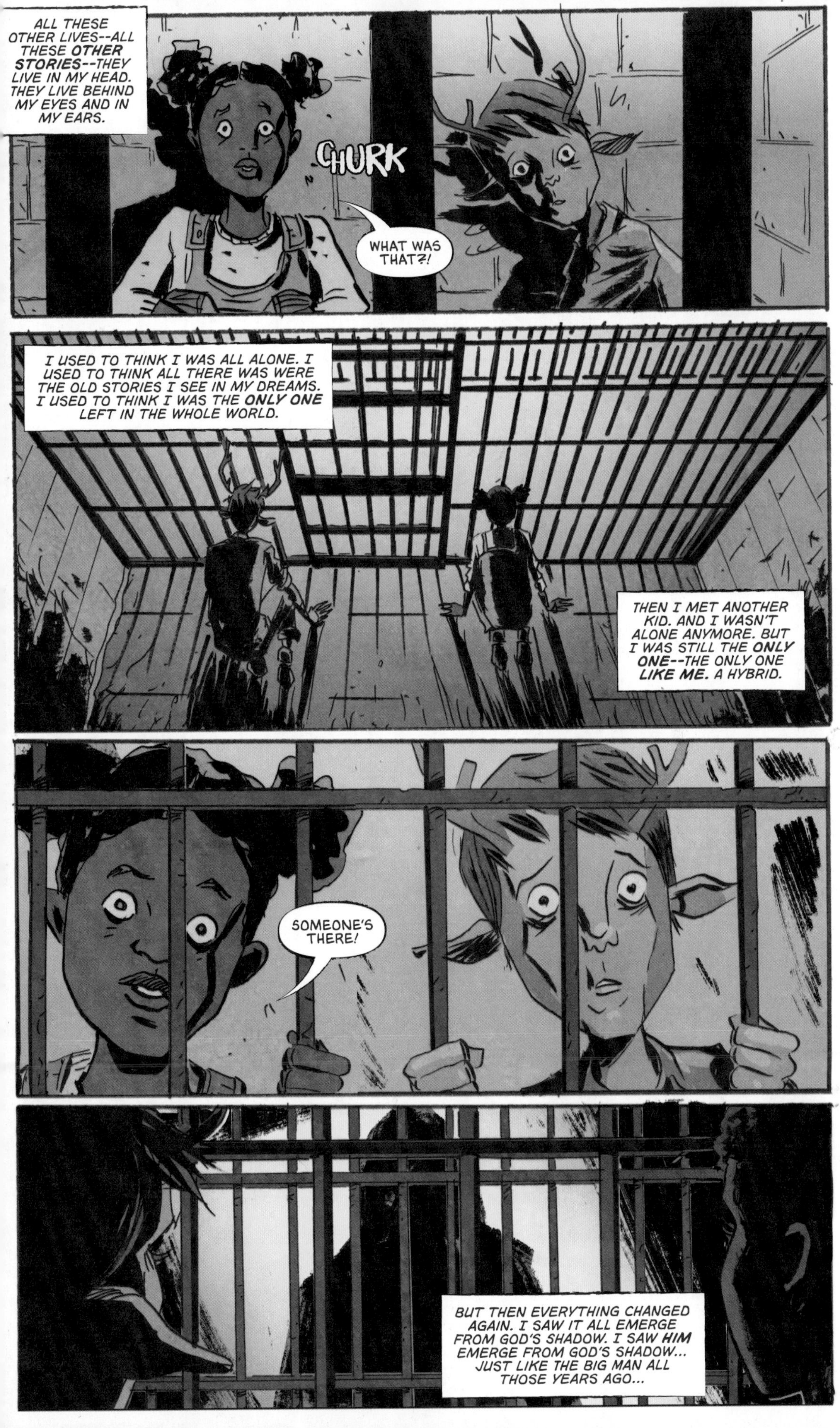
ALL THESE OTHER LIVES--ALL THESE OTHER STORIES--THEY LIVE IN MY HEAD. THEY LIVE BEHIND MY EYES AND IN MY EARS.
CHURK
WHAT WAS THAT?!
I USED TO THINK I WAS ALL ALONE. I USED TO THINK ALL THERE WAS WERE THE OLD STORIES I SEE IN MY DREAMS. I USED TO THINK I WAS THE ONLY ONE LEFT IN THE WHOLE WORLD.
THEN I MET ANOTHER KID. AND I WASN'T ALONE ANYMORE. BUT I WAS STILL THE ONLY ONE--THE ONLY ONE LIKE ME. A HYBRID.
SOMEONE'S THERE!
BUT THEN EVERYTHING CHANGED AGAIN. I SAW IT ALL EMERGE FROM GOD'S SHADOW. I SAW HIM EMERGE FROM GOD'S SHADOW... JUST LIKE THE BIG MAN ALL THOSE YEARS AGO...

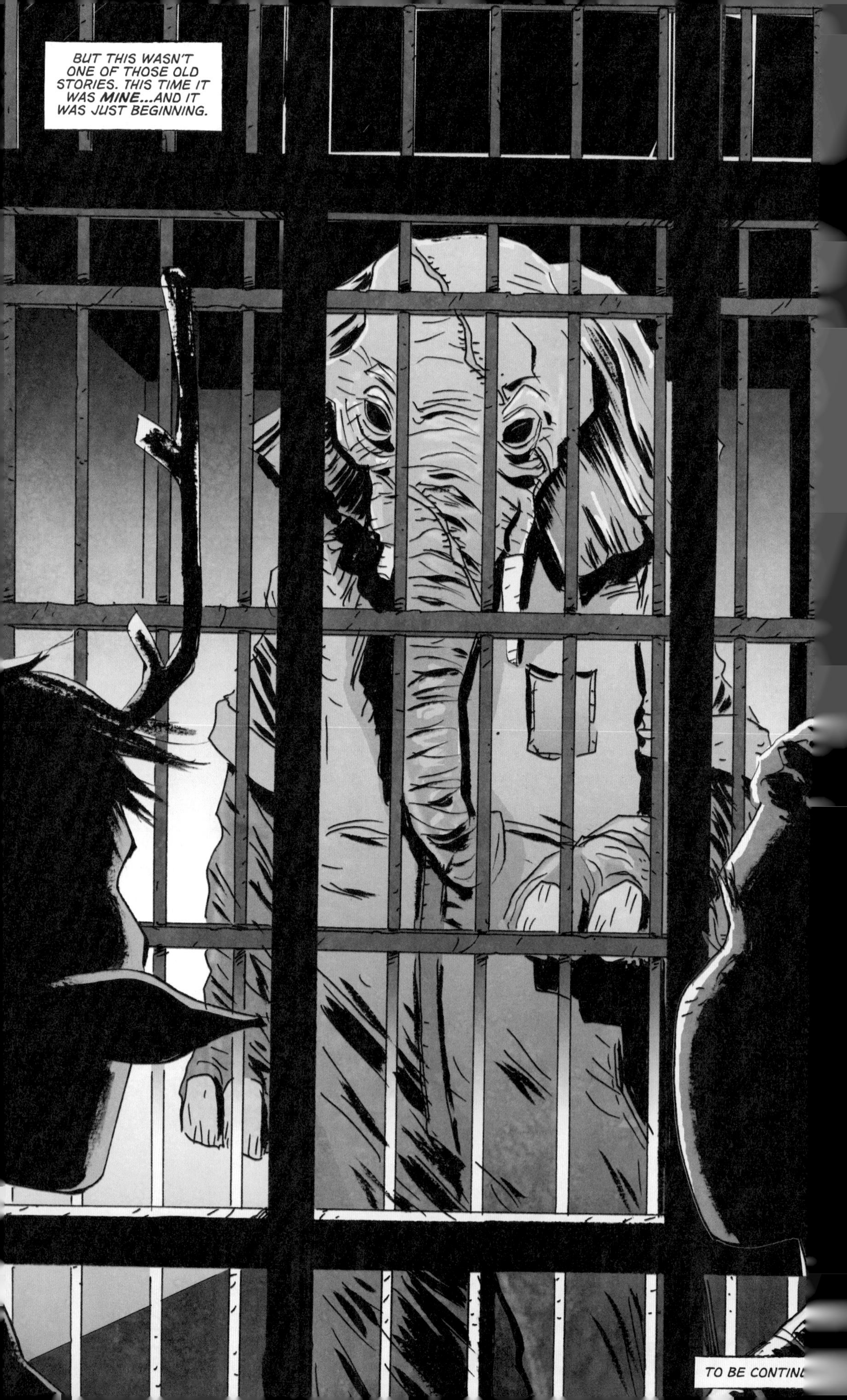
BUT THIS WASN'T ONE OF THOSE OLD STORIES. THIS TIME IT WAS MINE...AND IT WAS JUST BEGINNING.
TO BE CONTIN

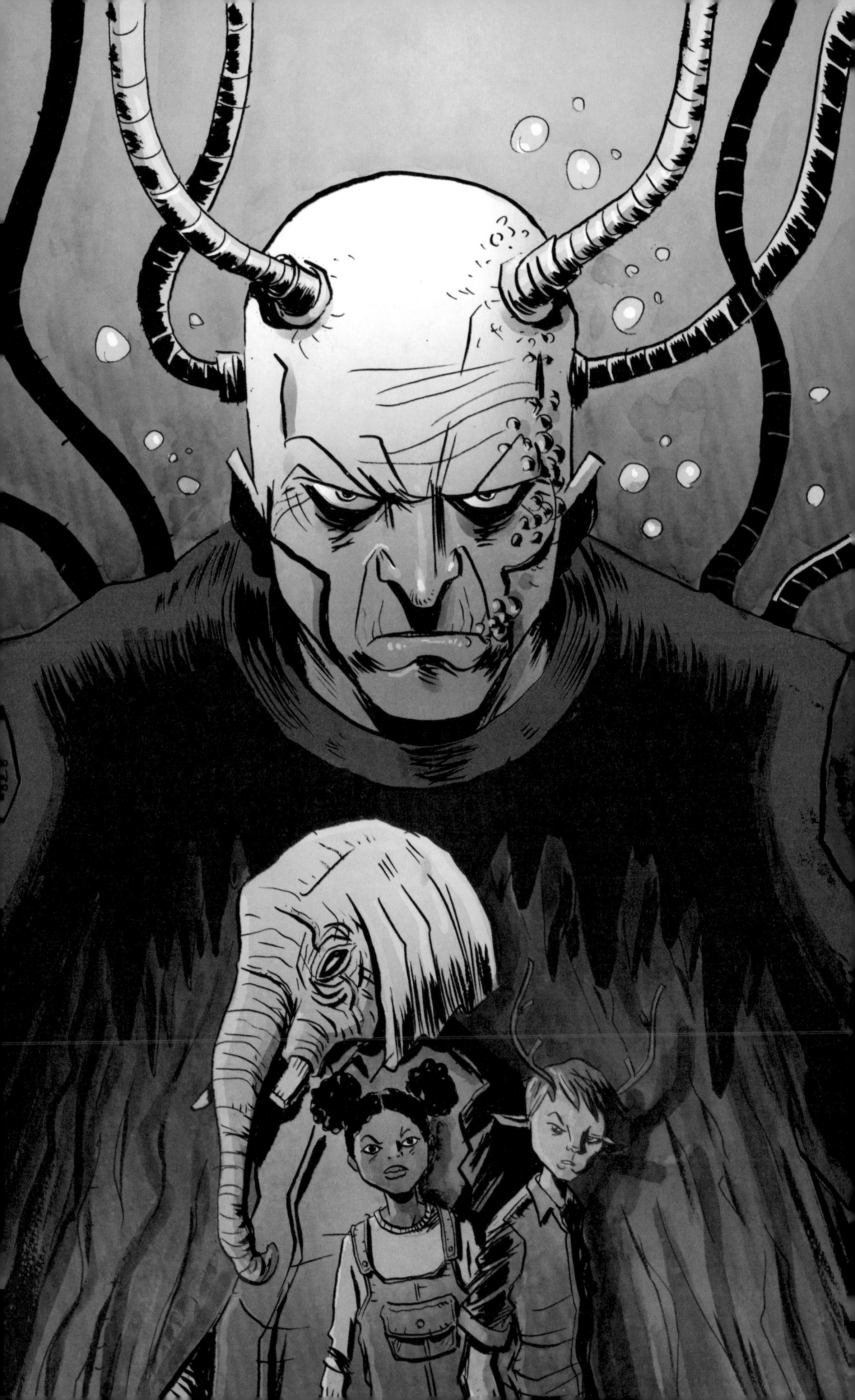

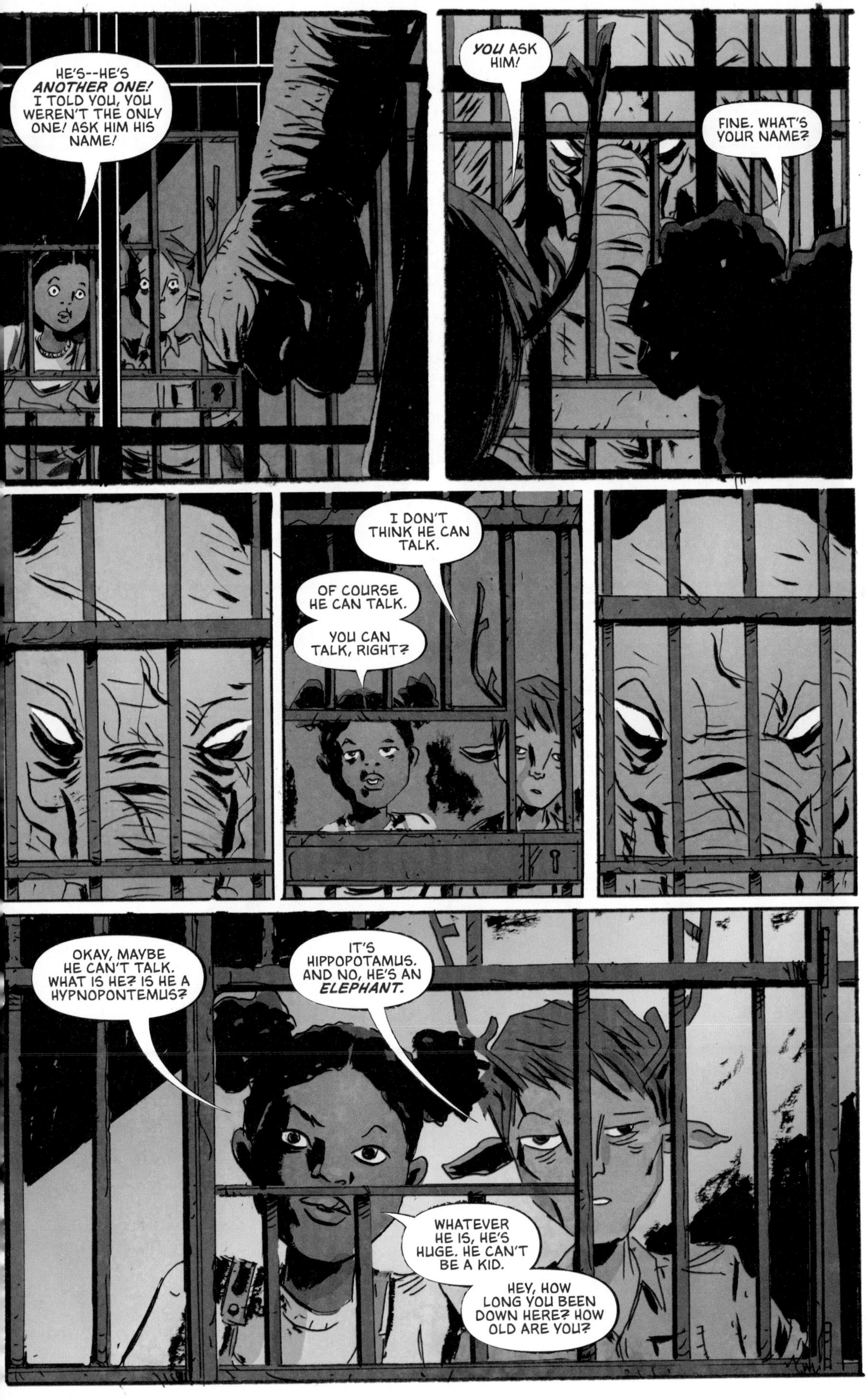
HE'S--HE'S ANOTHER ONE! I TOLD YOU, YOU WEREN'T THE ONLY ONE! ASK HIM HIS NAME!
YOU ASK HIM!
FINE. WHAT'S YOUR NAME?
I DON'T THINK HE CAN TALK.
OF COURSE HE CAN TALK.
YOU CAN TALK, RIGHT?
OKAY, MAYBE HE CAN'T TALK. WHAT IS HE? IS HE A HYPNOPONTEMUS?
IT'S HIPPOPOTAMUS. AND NO, HE'S AN ELEPHANT.
WHATEVER HE IS, HE'S HUGE. HE CAN'T BE A KID.
HEY, HOW LONG YOU BEEN DOWN HERE? HOW OLD ARE YOU?

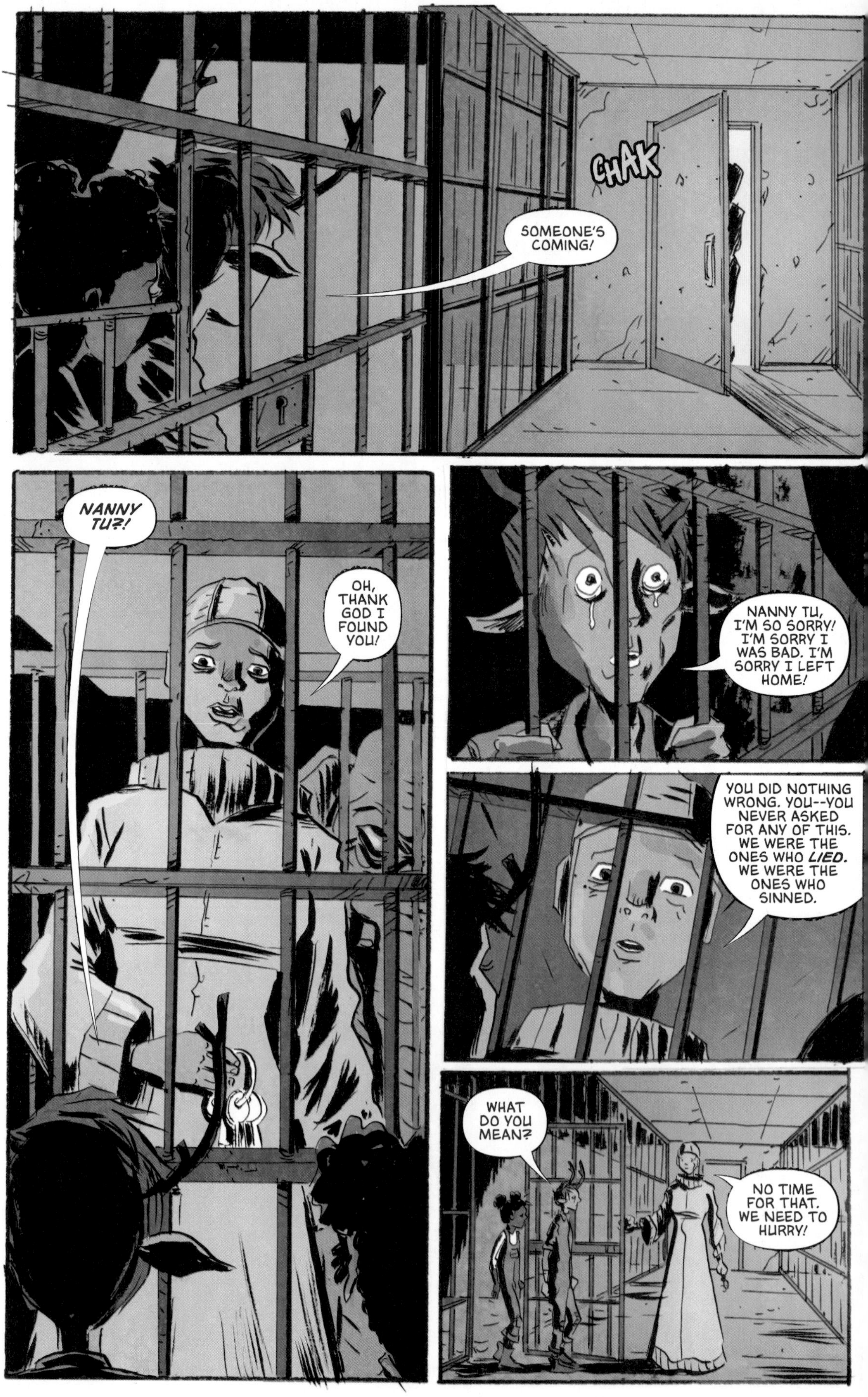
CHAK
SOMEONE'S COMING!
NANNY TU?!
OH, THANK GOD I FOUND YOU!
NANNY TU, I'M SO SORRY! I'M SORRY I WAS BAD. I'M SORRY I LEFT HOME!
YOU DID NOTHING WRONG. YOU--YOU NEVER ASKED FOR ANY OF THIS. WE WERE THE ONES WHO *LIED.* WE WERE THE ONES WHO SINNED.
WHAT DO YOU MEAN?
NO TIME FOR THAT. WE NEED TO HURRY!

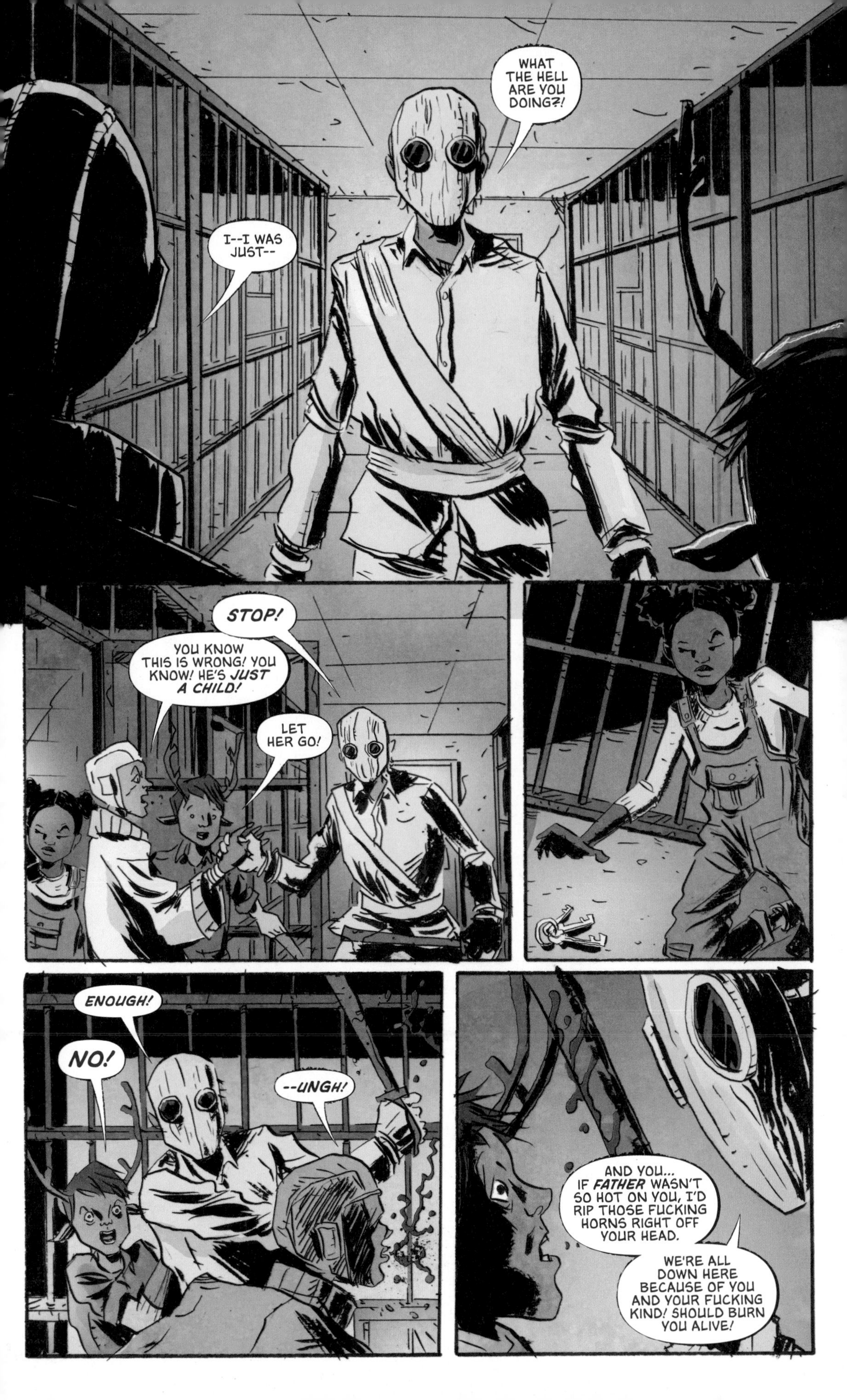
WHAT THE HELL ARE YOU DOING?!
I--I WAS JUST--
STOP!
YOU KNOW THIS IS WRONG! YOU KNOW! HE'S JUST A CHILD!
LET HER GO!
ENOUGH!
NO!
--UNGH!
AND YOU... IF FATHER WASN'T SO HOT ON YOU, I'D RIP THOSE FUCKING HORNS RIGHT OFF YOUR HEAD.
WE'RE ALL DOWN HERE BECAUSE OF YOU AND YOUR FUCKING KIND! SHOULD BURN YOU ALIVE!

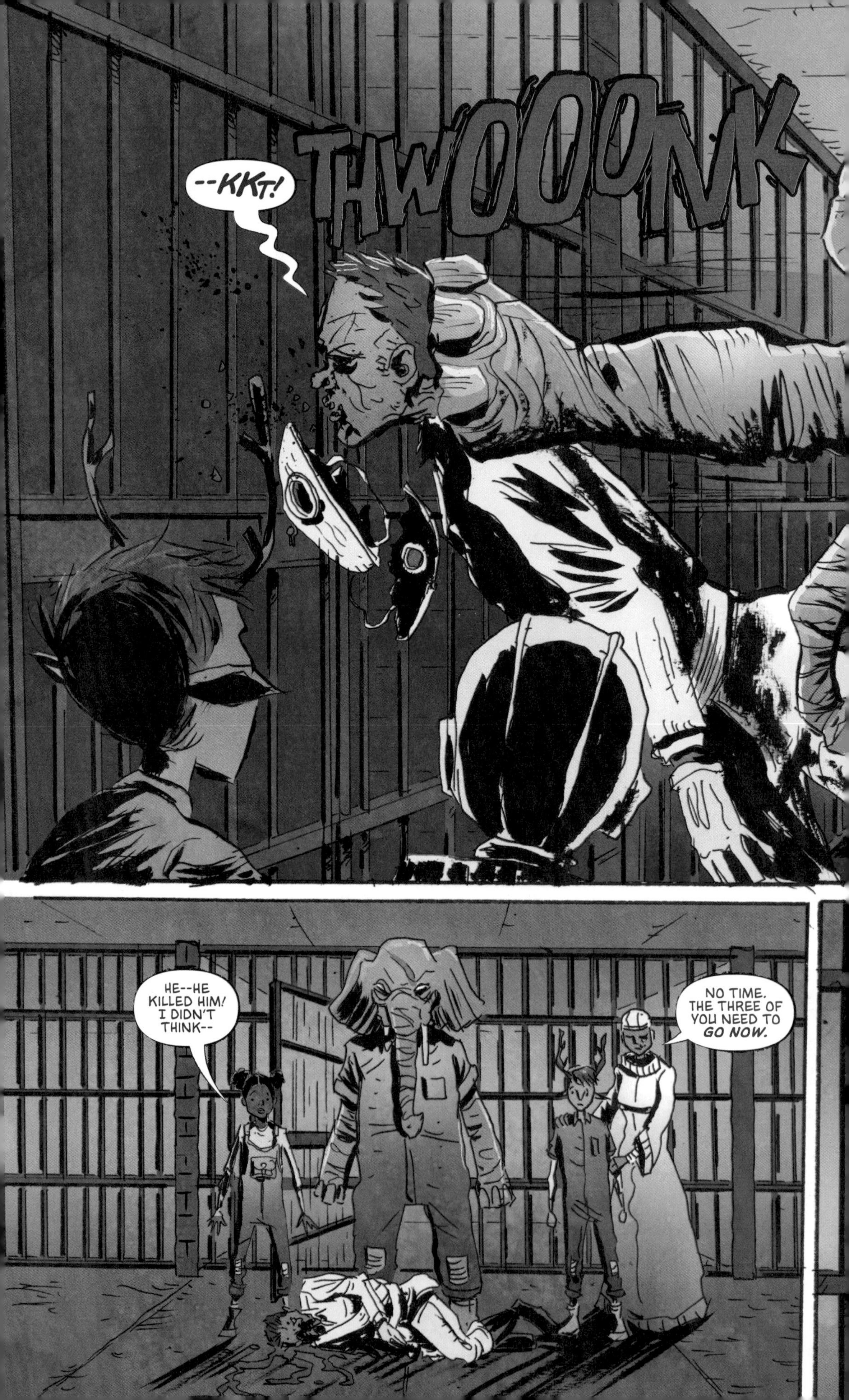
THWOOOONK
--KKT!
HE--HE KILLED HIM! I DIDN'T THINK--
NO TIME. THE THREE OF YOU NEED TO *GO NOW.*

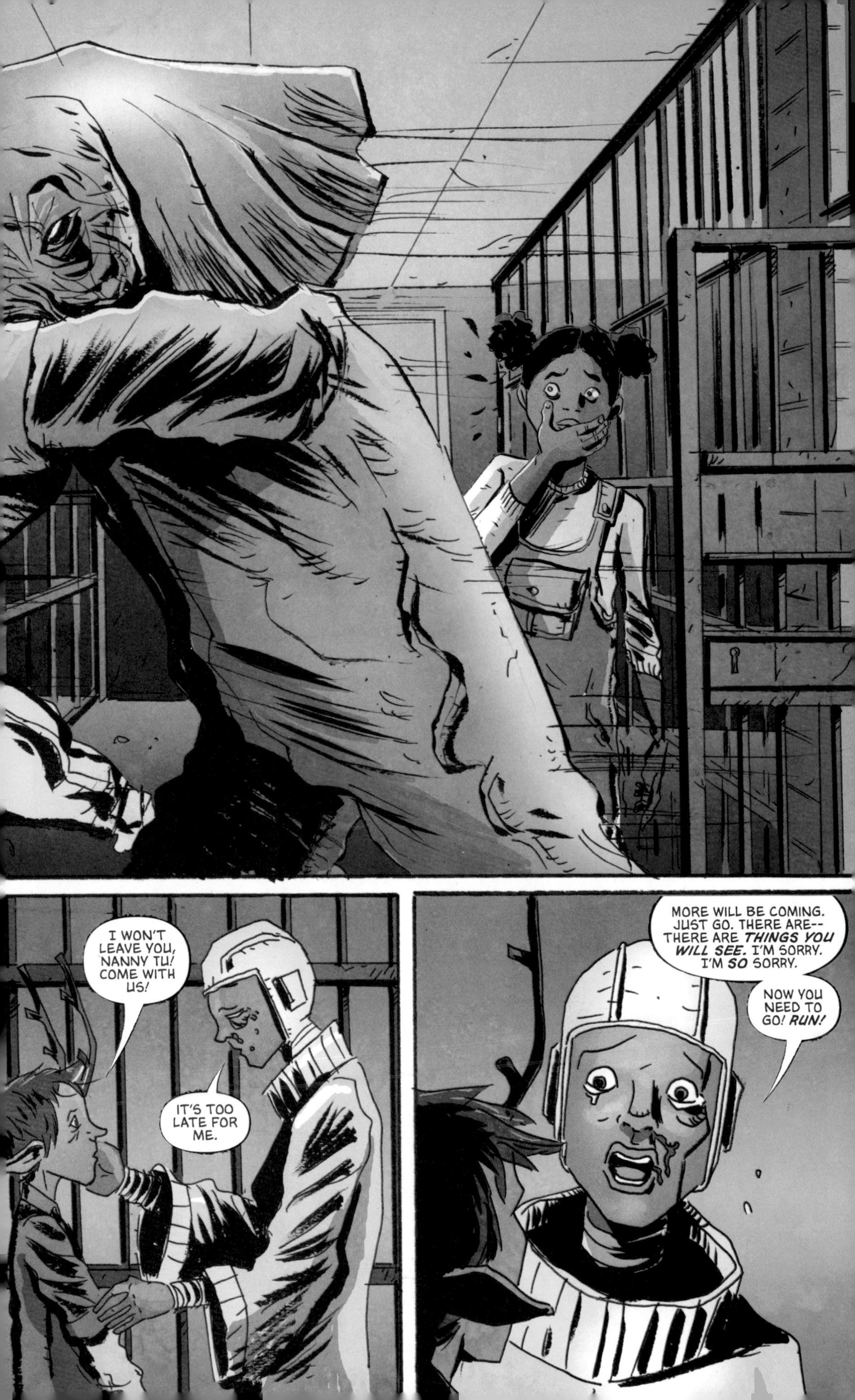
I WON'T LEAVE YOU, NANNY TU! COME WITH US!
IT'S TOO LATE FOR ME.
MORE WILL BE COMING. JUST GO. THERE ARE-- THERE ARE *THINGS YOU WILL SEE.* I'M SORRY. I'M *SO* SORRY.
NOW YOU NEED TO GO! *RUN!*

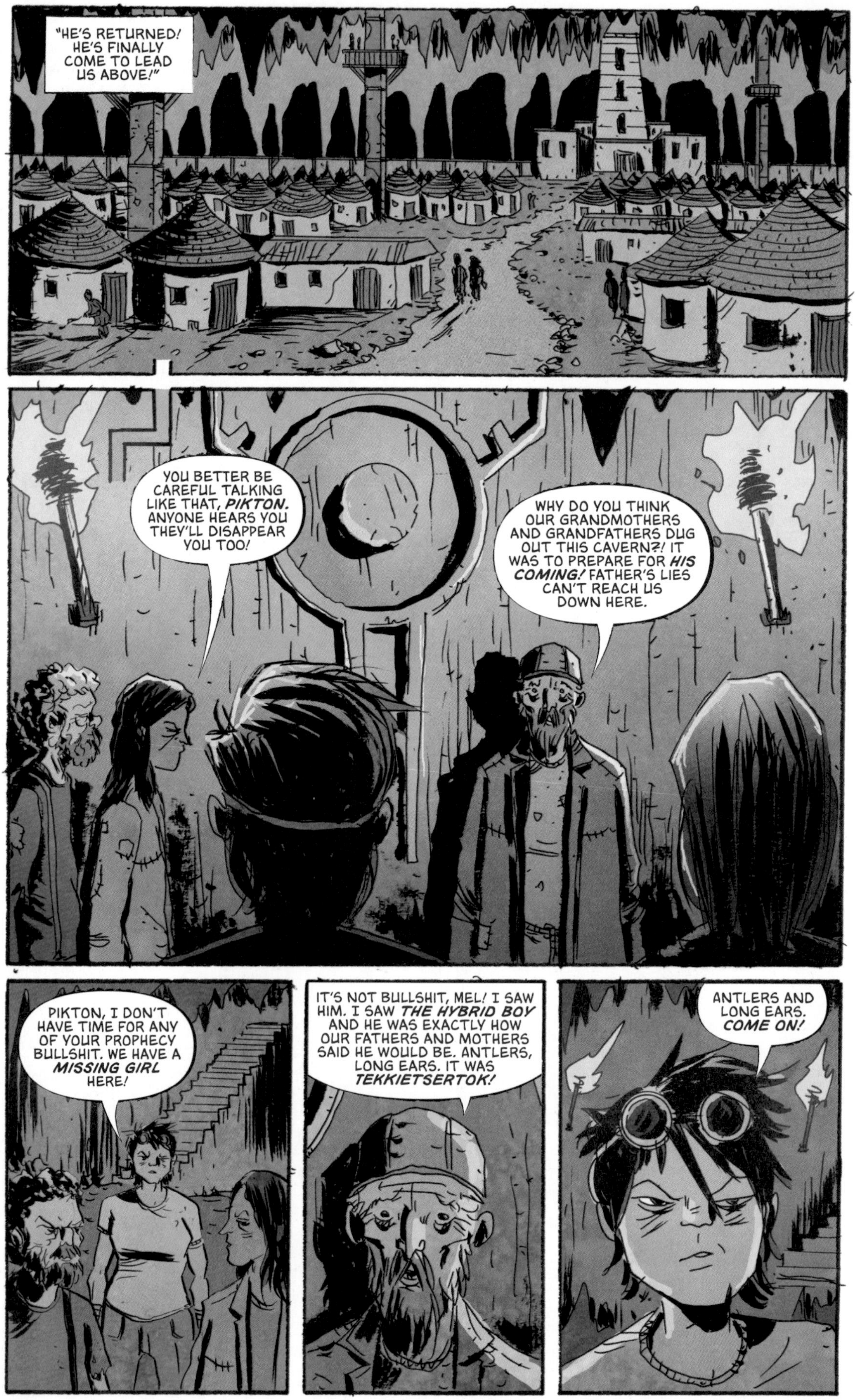
"HE'S RETURNED! HE'S FINALLY COME TO LEAD US ABOVE!"
YOU BETTER BE CAREFUL TALKING LIKE THAT, PIKTON. ANYONE HEARS YOU THEY'LL DISAPPEAR YOU TOO!
WHY DO YOU THINK OUR GRANDMOTHERS AND GRANDFATHERS DUG OUT THIS CAVERN?! IT WAS TO PREPARE FOR HIS COMING! FATHER'S LIES CAN'T REACH US DOWN HERE.
PIKTON, I DON'T HAVE TIME FOR ANY OF YOUR PROPHECY BULLSHIT. WE HAVE A MISSING GIRL HERE!
IT'S NOT BULLSHIT, MEL! I SAW HIM. I SAW THE HYBRID BOY AND HE WAS EXACTLY HOW OUR FATHERS AND MOTHERS SAID HE WOULD BE. ANTLERS, LONG EARS. IT WAS TEKKIETSERTOK!
ANTLERS AND LONG EARS. COME ON!

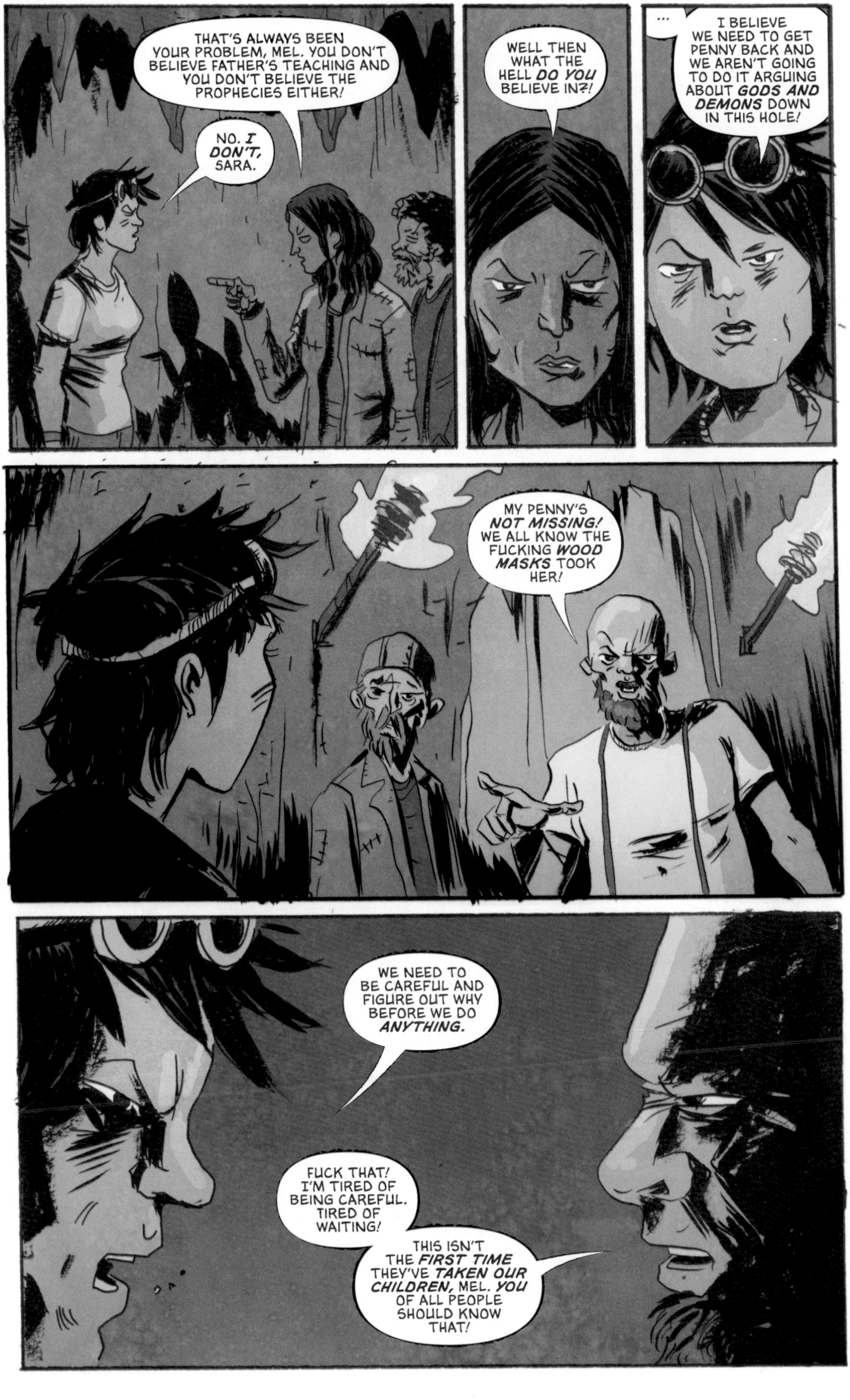
THAT'S ALWAYS BEEN YOUR PROBLEM, MEL. YOU DON'T BELIEVE FATHER'S TEACHING AND YOU DON'T BELIEVE THE PROPHECIES EITHER!
NO. I DON'T, SARA.
WELL THEN WHAT THE HELL DO YOU BELIEVE IN?!
...
I BELIEVE WE NEED TO GET PENNY BACK AND WE AREN'T GOING TO DO IT ARGUING ABOUT GODS AND DEMONS DOWN IN THIS HOLE!
MY PENNY'S NOT MISSING! WE ALL KNOW THE FUCKING WOOD MASKS TOOK HER!
WE NEED TO BE CAREFUL AND FIGURE OUT WHY BEFORE WE DO ANYTHING.
FUCK THAT! I'M TIRED OF BEING CAREFUL. TIRED OF WAITING!
THIS ISN'T THE FIRST TIME THEY'VE TAKEN OUR CHILDREN, MEL. YOU OF ALL PEOPLE SHOULD KNOW THAT!

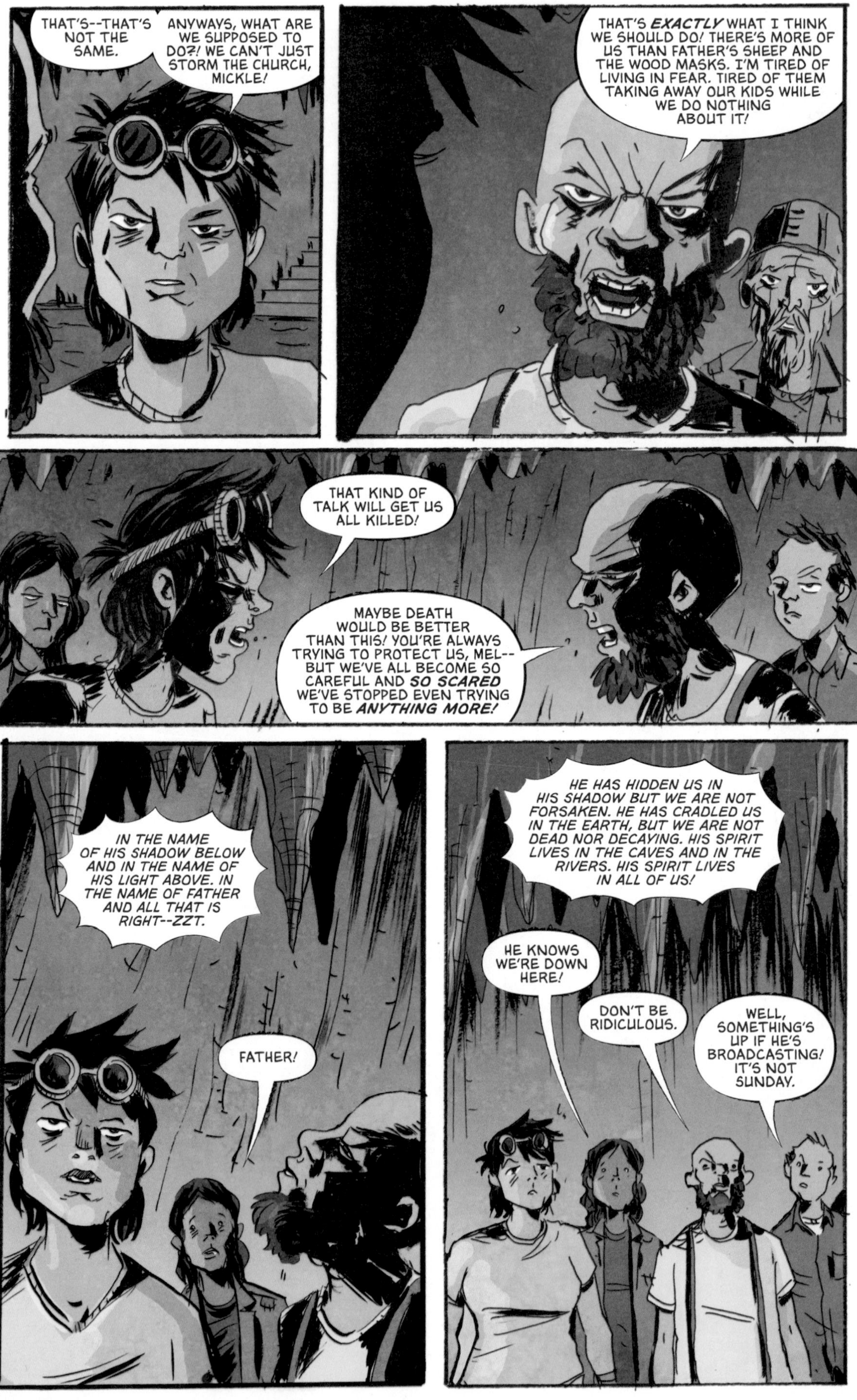
THAT'S--THAT'S NOT THE SAME.
ANYWAYS, WHAT ARE WE SUPPOSED TO DO?! WE CAN'T JUST STORM THE CHURCH, MICKLE!
THAT'S EXACTLY WHAT I THINK WE SHOULD DO! THERE'S MORE OF US THAN FATHER'S SHEEP AND THE WOOD MASKS. I'M TIRED OF LIVING IN FEAR. TIRED OF THEM TAKING AWAY OUR KIDS WHILE WE DO NOTHING ABOUT IT!
THAT KIND OF TALK WILL GET US ALL KILLED!
MAYBE DEATH WOULD BE BETTER THAN THIS! YOU'RE ALWAYS TRYING TO PROTECT US, MEL-- BUT WE'VE ALL BECOME SO CAREFUL AND SO SCARED WE'VE STOPPED EVEN TRYING TO BE ANYTHING MORE!
IN THE NAME OF HIS SHADOW BELOW AND IN THE NAME OF HIS LIGHT ABOVE. IN THE NAME OF FATHER AND ALL THAT IS RIGHT--ZZT.
FATHER!
HE HAS HIDDEN US IN HIS SHADOW BUT WE ARE NOT FORSAKEN. HE HAS CRADLED US IN THE EARTH, BUT WE ARE NOT DEAD NOR DECAYING. HIS SPIRIT LIVES IN THE CAVES AND IN THE RIVERS. HIS SPIRIT LIVES IN ALL OF US!
HE KNOWS WE'RE DOWN HERE!
DON'T BE RIDICULOUS.
WELL, SOMETHING'S UP IF HE'S BROADCASTING! IT'S NOT SUNDAY.

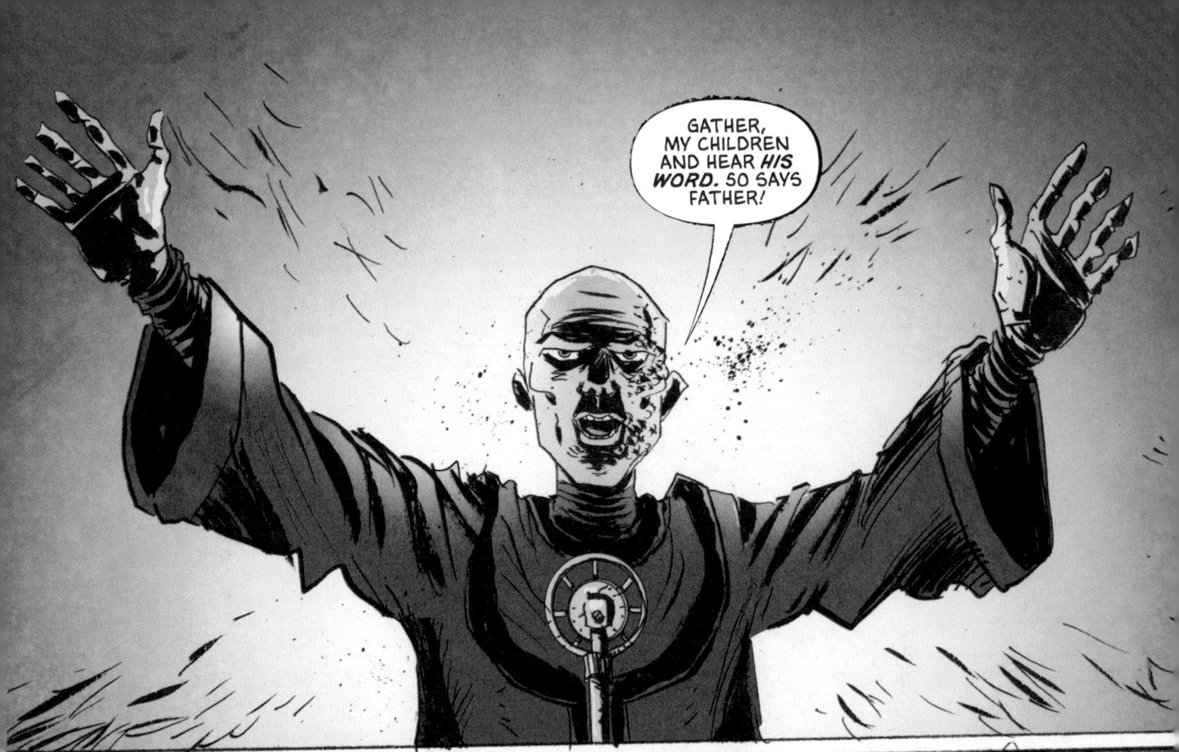
GATHER, MY CHILDREN AND HEAR HIS WORD. SO SAYS FATHER!

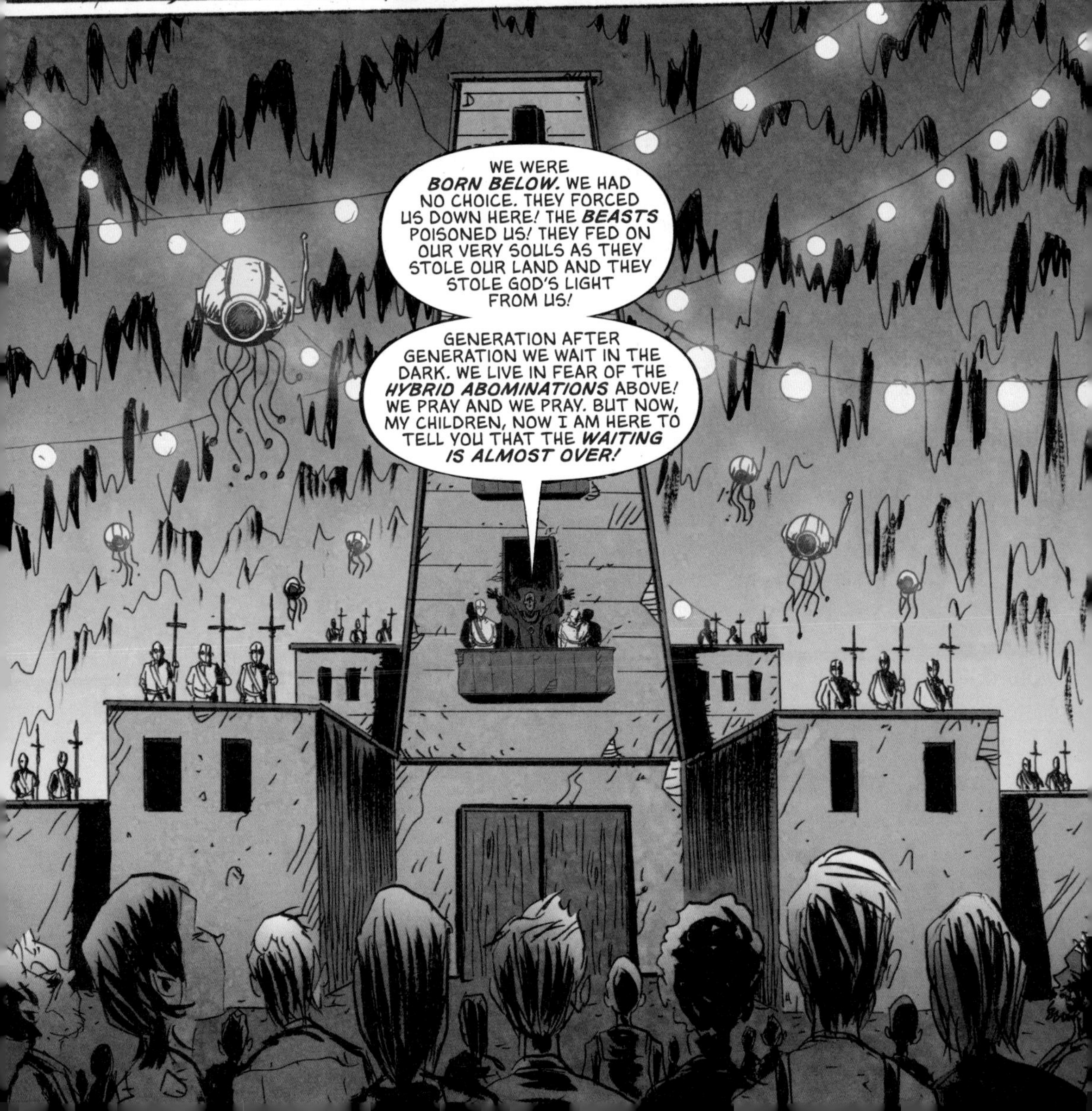
WE WERE BORN BELOW. WE HAD NO CHOICE. THEY FORCED US DOWN HERE! THE BEASTS POISONED US! THEY FED ON OUR VERY SOULS AS THEY STOLE OUR LAND AND THEY STOLE GOD'S LIGHT FROM US!
GENERATION AFTER GENERATION WE WAIT IN THE DARK. WE LIVE IN FEAR OF THE HYBRID ABOMINATIONS ABOVE! WE PRAY AND WE PRAY. BUT NOW, MY CHILDREN, NOW I AM HERE TO TELL YOU THAT THE WAITING IS ALMOST OVER!

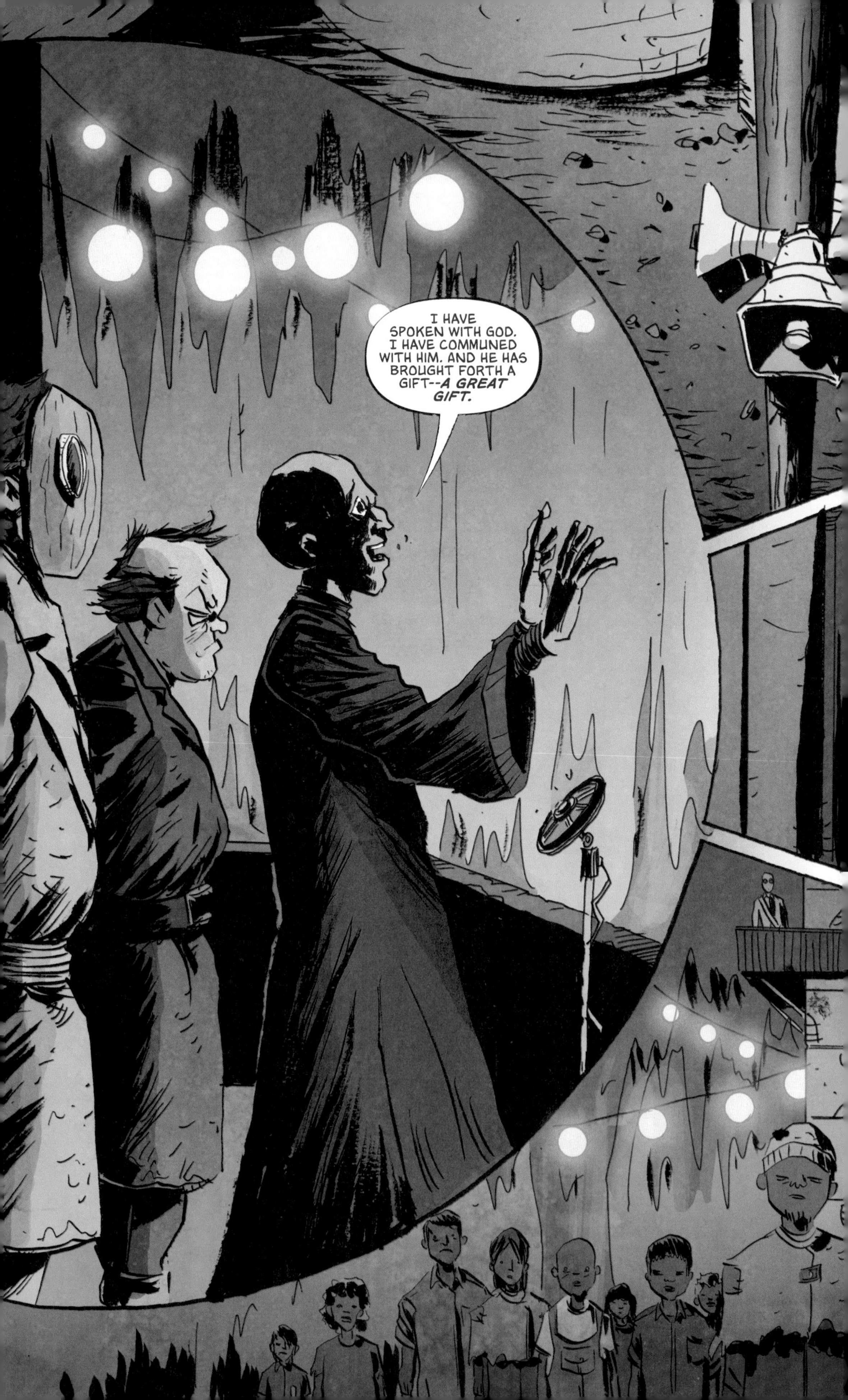
I HAVE SPOKEN WITH GOD. I HAVE COMMUNED WITH HIM. AND HE HAS BROUGHT FORTH A GIFT--*A GREAT GIFT.*

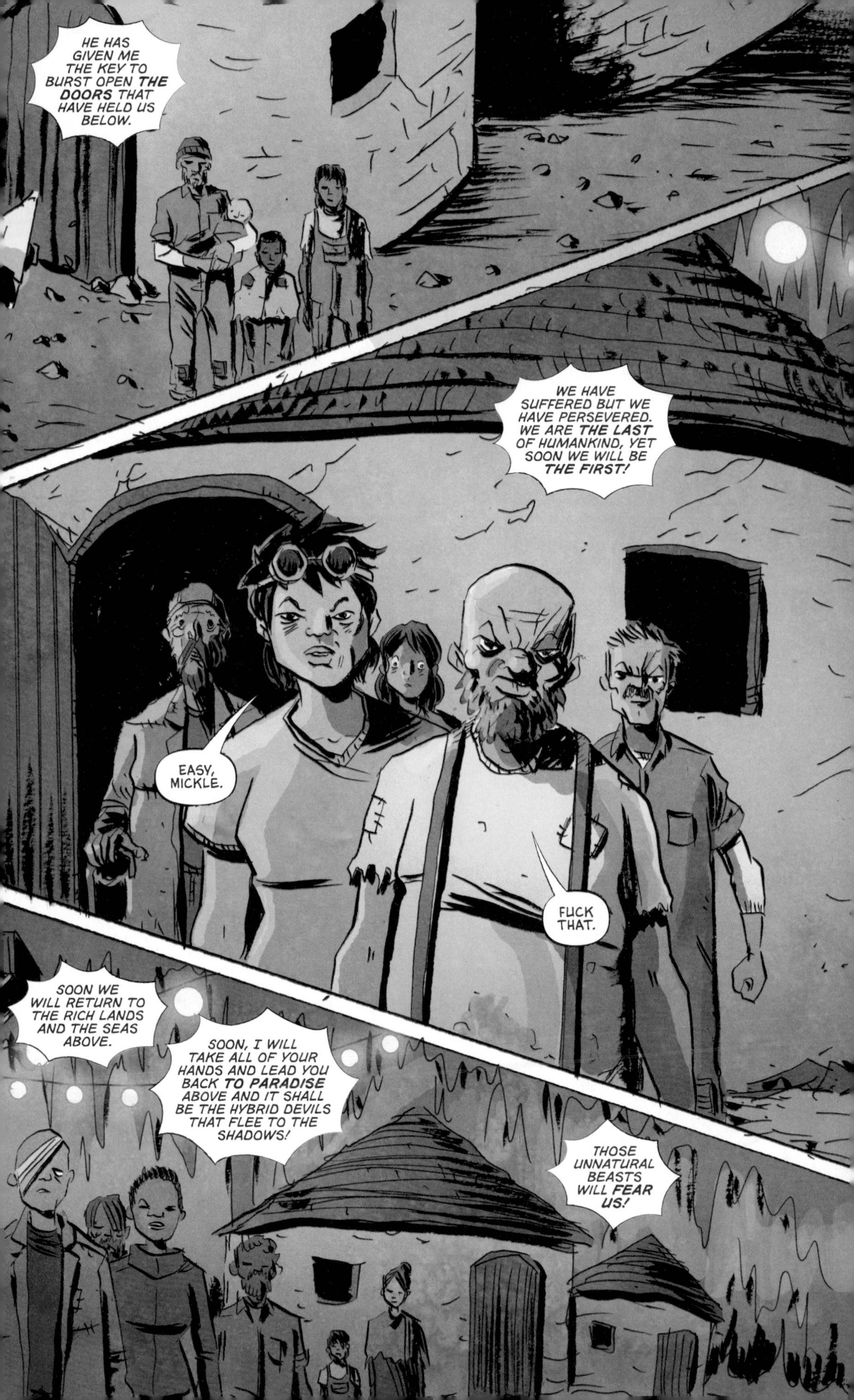
HE HAS GIVEN ME THE KEY TO BURST OPEN THE DOORS THAT HAVE HELD US BELOW.
WE HAVE SUFFERED BUT WE HAVE PERSEVERED. WE ARE THE LAST OF HUMANKIND, YET SOON WE WILL BE THE FIRST!
EASY, MICKLE.
FUCK THAT.
SOON WE WILL RETURN TO THE RICH LANDS AND THE SEAS ABOVE.
SOON, I WILL TAKE ALL OF YOUR HANDS AND LEAD YOU BACK TO PARADISE ABOVE AND IT SHALL BE THE HYBRID DEVILS THAT FLEE TO THE SHADOWS!
THOSE UNNATURAL BEASTS WILL FEAR US!

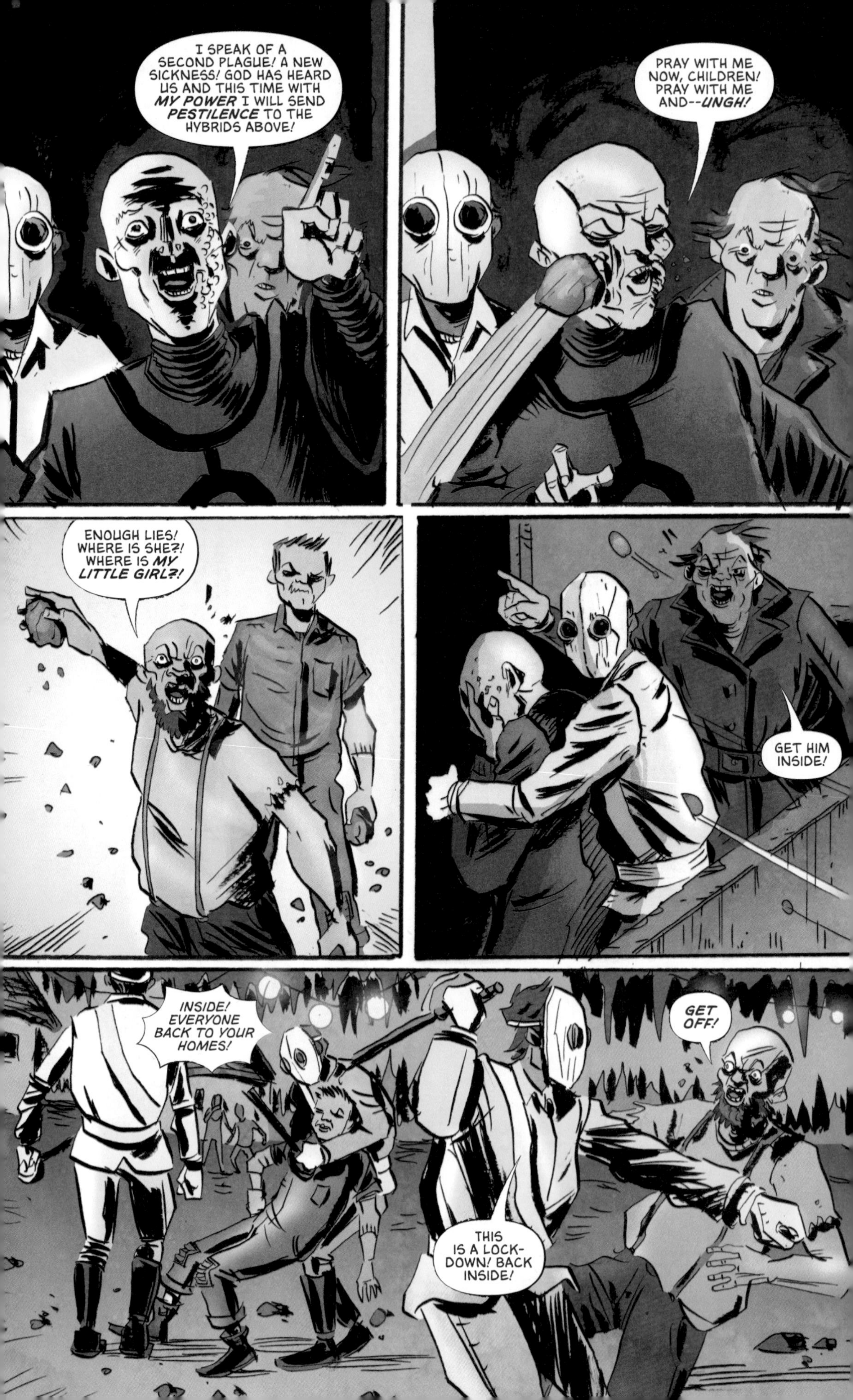
I SPEAK OF A SECOND PLAGUE! A NEW SICKNESS! GOD HAS HEARD US AND THIS TIME WITH *MY POWER* I WILL SEND *PESTILENCE* TO THE HYBRIDS ABOVE!
PRAY WITH ME NOW, CHILDREN! PRAY WITH ME AND--*UNGH!*
ENOUGH LIES! WHERE IS SHE?! WHERE IS *MY LITTLE GIRL?!*
GET HIM INSIDE!
INSIDE! EVERYONE BACK TO YOUR HOMES!
GET OFF!
THIS IS A LOCK-DOWN! BACK INSIDE!

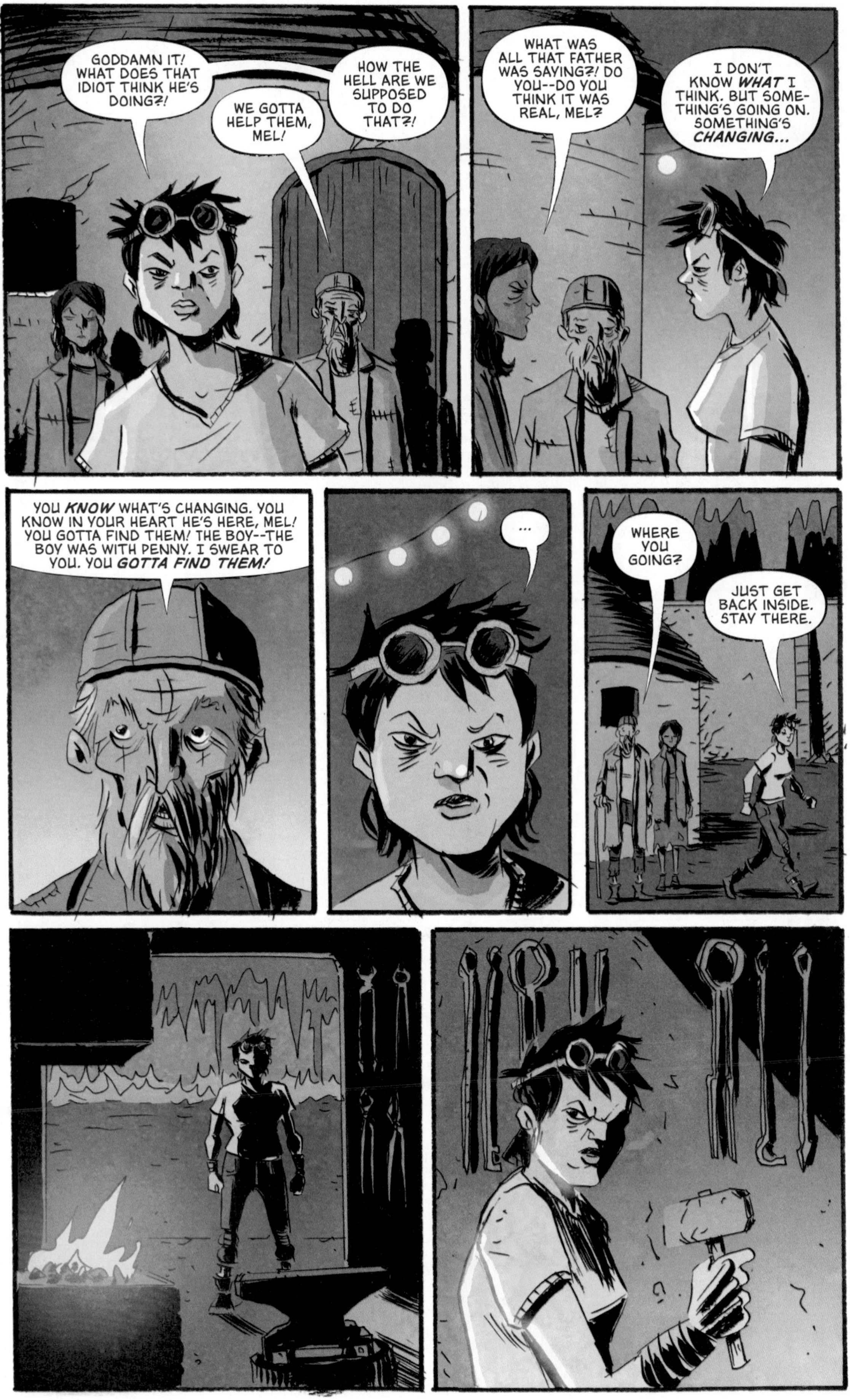
GODDAMN IT! WHAT DOES THAT IDIOT THINK HE'S DOING?!
HOW THE HELL ARE WE SUPPOSED TO DO THAT?!
WE GOTTA HELP THEM, MEL!
WHAT WAS ALL THAT FATHER WAS SAYING?! DO YOU--DO YOU THINK IT WAS REAL, MEL?
I DON'T KNOW WHAT I THINK. BUT SOMETHING'S GOING ON. SOMETHING'S CHANGING...
YOU KNOW WHAT'S CHANGING. YOU KNOW IN YOUR HEART HE'S HERE, MEL! YOU GOTTA FIND THEM! THE BOY--THE BOY WAS WITH PENNY. I SWEAR TO YOU. YOU GOTTA FIND THEM!
...
WHERE YOU GOING?
JUST GET BACK INSIDE. STAY THERE.

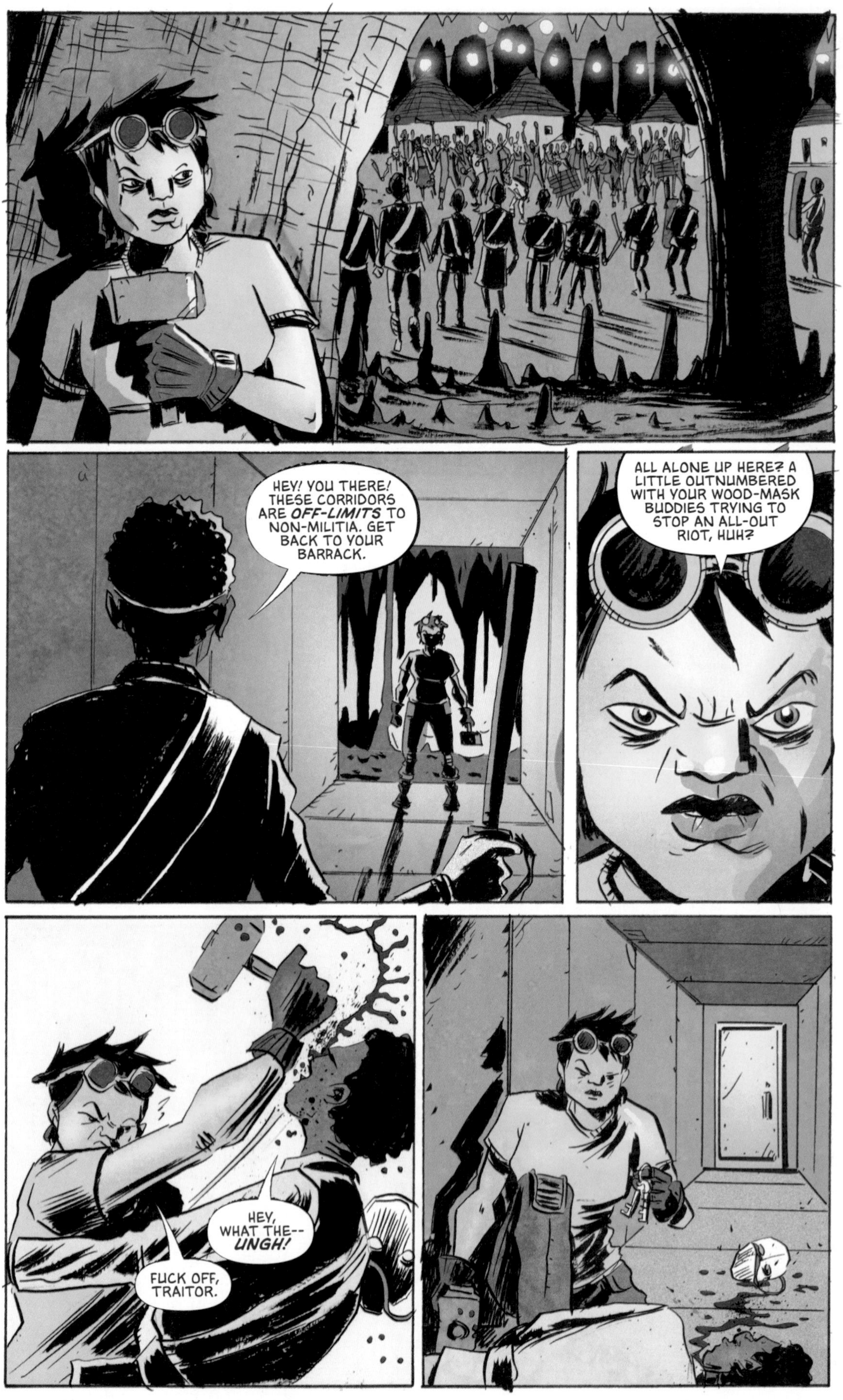
HEY! YOU THERE! THESE CORRIDORS ARE *OFF-LIMITS* TO NON-MILITIA. GET BACK TO YOUR BARRACK.
ALL ALONE UP HERE? A LITTLE OUTNUMBERED WITH YOUR WOOD-MASK BUDDIES TRYING TO STOP AN ALL-OUT RIOT, HUH?
HEY, WHAT THE-- *UNGH!*
FUCK OFF, TRAITOR.

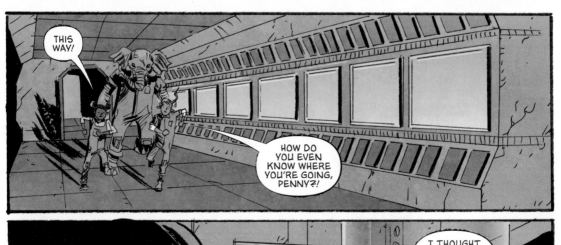

THIS WAY!

HOW DO YOU EVEN KNOW WHERE YOU'RE GOING, PENNY?!

I THOUGHT THIS WAS THE WAY THEY BROUGHT US IN?

WHAT IS ALL OF THIS?

NEVER SEEN NOTHING LIKE THIS.

WHAT IS IT? WHAT'S WRONG?

I DON'T-- I DON'T KNOW. I JUST. I'M SACRED. I JUST *WANT TO GO HOME.*

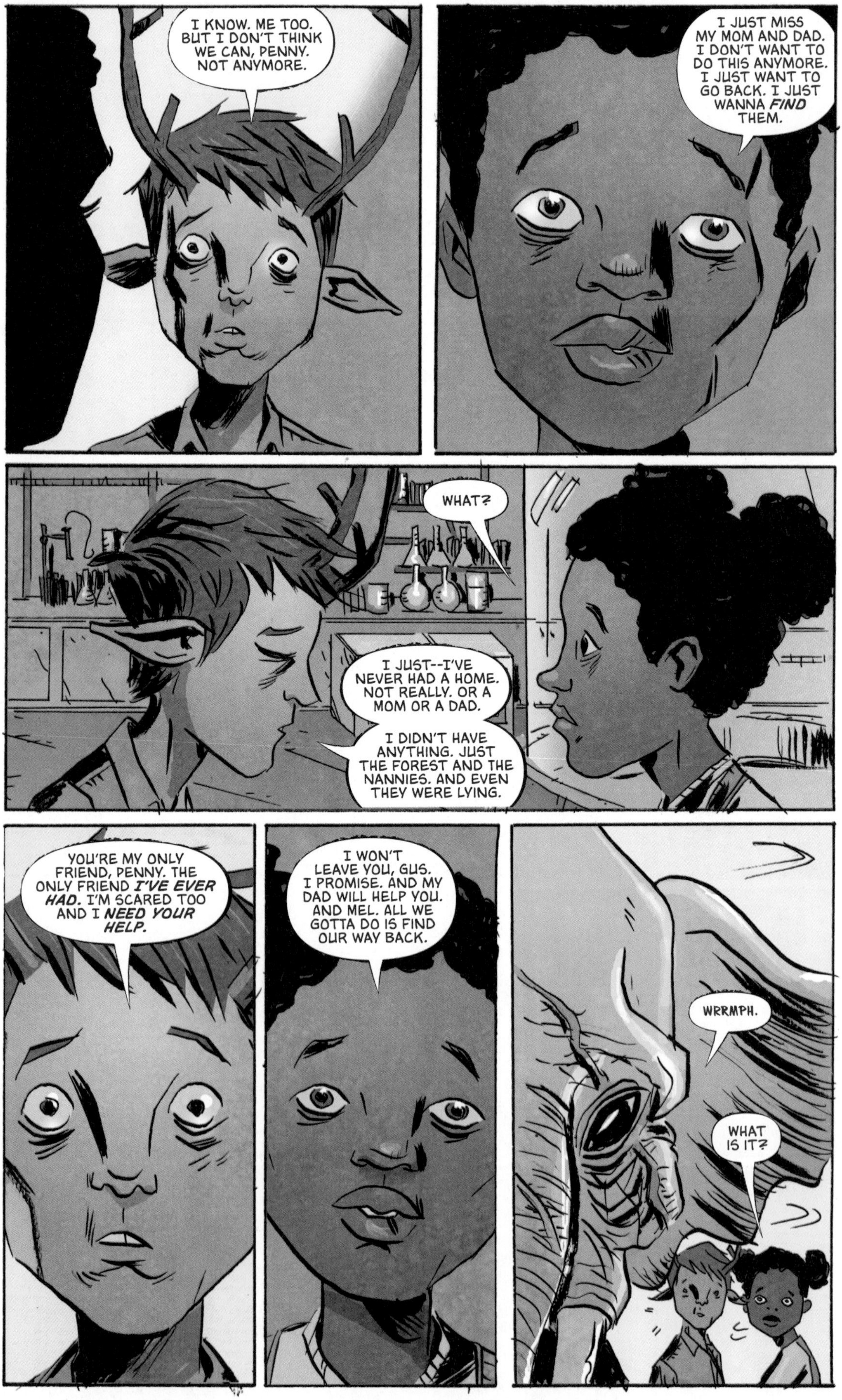
I KNOW. ME TOO. BUT I DON'T THINK WE CAN, PENNY. NOT ANYMORE.
I JUST MISS MY MOM AND DAD. I DON'T WANT TO DO THIS ANYMORE. I JUST WANT TO GO BACK. I JUST WANNA *FIND* THEM.
WHAT?
I JUST--I'VE NEVER HAD A HOME. NOT REALLY. OR A MOM OR A DAD.
I DIDN'T HAVE ANYTHING. JUST THE FOREST AND THE NANNIES. AND EVEN THEY WERE LYING.
YOU'RE MY ONLY FRIEND, PENNY. THE ONLY FRIEND ***I'VE EVER HAD.*** I'M SCARED TOO AND I ***NEED YOUR HELP.***
I WON'T LEAVE YOU, GUS. I PROMISE. AND MY DAD WILL HELP YOU. AND MEL. ALL WE GOTTA DO IS FIND OUR WAY BACK.
WRRMPH.
WHAT IS IT?

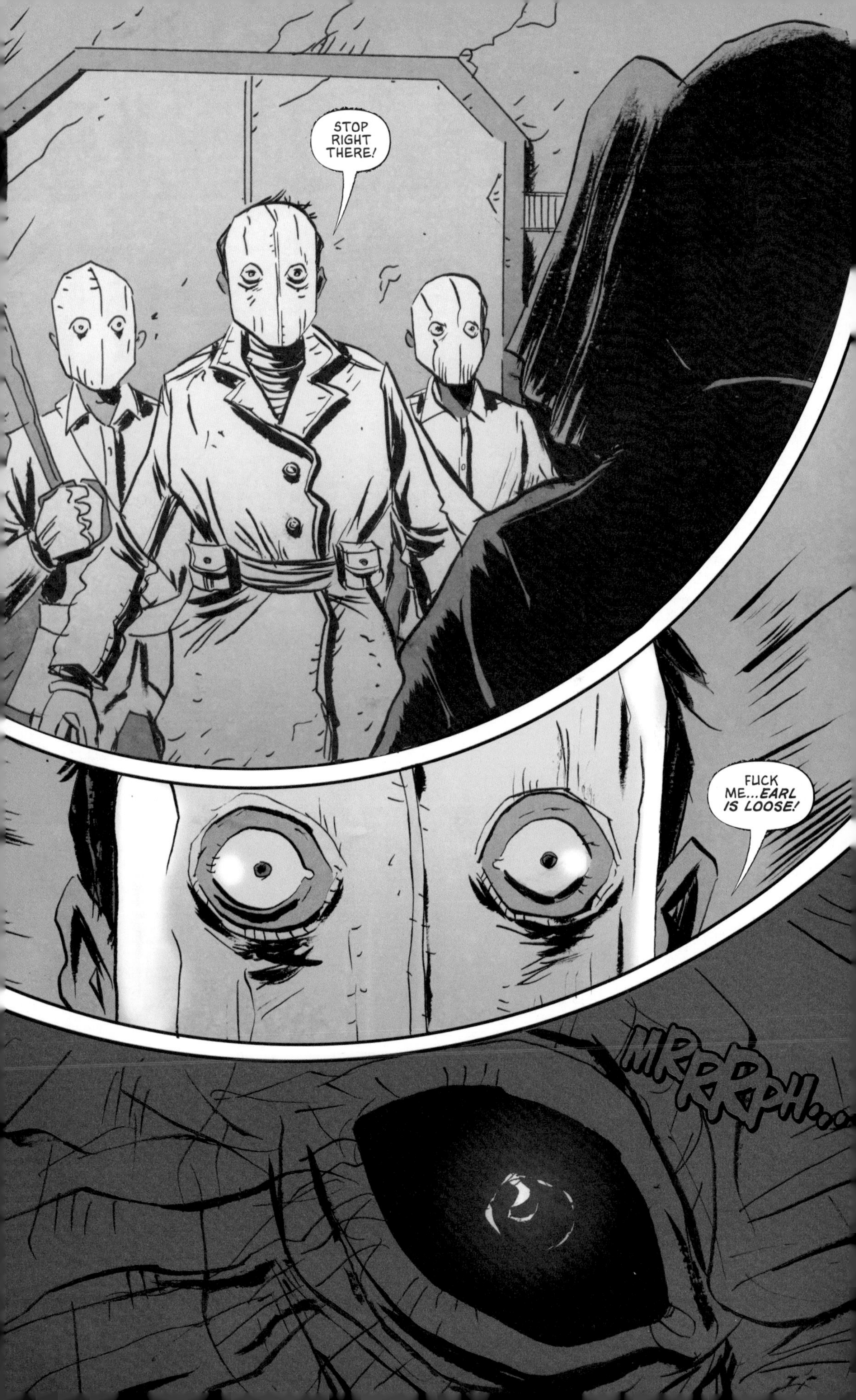
STOP RIGHT THERE!
FUCK ME...EARL IS LOOSE!
MRRRRPH...

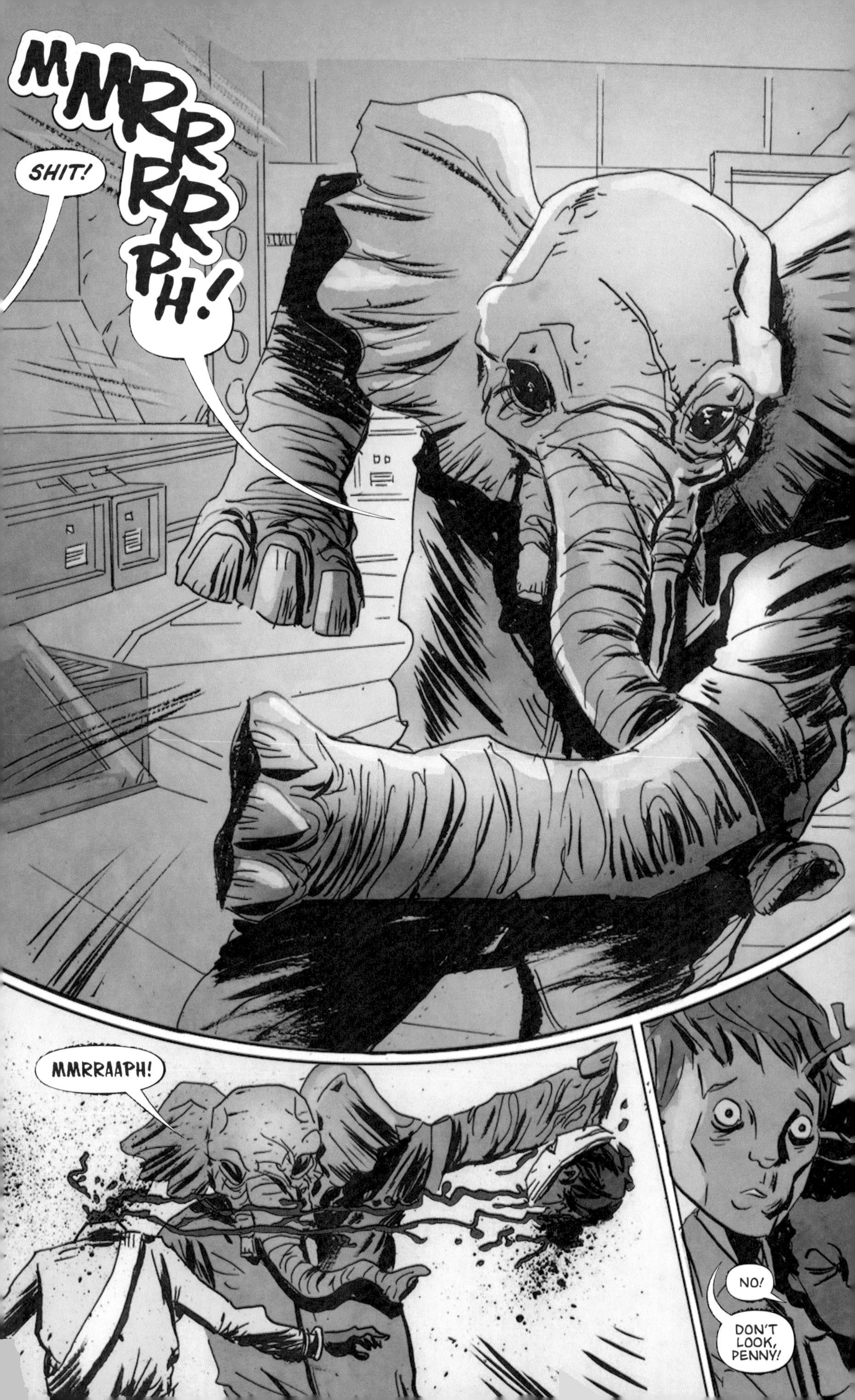
MMRRRRPH!
SHIT!
MMRRAAPH!
NO!
DON'T LOOK, PENNY!

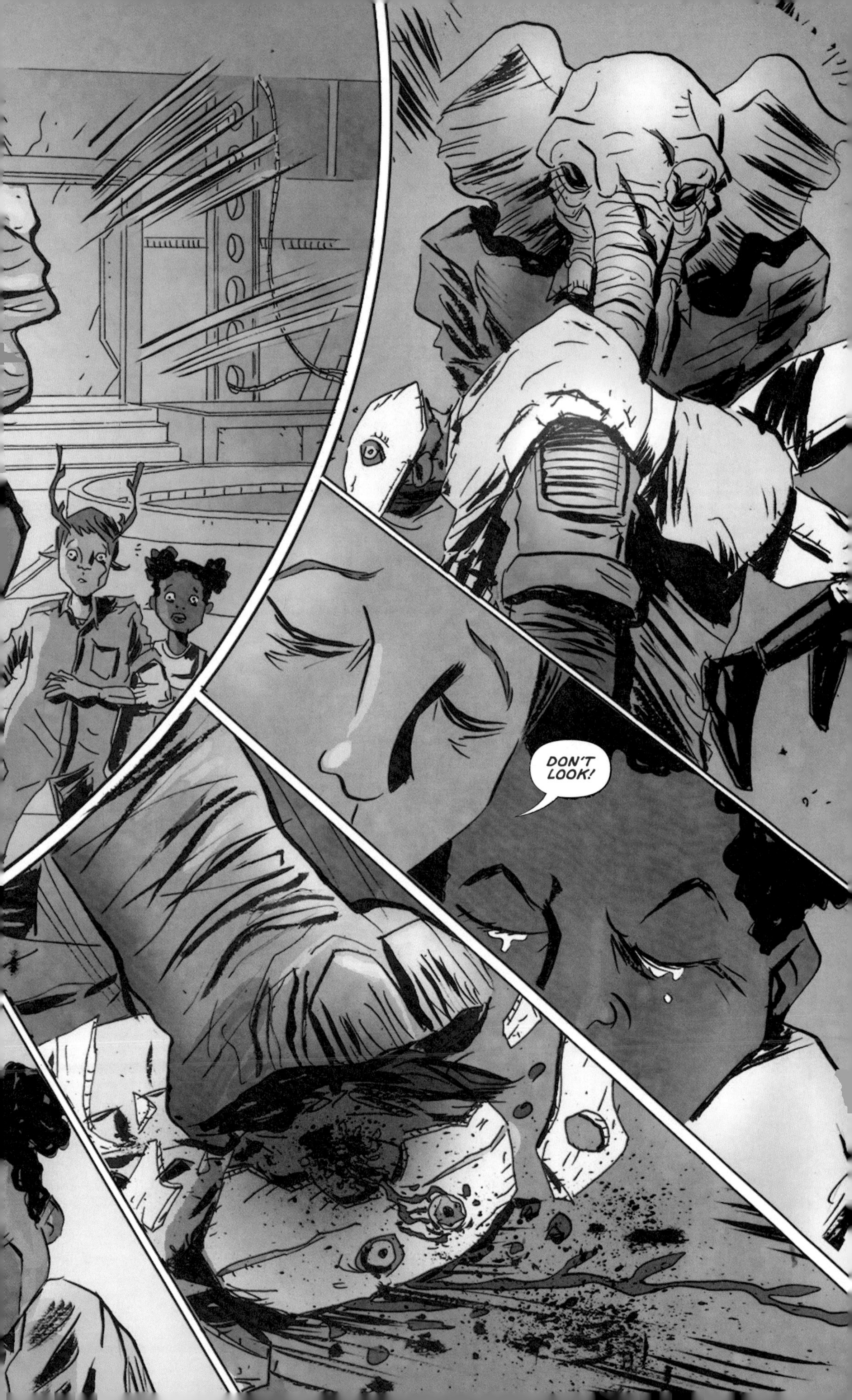
DON'T LOOK!

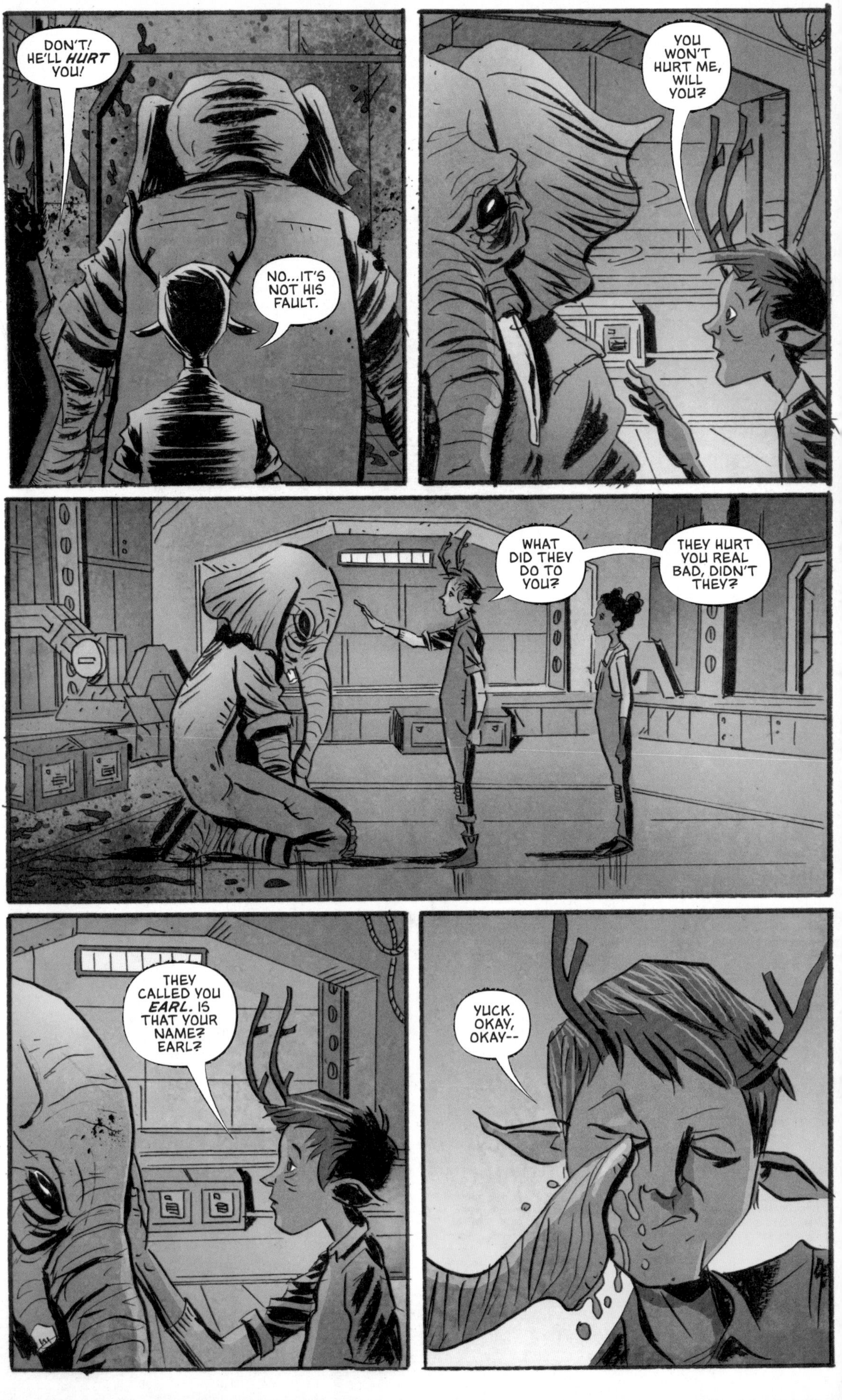
DON'T! HE'LL HURT YOU!
NO...IT'S NOT HIS FAULT.
YOU WON'T HURT ME, WILL YOU?
WHAT DID THEY DO TO YOU?
THEY HURT YOU REAL BAD, DIDN'T THEY?
THEY CALLED YOU EARL. IS THAT YOUR NAME? EARL?
YUCK. OKAY, OKAY--

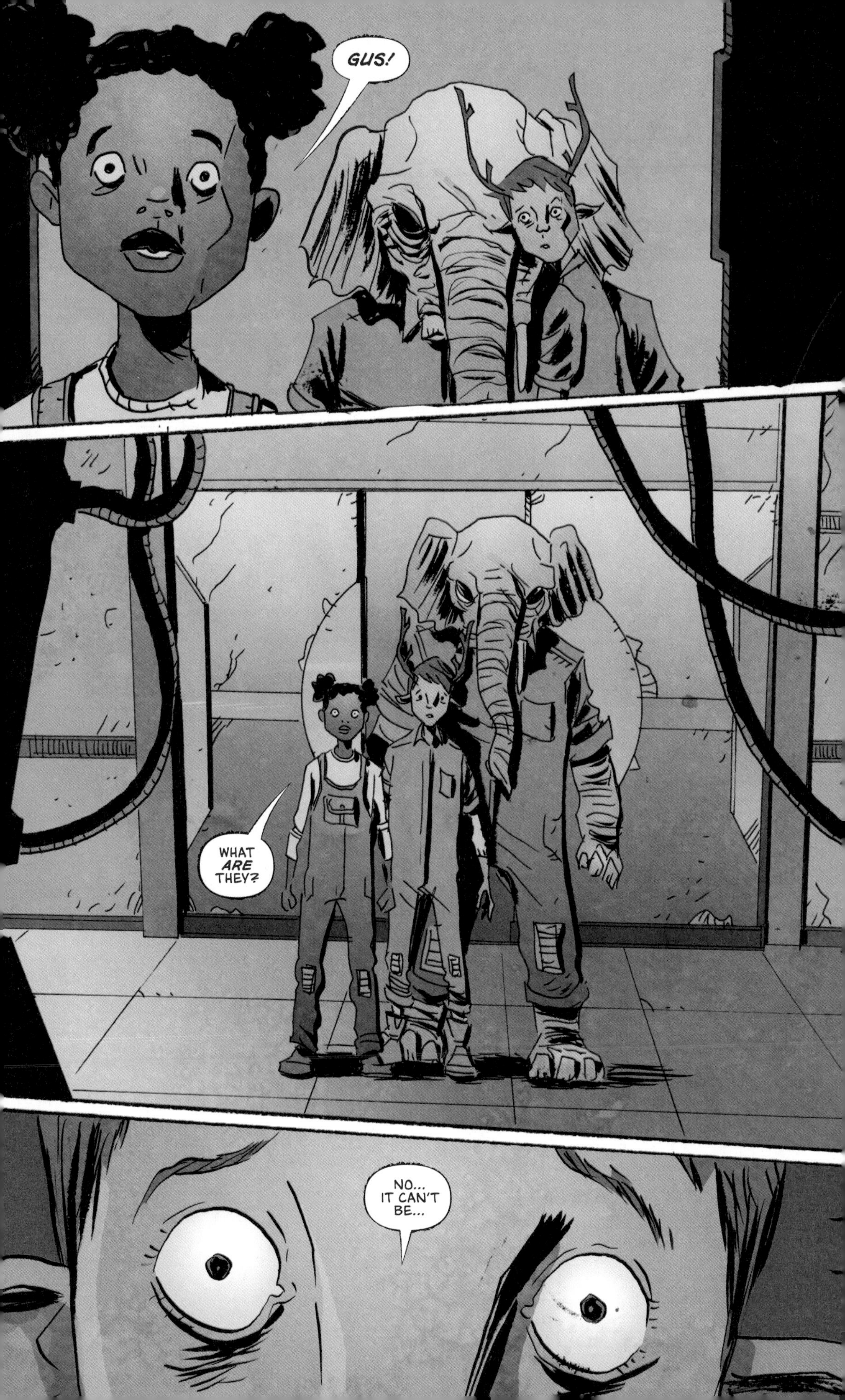
GUS!
WHAT ARE THEY?
NO... IT CAN'T BE...

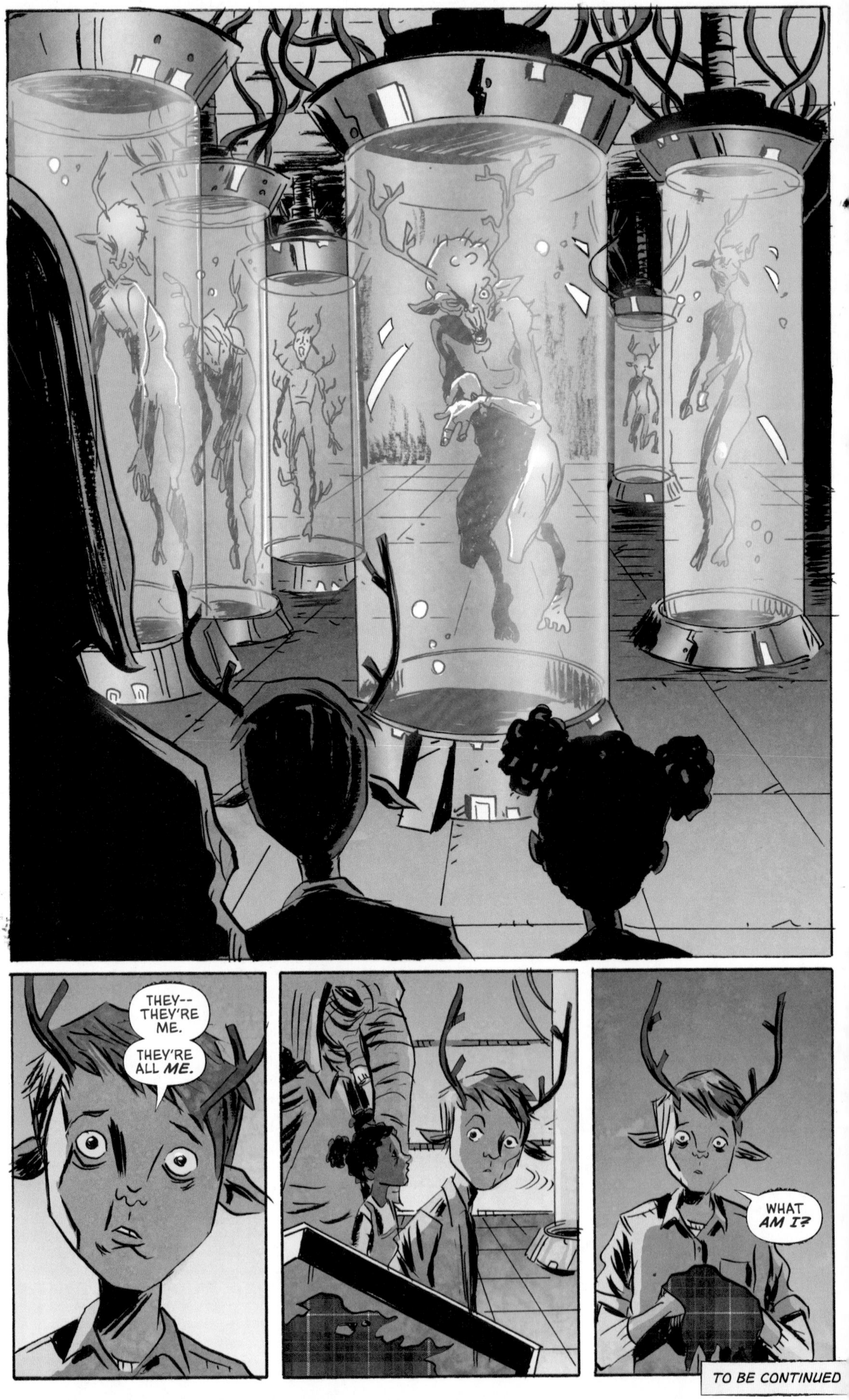
THEY-- THEY'RE ME.
THEY'RE ALL *ME.*
WHAT *AM I?*
TO BE CONTINUED

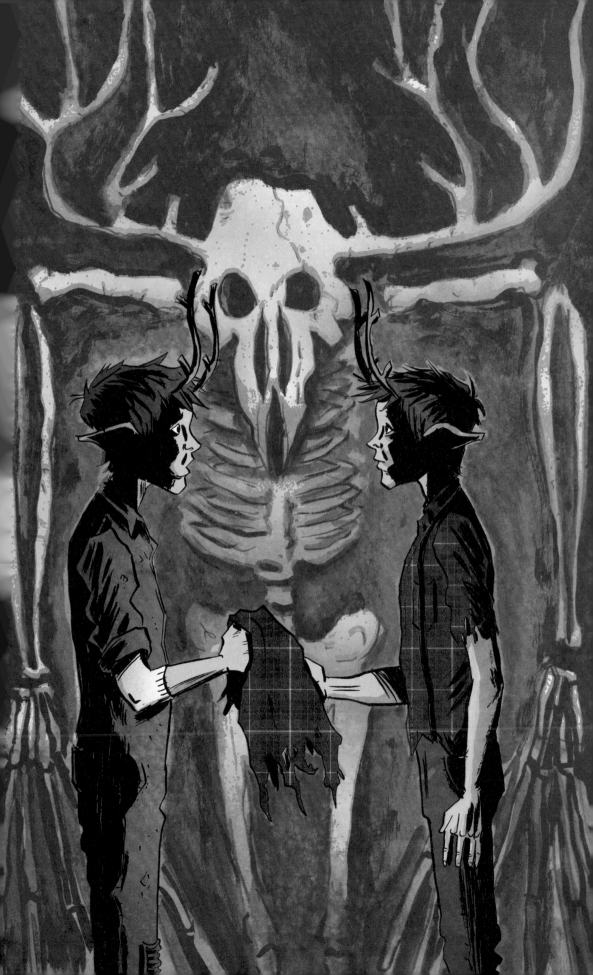

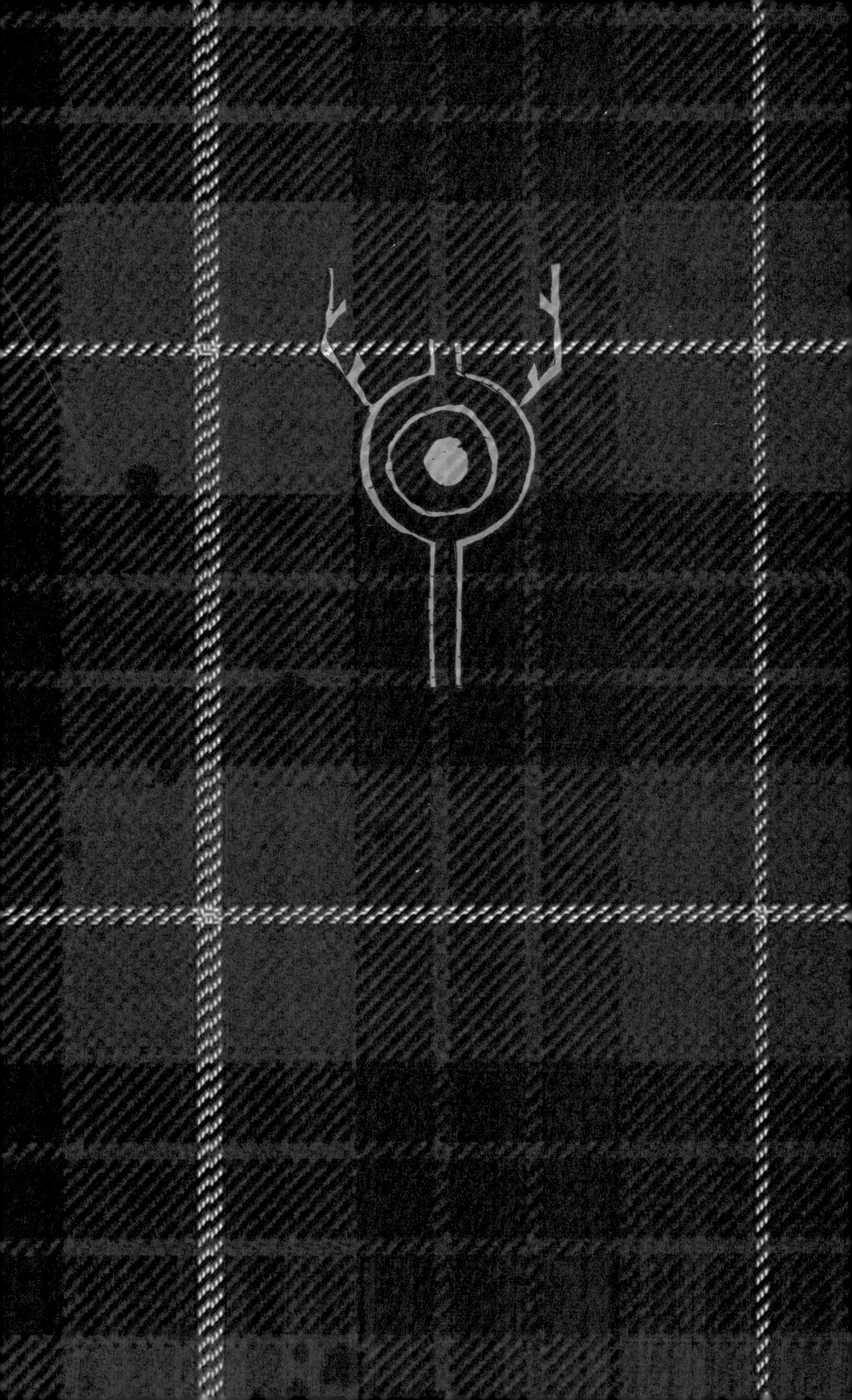

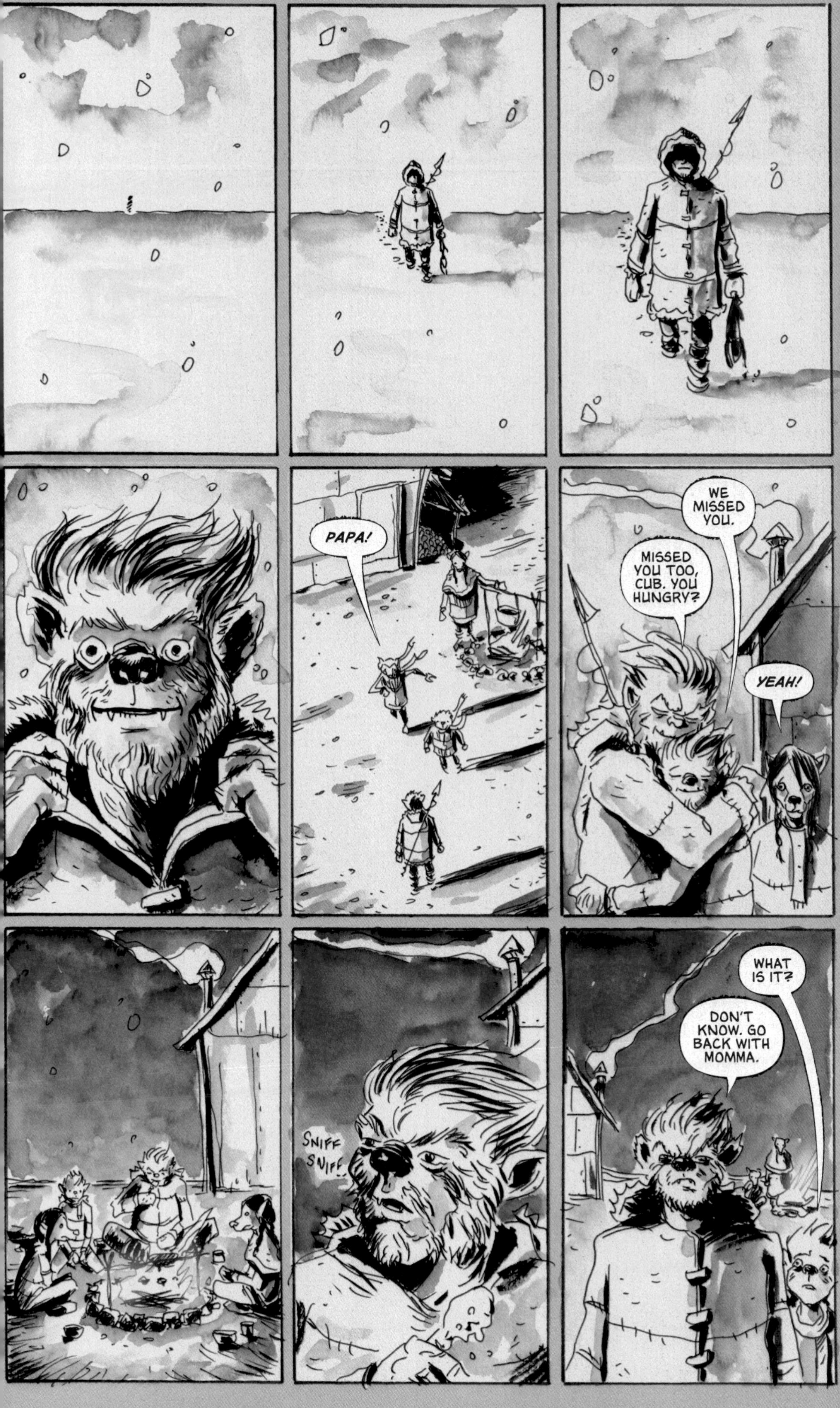
PAPA!
WE MISSED YOU.
MISSED YOU TOO, CUB. YOU HUNGRY?
YEAH!
SNIFF SNIFF
WHAT IS IT?
DON'T KNOW. GO BACK WITH MOMMA.

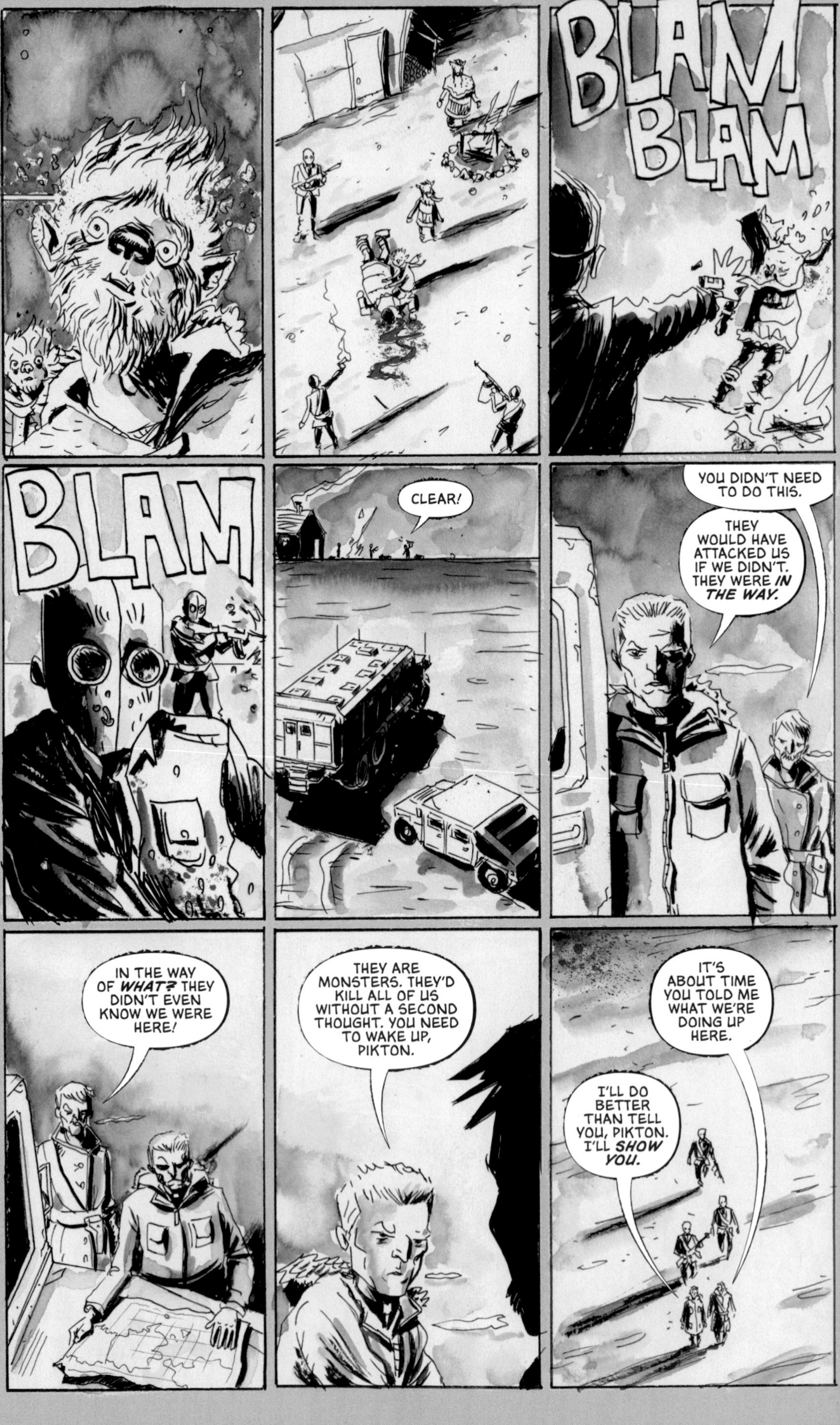
BLAM
BLAM
BLAM
CLEAR!
YOU DIDN'T NEED TO DO THIS.
THEY WOULD HAVE ATTACKED US IF WE DIDN'T. THEY WERE IN THE WAY.
IN THE WAY OF WHAT? THEY DIDN'T EVEN KNOW WE WERE HERE!
THEY ARE MONSTERS. THEY'D KILL ALL OF US WITHOUT A SECOND THOUGHT. YOU NEED TO WAKE UP, PIKTON.
IT'S ABOUT TIME YOU TOLD ME WHAT WE'RE DOING UP HERE.
I'LL DO BETTER THAN TELL YOU, PIKTON. I'LL SHOW YOU.

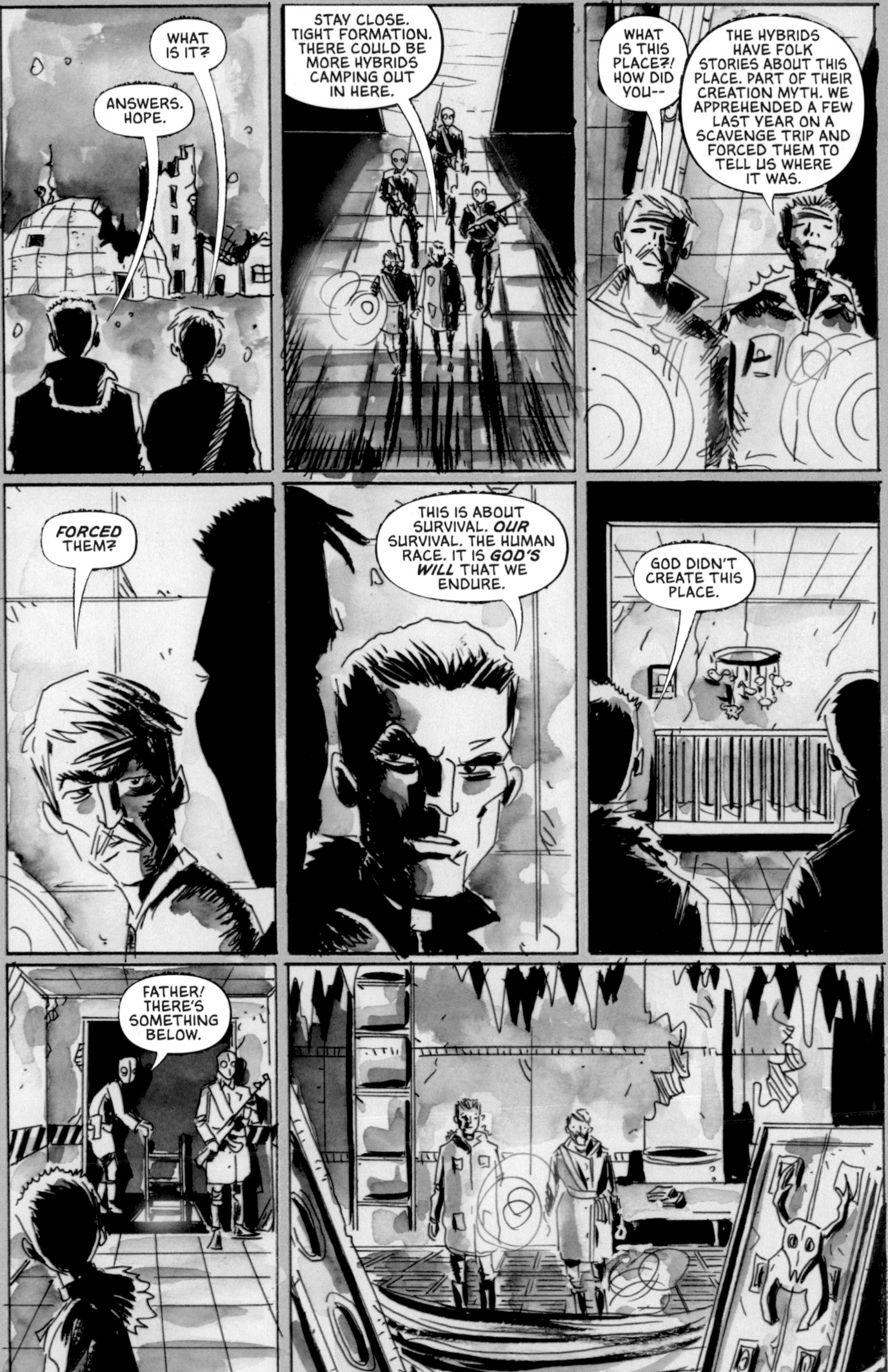
WHAT IS IT?
ANSWERS. HOPE.
STAY CLOSE. TIGHT FORMATION. THERE COULD BE MORE HYBRIDS CAMPING OUT IN HERE.
WHAT IS THIS PLACE?! HOW DID YOU--
THE HYBRIDS HAVE FOLK STORIES ABOUT THIS PLACE. PART OF THEIR CREATION MYTH. WE APPREHENDED A FEW LAST YEAR ON A SCAVENGE TRIP AND FORCED THEM TO TELL US WHERE IT WAS.
FORCED THEM?
THIS IS ABOUT SURVIVAL. OUR SURVIVAL. THE HUMAN RACE. IT IS GOD'S WILL THAT WE ENDURE.
GOD DIDN'T CREATE THIS PLACE.
FATHER! THERE'S SOMETHING BELOW.

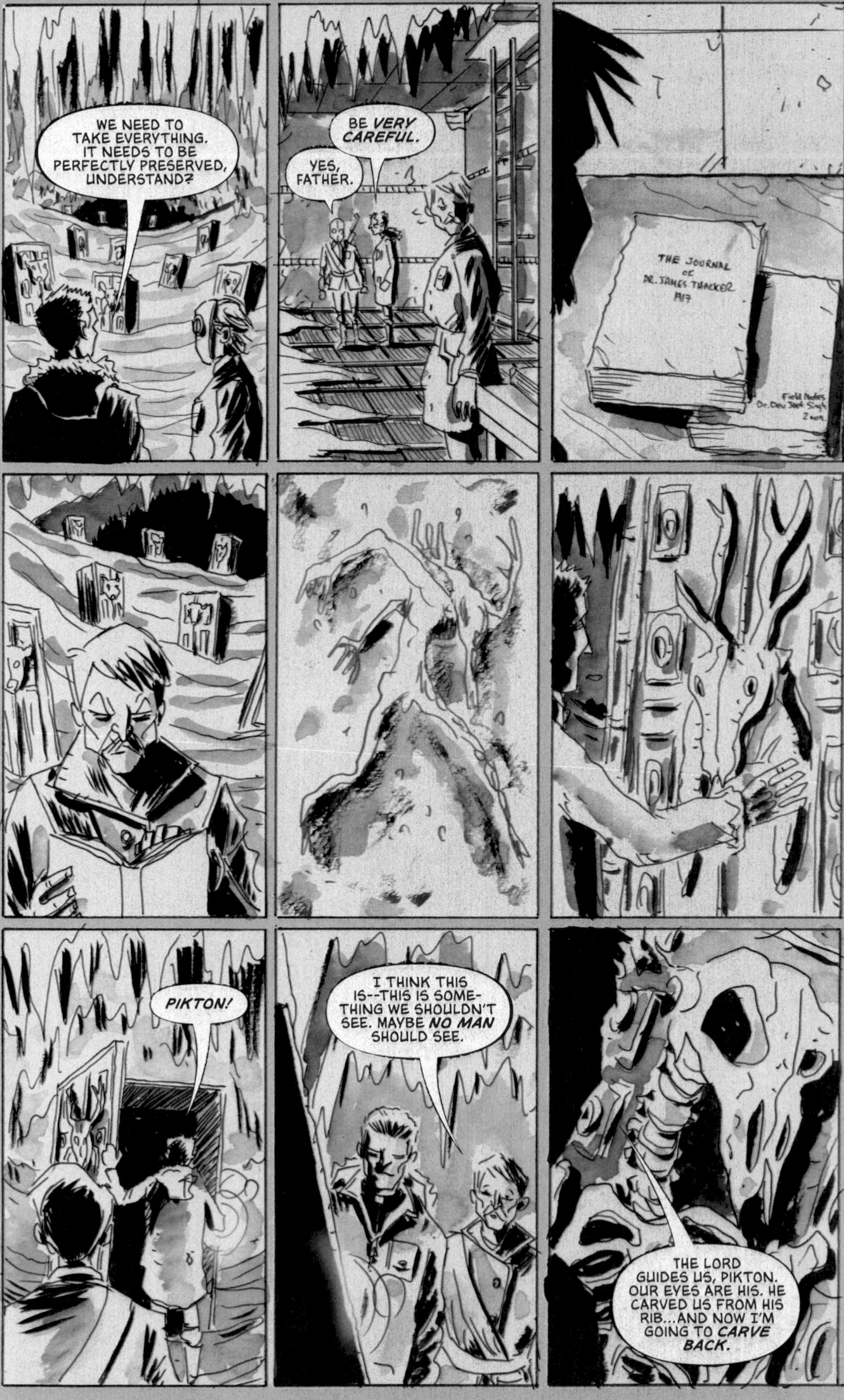
WE NEED TO TAKE EVERYTHING. IT NEEDS TO BE PERFECTLY PRESERVED, UNDERSTAND?
BE VERY CAREFUL.
YES, FATHER.
THE JOURNAL OF DR. JAMES THACKER 1917
PIKTON!
I THINK THIS IS--THIS IS SOMETHING WE SHOULDN'T SEE. MAYBE NO MAN SHOULD SEE.
THE LORD GUIDES US, PIKTON. OUR EYES ARE HIS. HE CARVED US FROM HIS RIB...AND NOW I'M GOING TO CARVE BACK.

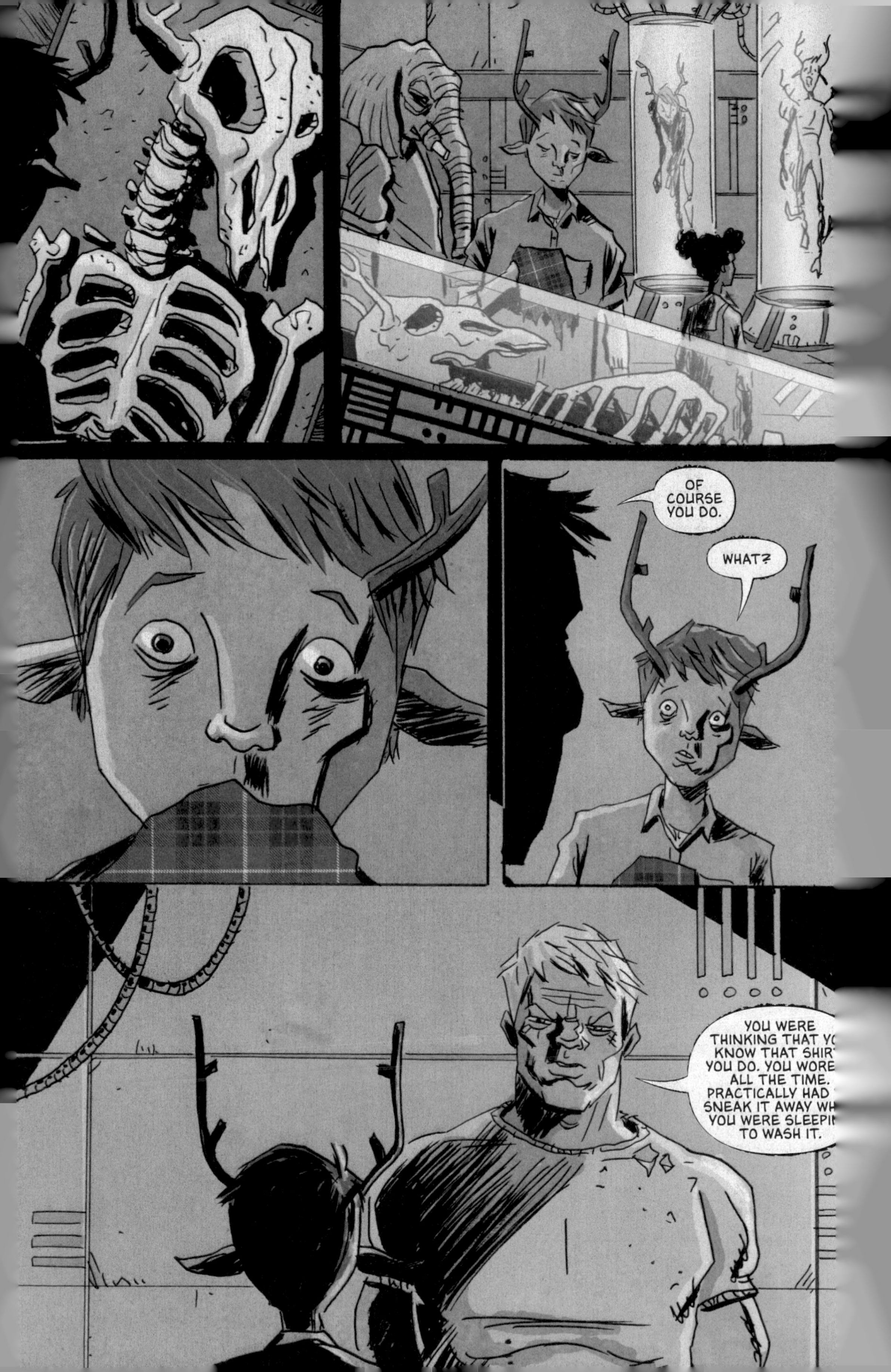
OF COURSE YOU DO.
WHAT?
YOU WERE THINKING THAT YO KNOW THAT SHIR YOU DO. YOU WORE ALL THE TIME. PRACTICALLY HAD SNEAK IT AWAY WH YOU WERE SLEEPIN TO WASH IT.

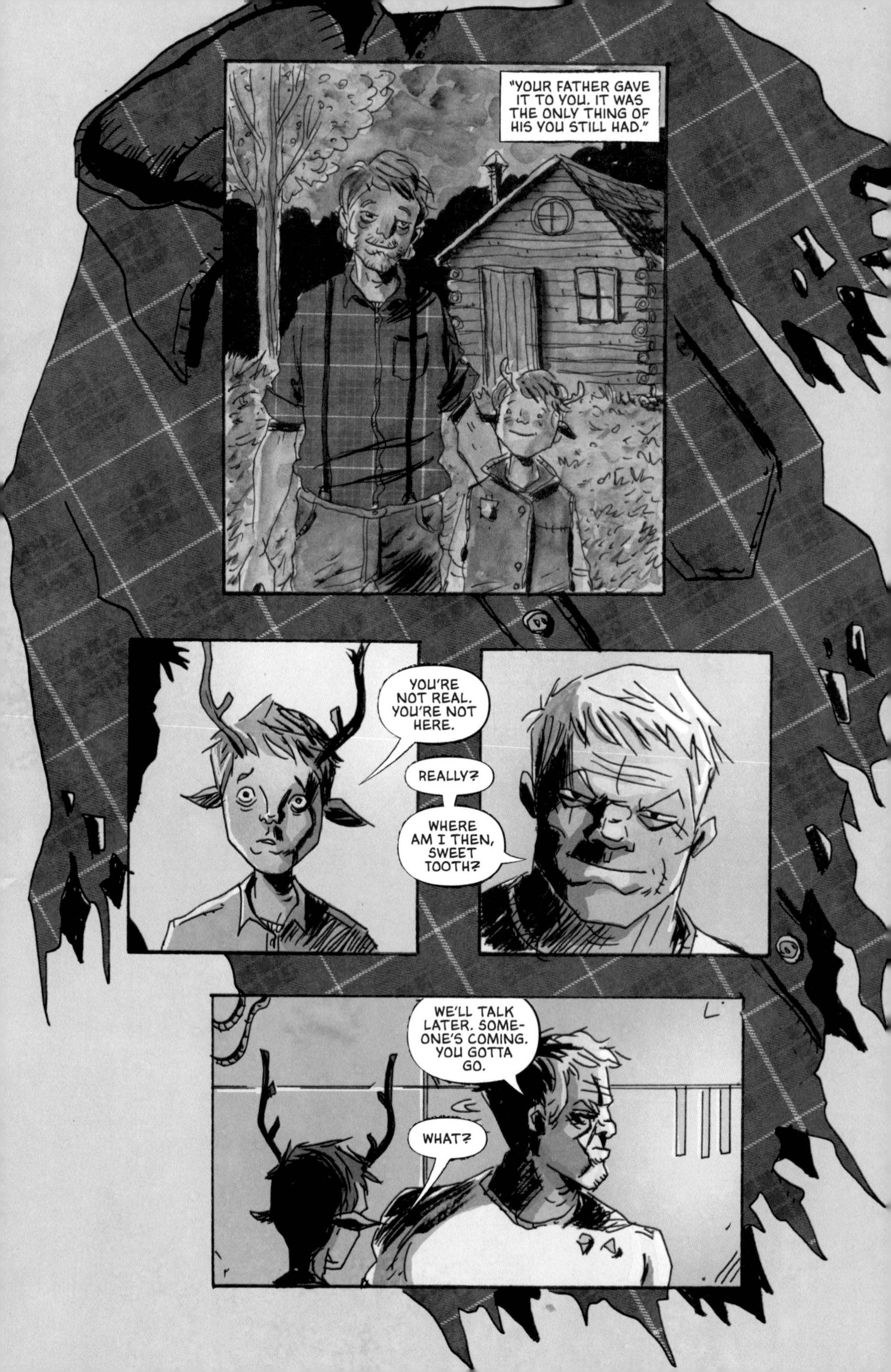
"YOUR FATHER GAVE IT TO YOU. IT WAS THE ONLY THING OF HIS YOU STILL HAD."
YOU'RE NOT REAL. YOU'RE NOT HERE.
REALLY?
WHERE AM I THEN, SWEET TOOTH?
WE'LL TALK LATER. SOME-ONE'S COMING. YOU GOTTA GO.
WHAT?

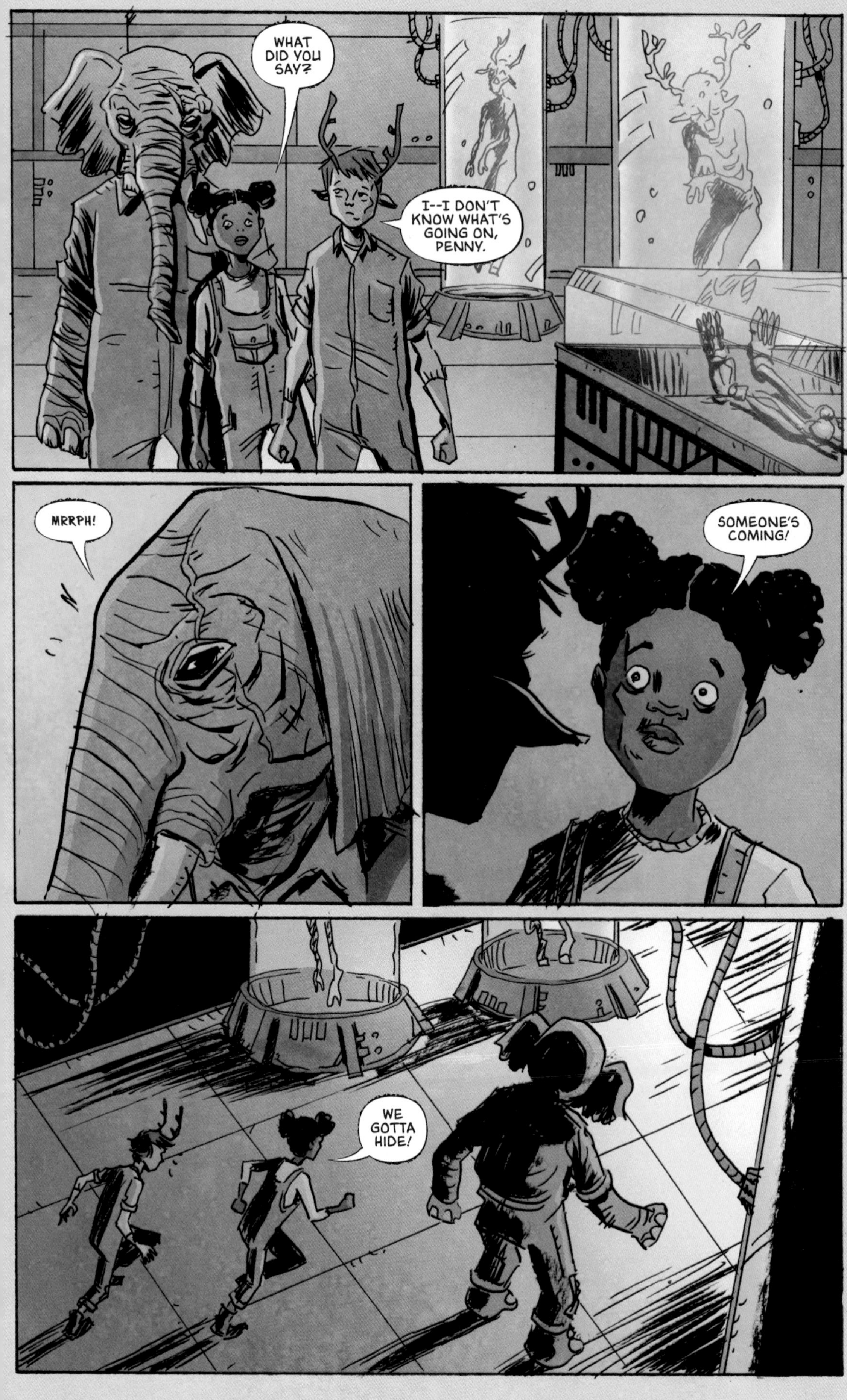
WHAT DID YOU SAY?
I--I DON'T KNOW WHAT'S GOING ON, PENNY.
MRRPH!
SOMEONE'S COMING!
WE GOTTA HIDE!

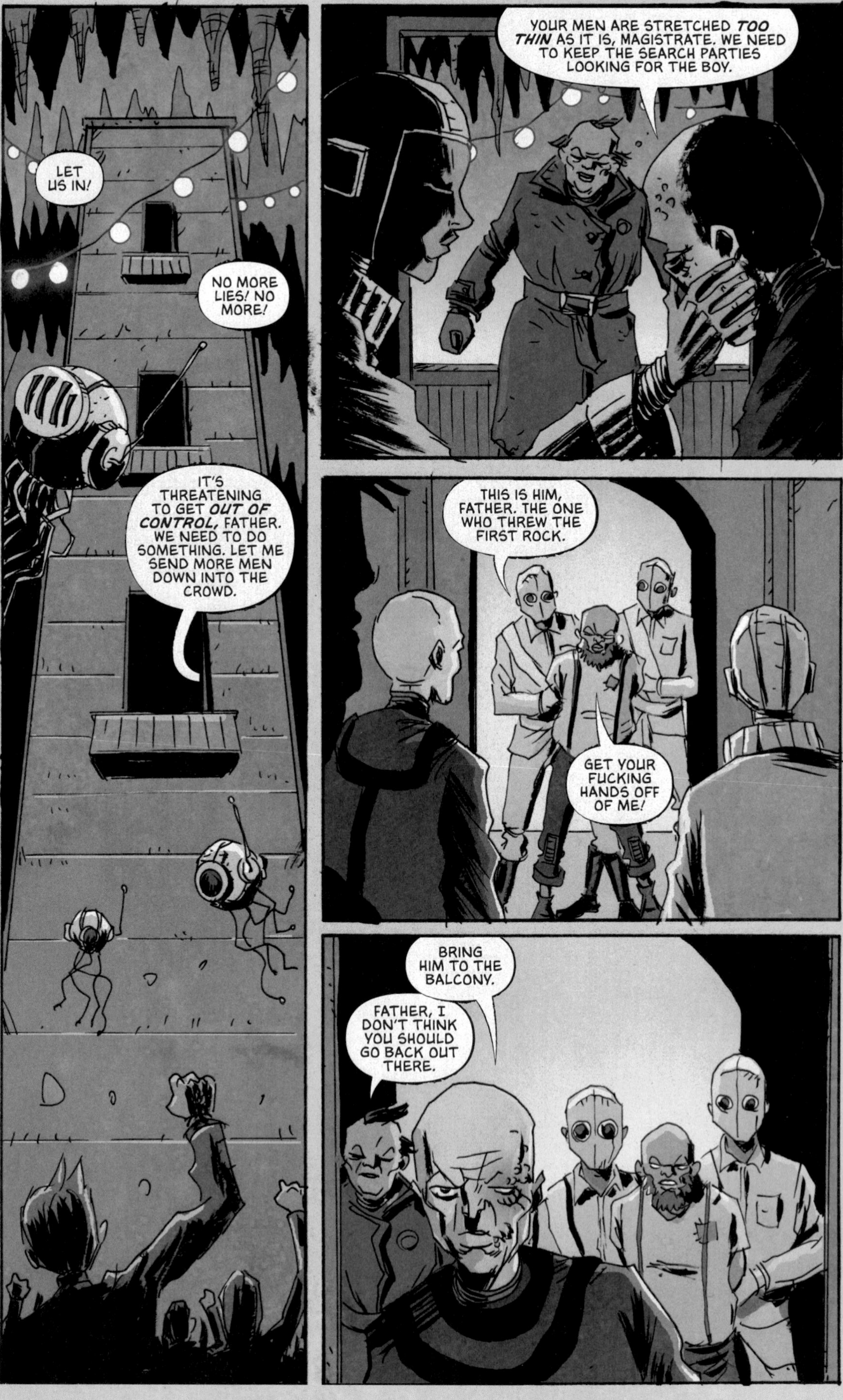
LET US IN!
NO MORE LIES! NO MORE!
IT'S THREATENING TO GET OUT OF CONTROL, FATHER. WE NEED TO DO SOMETHING. LET ME SEND MORE MEN DOWN INTO THE CROWD.
YOUR MEN ARE STRETCHED TOO THIN AS IT IS, MAGISTRATE. WE NEED TO KEEP THE SEARCH PARTIES LOOKING FOR THE BOY.
THIS IS HIM, FATHER. THE ONE WHO THREW THE FIRST ROCK.
GET YOUR FUCKING HANDS OFF OF ME!
BRING HIM TO THE BALCONY.
FATHER, I DON'T THINK YOU SHOULD GO BACK OUT THERE.

NONSENSE! YOU WANTED ME TO DO SOMETHING, SO *I'M DOING SOMETHING.* I WON'T LET THIS RUIN EVERYTHING I'VE WORKED SO HARD FOR. NOT NOW.

LISTEN! THIS HAS TO STOP! I TOLD YOU ALL WE ARE ON THE VERGE OF *FREEDOM!* WE ARE ON THE VERGE OF FINALLY SEEING *THE LIGHT ABOVE!*

I *WILL NOT* TOLERATE THIS!

WHERE IS SHE, YOU MONSTER! WHERE IS MY DAUGHTER?

LET ME SHOW YOU...

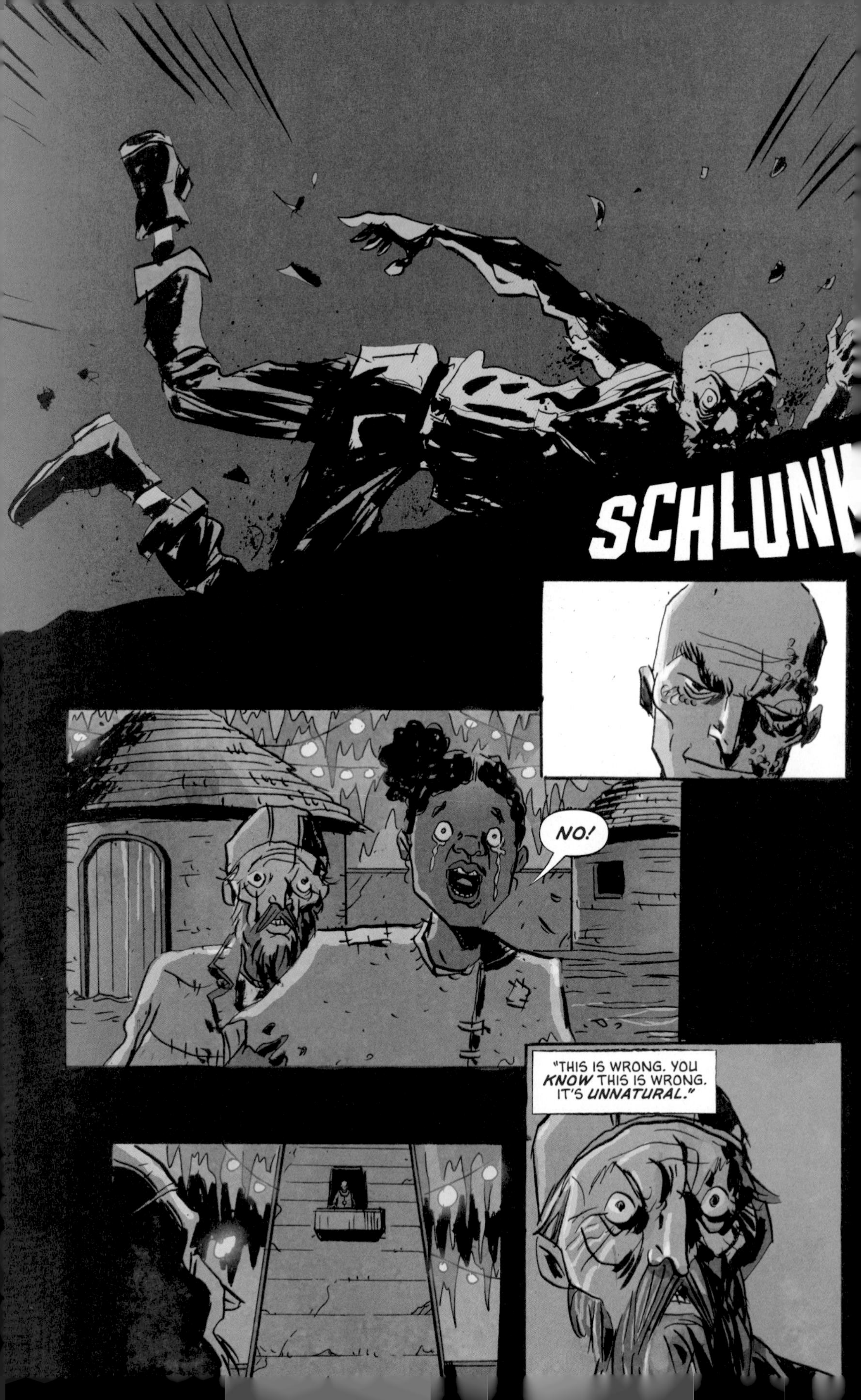
SCHLUNK
NO!
"THIS IS WRONG. YOU KNOW THIS IS WRONG. IT'S UNNATURAL."

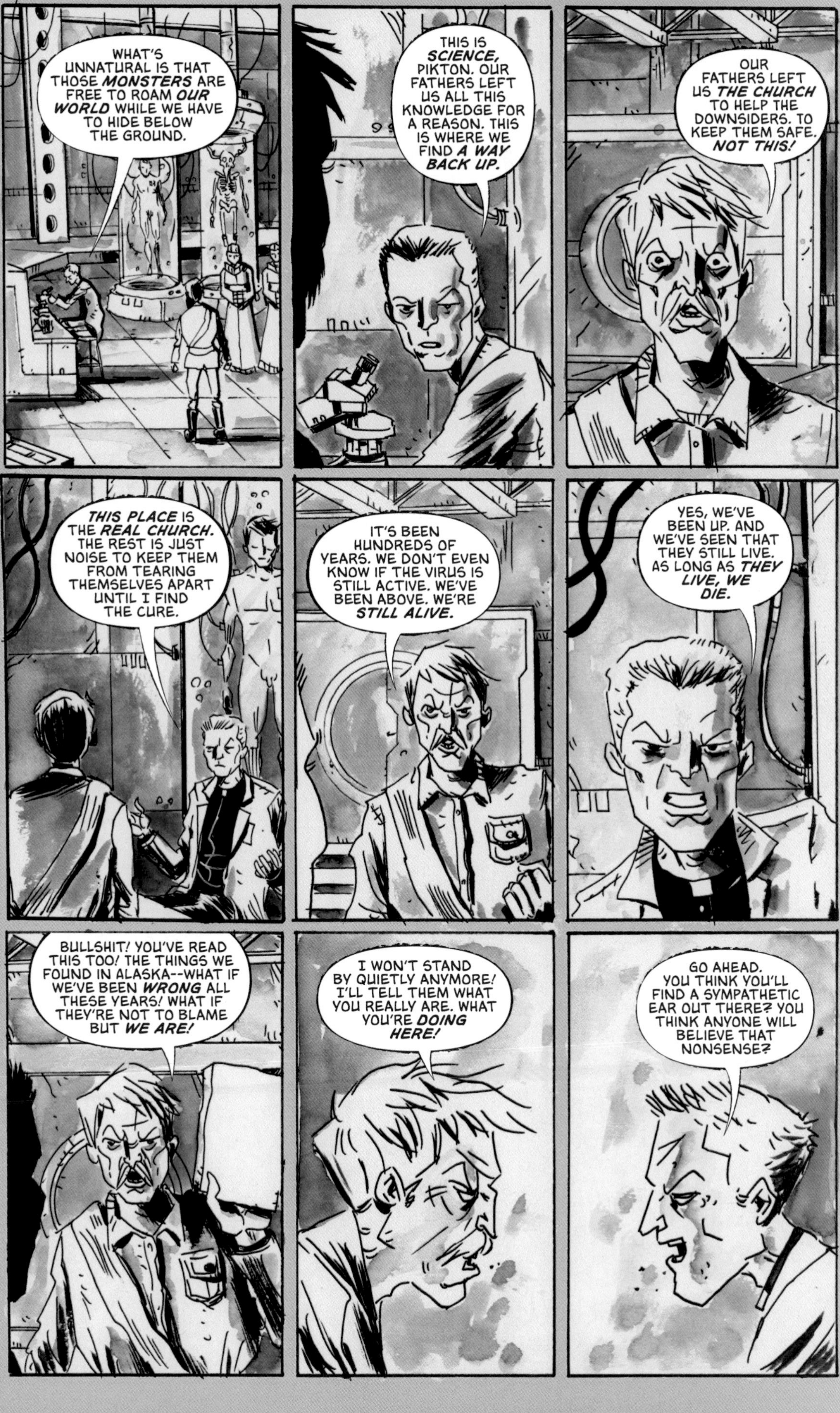
WHAT'S UNNATURAL IS THAT THOSE MONSTERS ARE FREE TO ROAM OUR WORLD WHILE WE HAVE TO HIDE BELOW THE GROUND.
THIS IS SCIENCE, PIKTON. OUR FATHERS LEFT US ALL THIS KNOWLEDGE FOR A REASON. THIS IS WHERE WE FIND A WAY BACK UP.
OUR FATHERS LEFT US THE CHURCH TO HELP THE DOWNSIDERS. TO KEEP THEM SAFE. NOT THIS!
THIS PLACE IS THE REAL CHURCH. THE REST IS JUST NOISE TO KEEP THEM FROM TEARING THEMSELVES APART UNTIL I FIND THE CURE.
IT'S BEEN HUNDREDS OF YEARS. WE DON'T EVEN KNOW IF THE VIRUS IS STILL ACTIVE. WE'VE BEEN ABOVE. WE'RE STILL ALIVE.
YES, WE'VE BEEN UP. AND WE'VE SEEN THAT THEY STILL LIVE. AS LONG AS THEY LIVE, WE DIE.
BULLSHIT! YOU'VE READ THIS TOO! THE THINGS WE FOUND IN ALASKA--WHAT IF WE'VE BEEN WRONG ALL THESE YEARS! WHAT IF THEY'RE NOT TO BLAME BUT WE ARE!
I WON'T STAND BY QUIETLY ANYMORE! I'LL TELL THEM WHAT YOU REALLY ARE. WHAT YOU'RE DOING HERE!
GO AHEAD. YOU THINK YOU'LL FIND A SYMPATHETIC EAR OUT THERE? YOU THINK ANYONE WILL BELIEVE THAT NONSENSE?

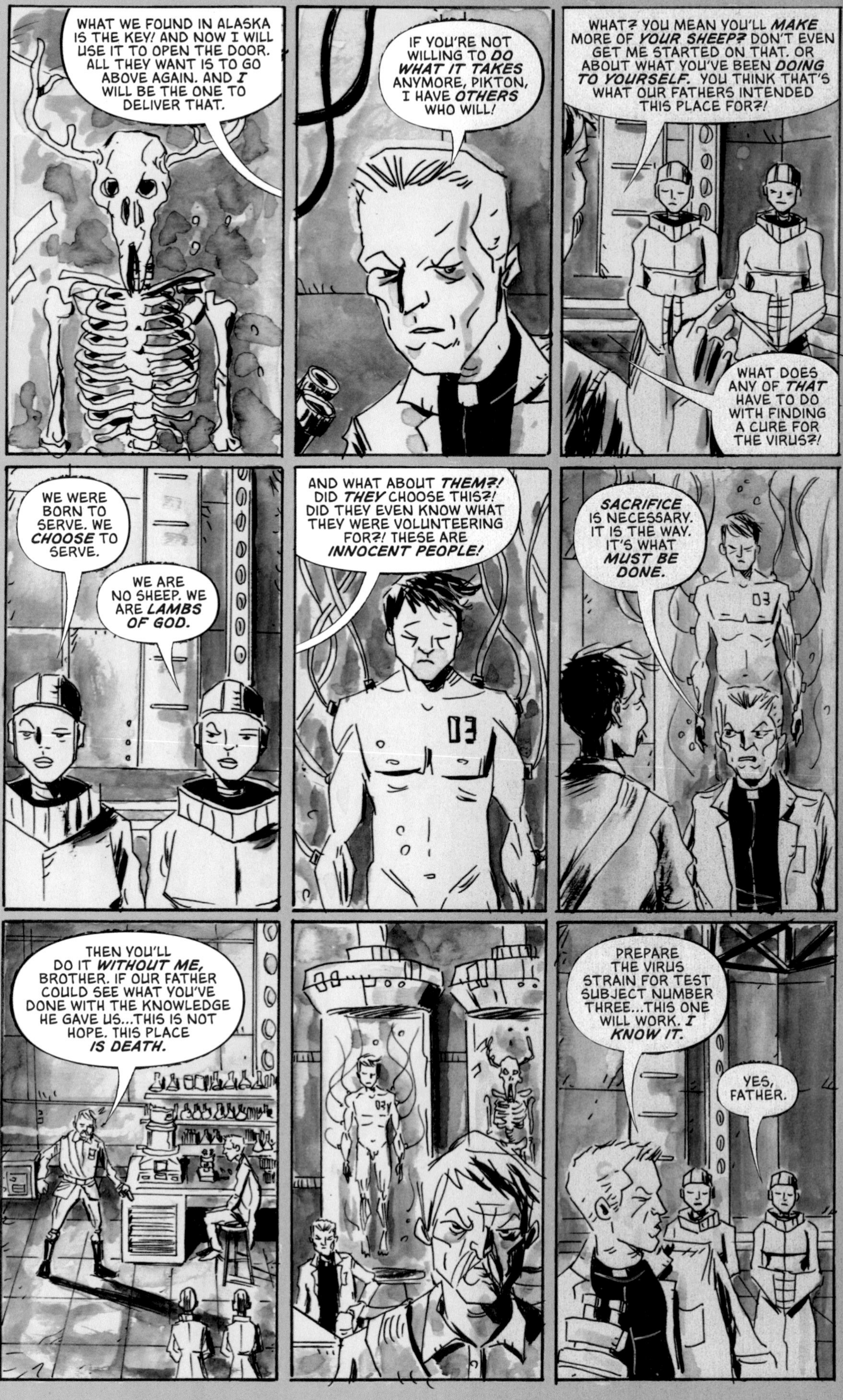
WHAT WE FOUND IN ALASKA IS THE KEY! AND NOW I WILL USE IT TO OPEN THE DOOR. ALL THEY WANT IS TO GO ABOVE AGAIN. AND I WILL BE THE ONE TO DELIVER THAT.
IF YOU'RE NOT WILLING TO DO WHAT IT TAKES ANYMORE, PIKTON, I HAVE OTHERS WHO WILL!
WHAT? YOU MEAN YOU'LL MAKE MORE OF YOUR SHEEP? DON'T EVEN GET ME STARTED ON THAT. OR ABOUT WHAT YOU'VE BEEN DOING TO YOURSELF. YOU THINK THAT'S WHAT OUR FATHERS INTENDED THIS PLACE FOR?!
WHAT DOES ANY OF THAT HAVE TO DO WITH FINDING A CURE FOR THE VIRUS?!
WE WERE BORN TO SERVE. WE CHOOSE TO SERVE.
WE ARE NO SHEEP. WE ARE LAMBS OF GOD.
AND WHAT ABOUT THEM?! DID THEY CHOOSE THIS?! DID THEY EVEN KNOW WHAT THEY WERE VOLUNTEERING FOR?! THESE ARE INNOCENT PEOPLE!
03
SACRIFICE IS NECESSARY. IT IS THE WAY. IT'S WHAT MUST BE DONE.
03
THEN YOU'LL DO IT WITHOUT ME, BROTHER. IF OUR FATHER COULD SEE WHAT YOU'VE DONE WITH THE KNOWLEDGE HE GAVE US...THIS IS NOT HOPE. THIS PLACE IS DEATH.
PREPARE THE VIRUS STRAIN FOR TEST SUBJECT NUMBER THREE...THIS ONE WILL WORK. I KNOW IT.
YES, FATHER.

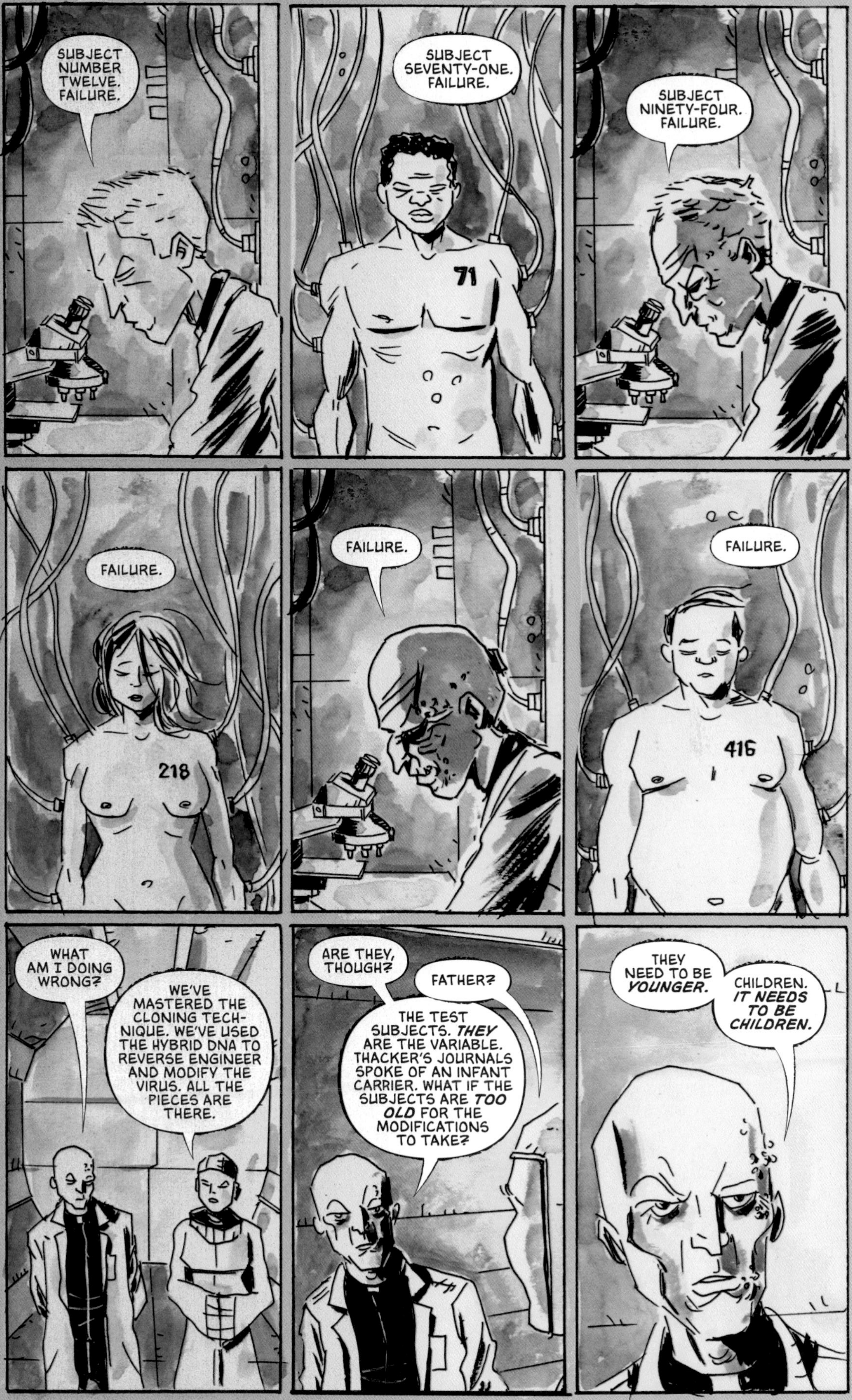
SUBJECT NUMBER TWELVE. FAILURE.
SUBJECT SEVENTY-ONE. FAILURE.
71
SUBJECT NINETY-FOUR. FAILURE.
FAILURE.
218
FAILURE.
FAILURE.
416
WHAT AM I DOING WRONG?
WE'VE MASTERED THE CLONING TECH-NIQUE. WE'VE USED THE HYBRID DNA TO REVERSE ENGINEER AND MODIFY THE VIRUS. ALL THE PIECES ARE THERE.
ARE THEY, THOUGH?
FATHER?
THE TEST SUBJECTS. *THEY* ARE THE VARIABLE. THACKER'S JOURNALS SPOKE OF AN INFANT CARRIER. WHAT IF THE SUBJECTS ARE *TOO OLD* FOR THE MODIFICATIONS TO TAKE?
THEY NEED TO BE *YOUNGER.*
CHILDREN. *IT NEEDS TO BE CHILDREN.*

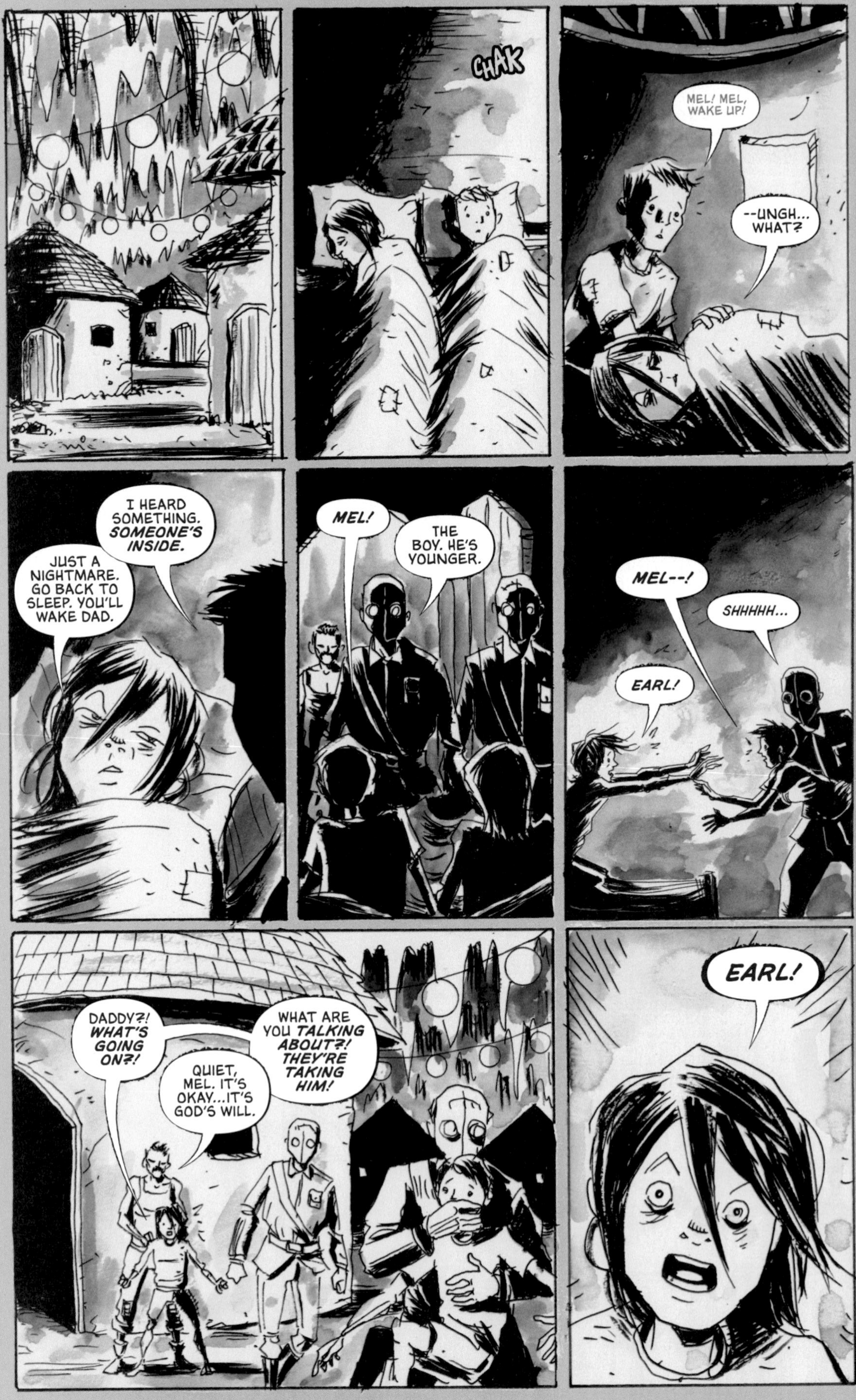
CHAK
MEL! MEL, WAKE UP!
--UNGH... WHAT?
I HEARD SOMETHING. SOMEONE'S INSIDE.
JUST A NIGHTMARE. GO BACK TO SLEEP. YOU'LL WAKE DAD.
MEL!
THE BOY. HE'S YOUNGER.
MEL--!
SHHHHH...
EARL!
DADDY?! WHAT'S GOING ON?!
WHAT ARE YOU TALKING ABOUT?! THEY'RE TAKING HIM!
QUIET, MEL. IT'S OKAY...IT'S GOD'S WILL.
EARL!

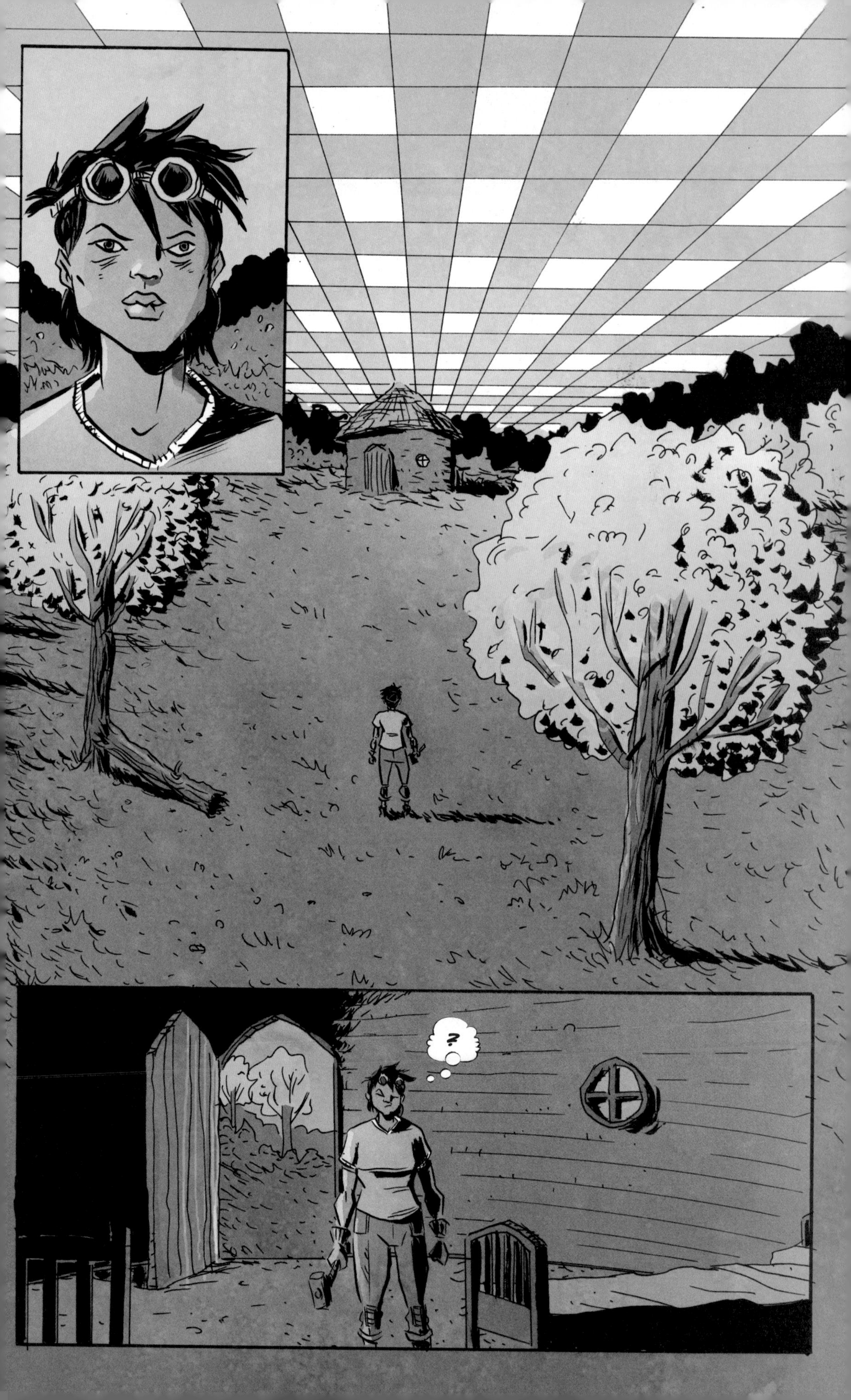
?

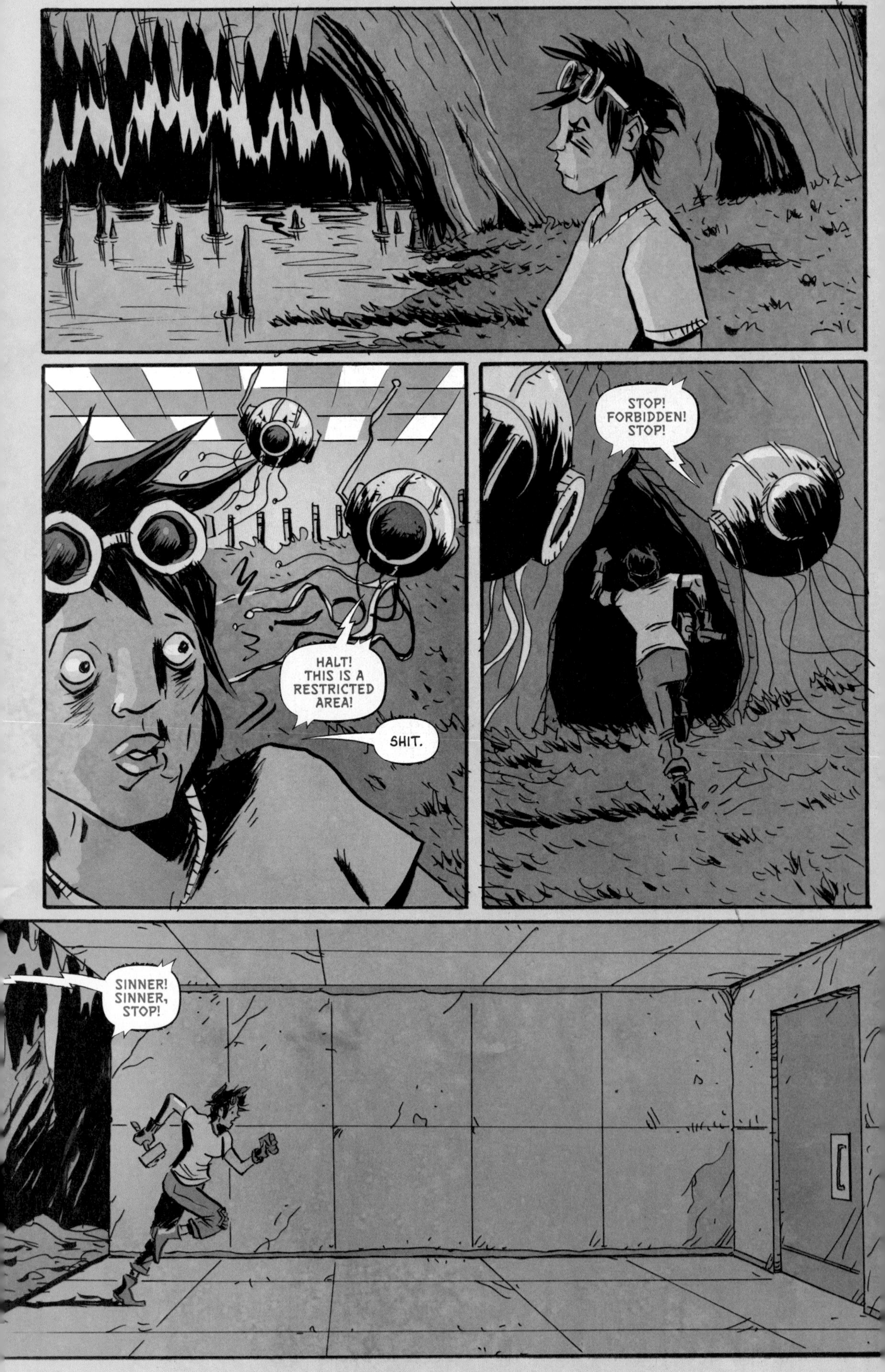
HALT! THIS IS A RESTRICTED AREA!
SHIT.
STOP! FORBIDDEN! STOP!
SINNER! SINNER, STOP!

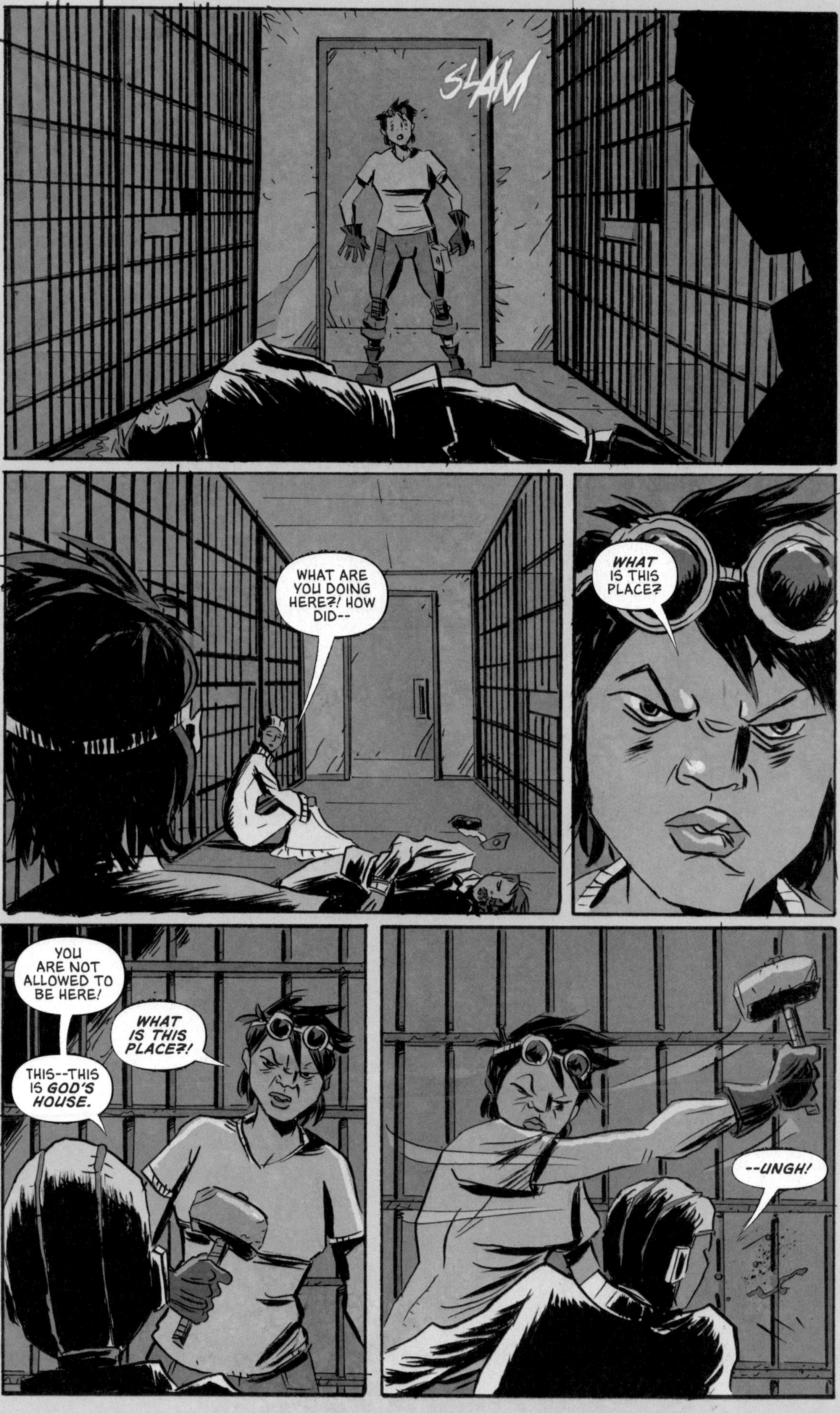

SLAM
WHAT ARE YOU DOING HERE?! HOW DID--
WHAT IS THIS PLACE?
YOU ARE NOT ALLOWED TO BE HERE!
WHAT IS THIS PLACE?!
THIS--THIS IS GOD'S HOUSE.
--UNGH!

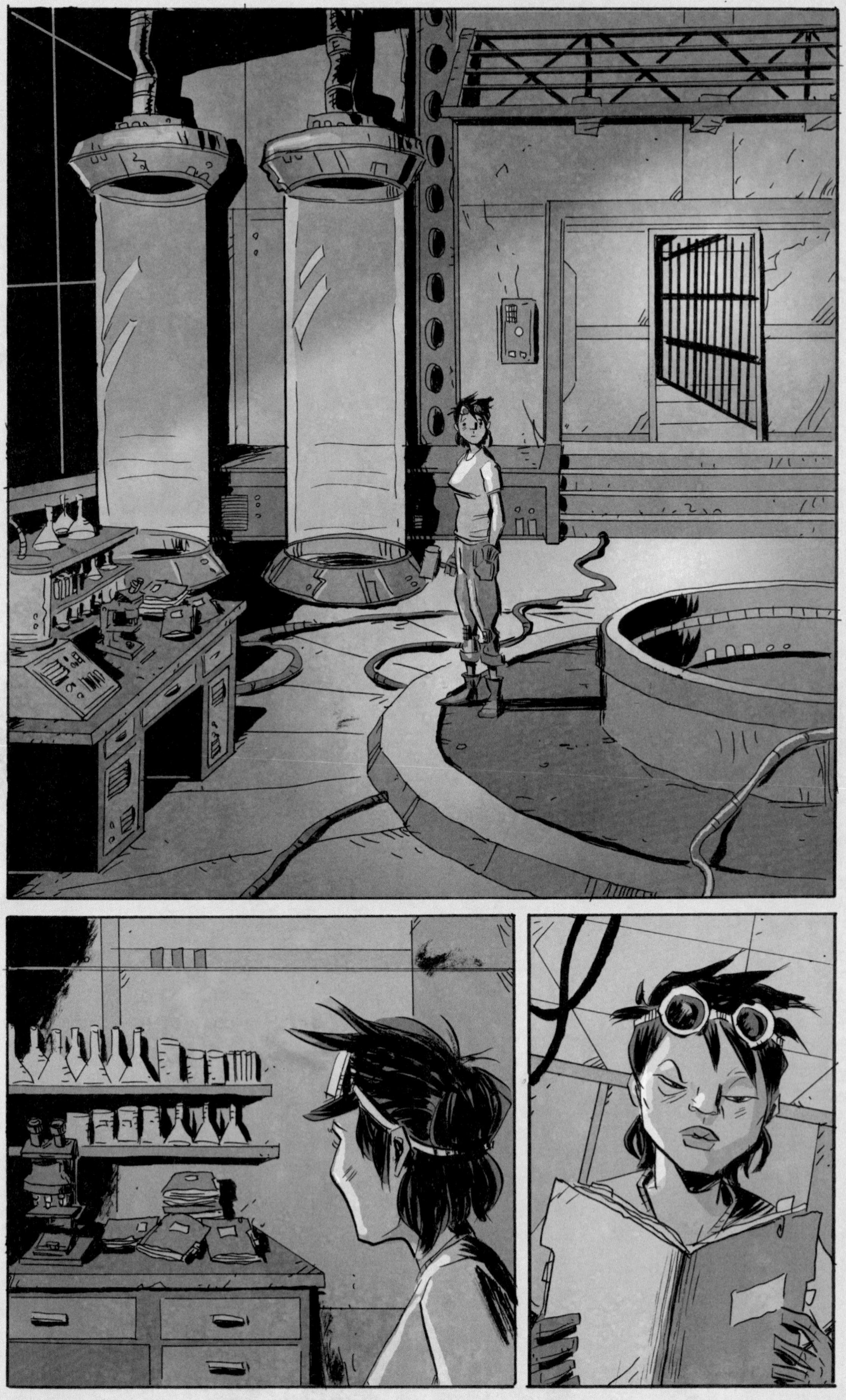

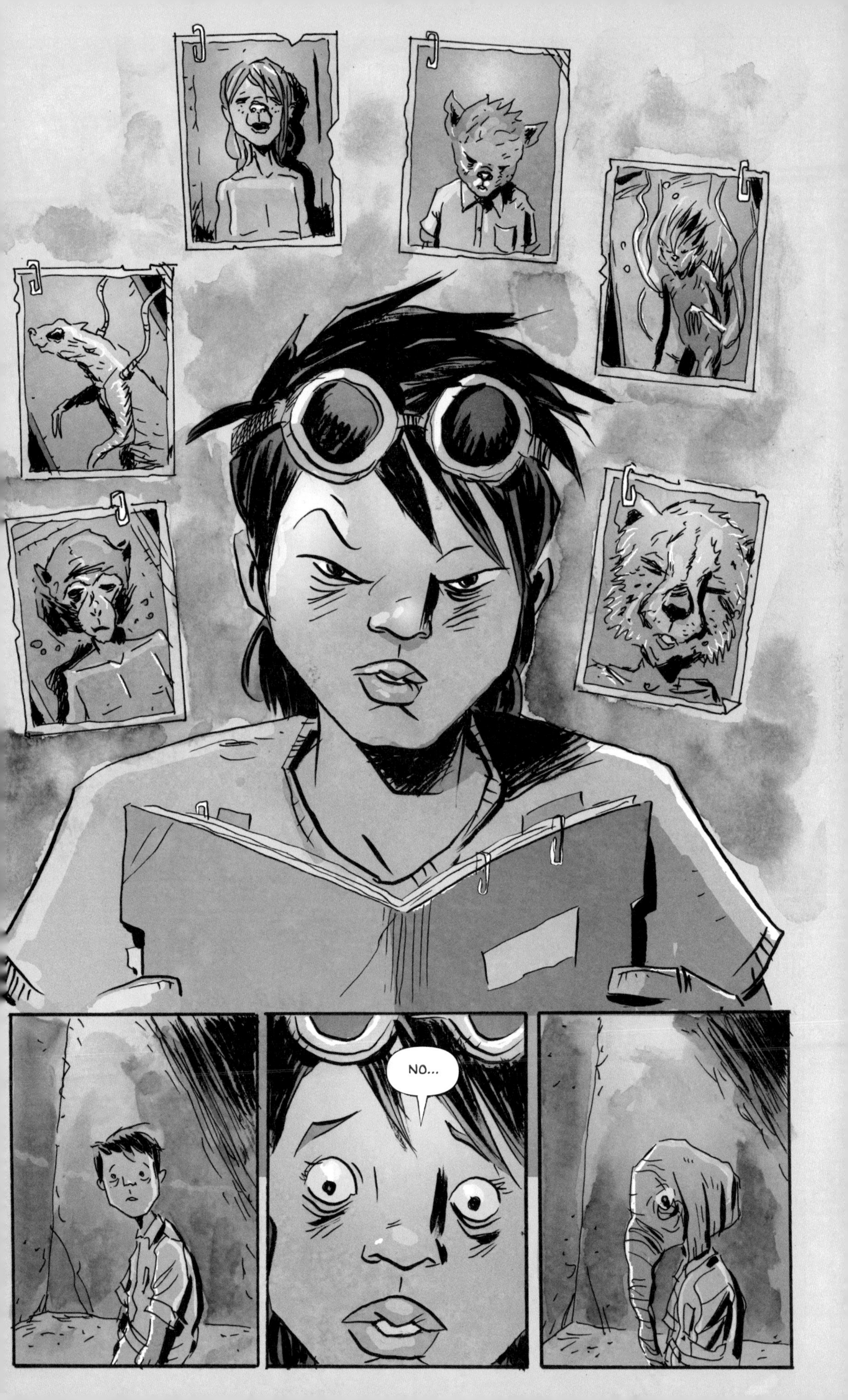
NO...

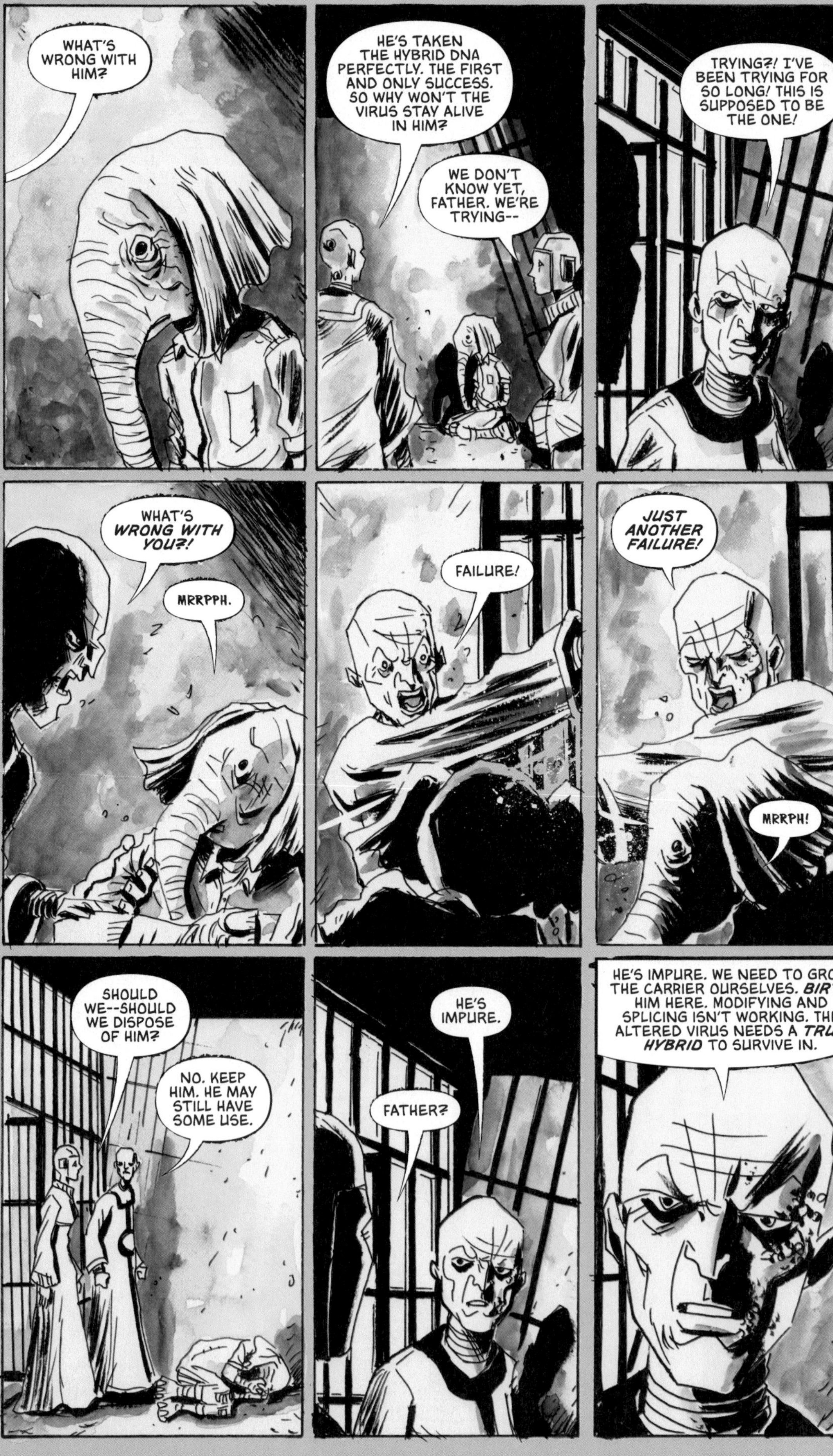
WHAT'S WRONG WITH HIM?
HE'S TAKEN THE HYBRID DNA PERFECTLY. THE FIRST AND ONLY SUCCESS. SO WHY WON'T THE VIRUS STAY ALIVE IN HIM?
WE DON'T KNOW YET, FATHER. WE'RE TRYING--
TRYING?! I'VE BEEN TRYING FOR SO LONG! THIS IS SUPPOSED TO BE THE ONE!
WHAT'S *WRONG WITH YOU?!*
MRRPPH.
FAILURE!
JUST ANOTHER FAILURE!
MRRPH!
SHOULD WE--SHOULD WE DISPOSE OF HIM?
NO. KEEP HIM. HE MAY STILL HAVE SOME USE.
HE'S IMPURE.
FATHER?
HE'S IMPURE. WE NEED TO GROW THE CARRIER OURSELVES. *BIRTH* HIM HERE. MODIFYING AND SPLICING ISN'T WORKING. THE ALTERED VIRUS NEEDS A *TRUE HYBRID* TO SURVIVE IN.

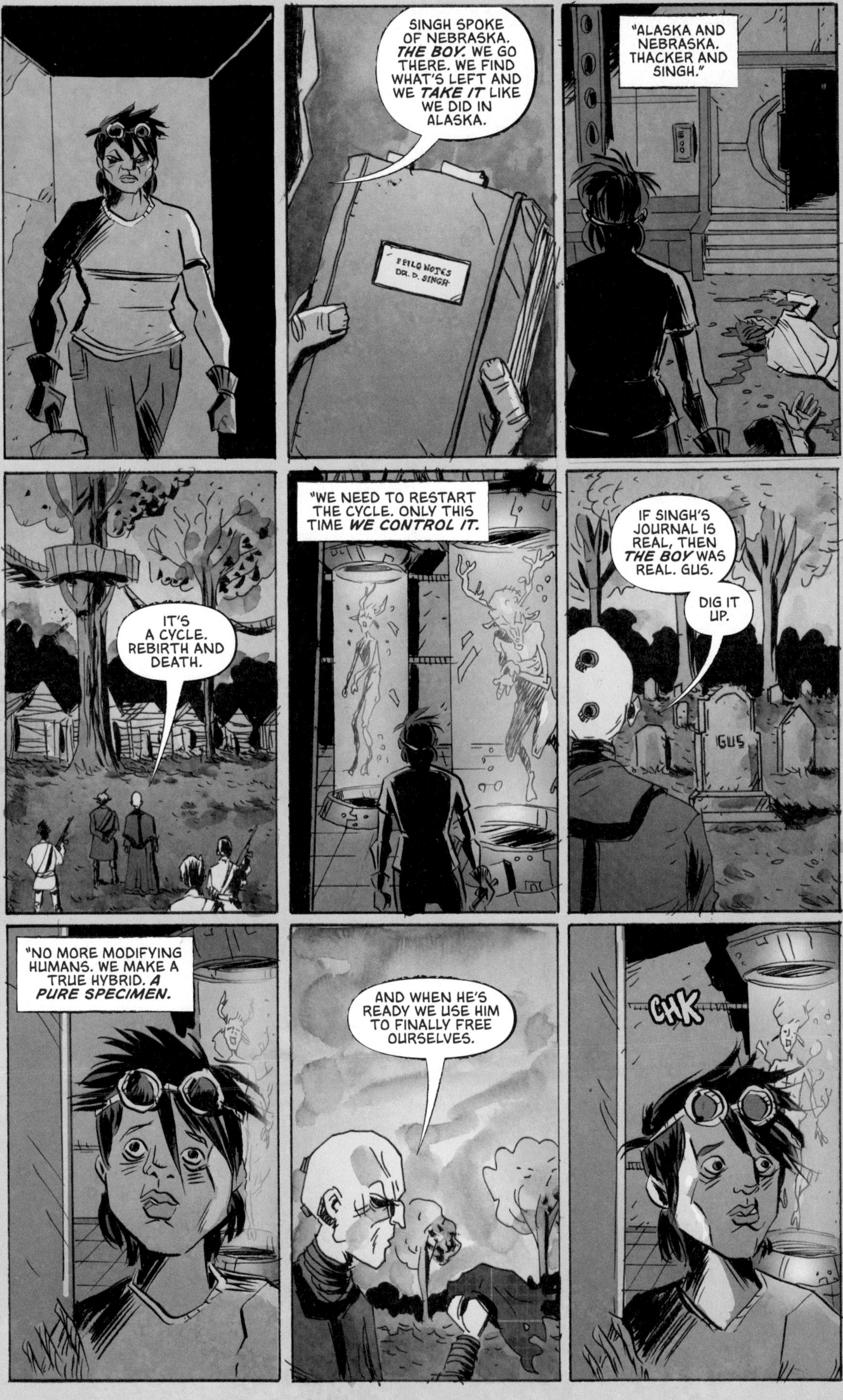
SINGH SPOKE OF NEBRASKA. *THE BOY.* WE GO THERE. WE FIND WHAT'S LEFT AND WE *TAKE IT* LIKE WE DID IN ALASKA.
FIELD NOTES DR. D. SINGH
"ALASKA AND NEBRASKA. THACKER AND SINGH."
IT'S A CYCLE. REBIRTH AND DEATH.
"WE NEED TO RESTART THE CYCLE. ONLY THIS TIME *WE CONTROL IT.*
IF SINGH'S JOURNAL IS REAL, THEN *THE BOY* WAS REAL. GUS.
DIG IT UP.
GUS
"NO MORE MODIFYING HUMANS. WE MAKE A TRUE HYBRID. *A PURE SPECIMEN.*
AND WHEN HE'S READY WE USE HIM TO FINALLY FREE OURSELVES.
CHK

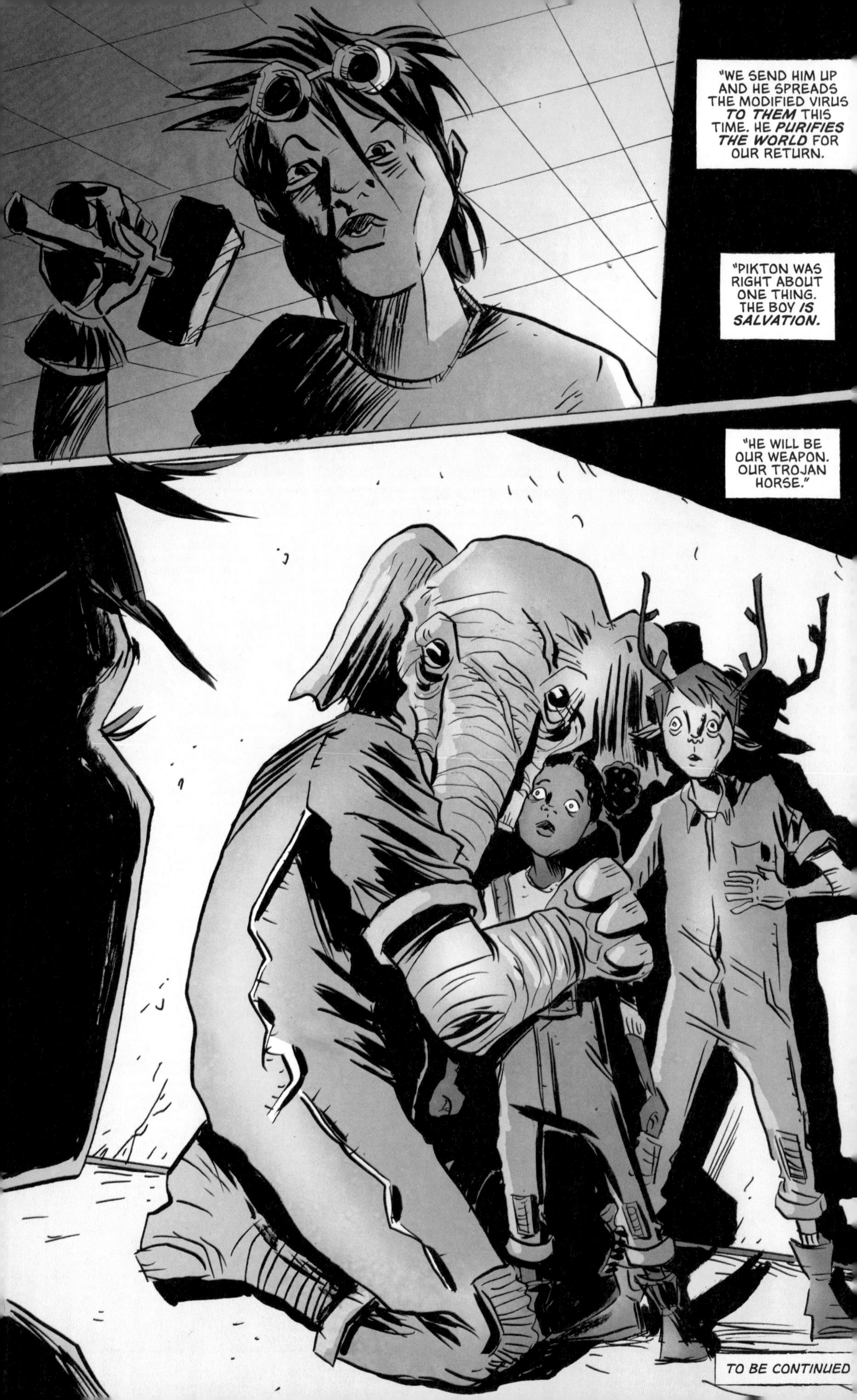
"WE SEND HIM UP AND HE SPREADS THE MODIFIED VIRUS *TO THEM* THIS TIME. HE *PURIFIES THE WORLD* FOR OUR RETURN.
"PIKTON WAS RIGHT ABOUT ONE THING. THE BOY *IS SALVATION.*
"HE WILL BE OUR WEAPON. OUR TROJAN HORSE."
TO BE CONTINUED

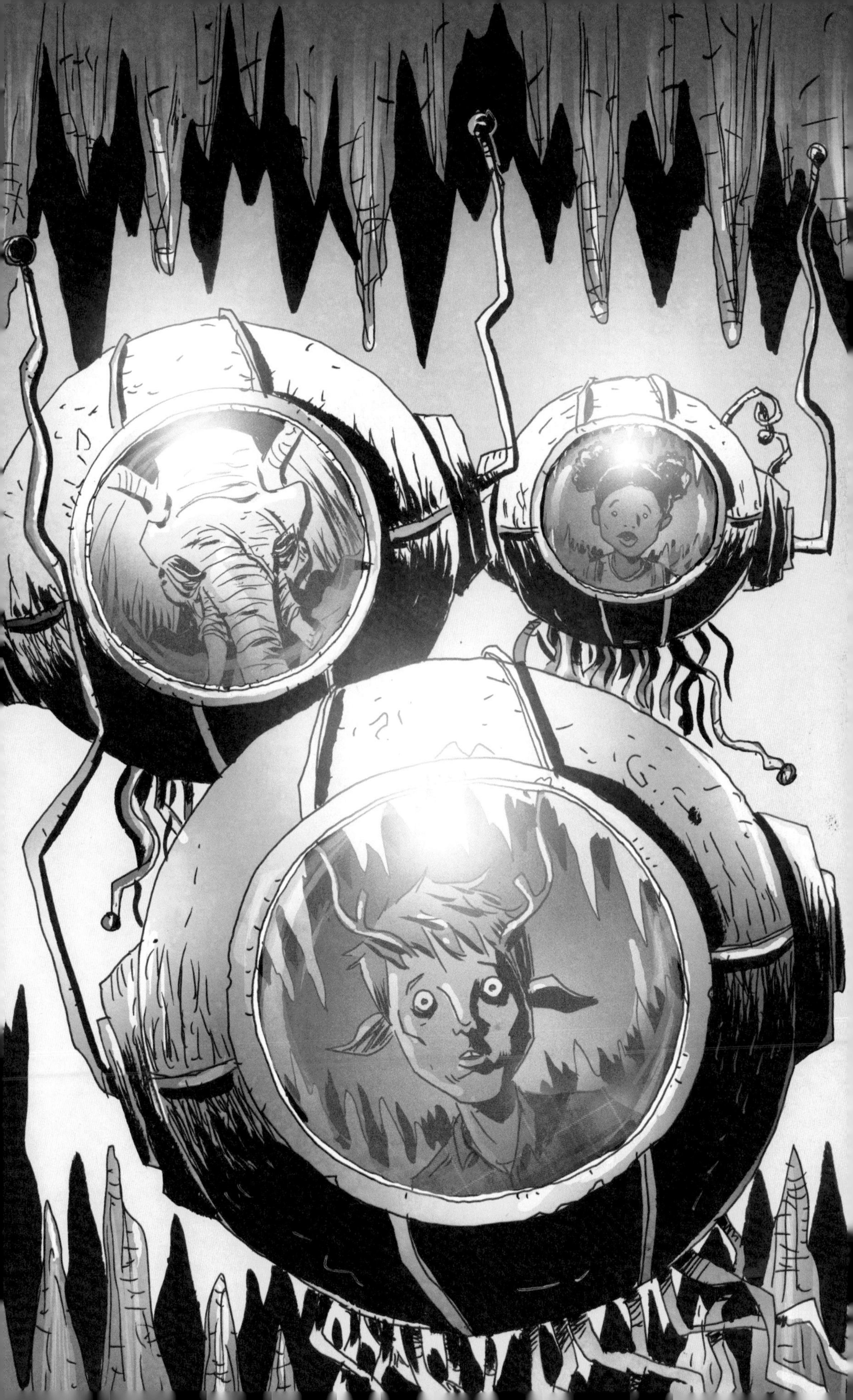

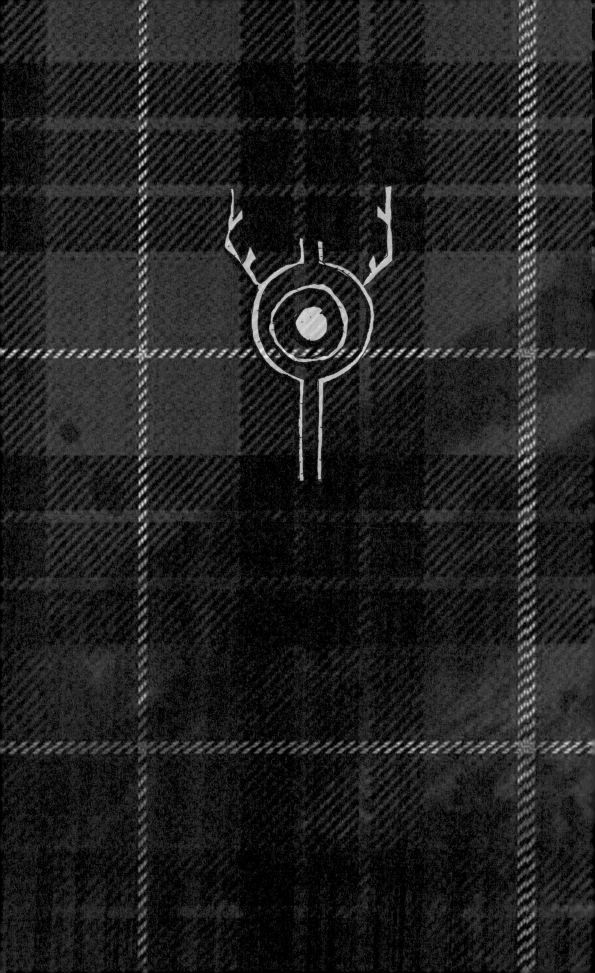

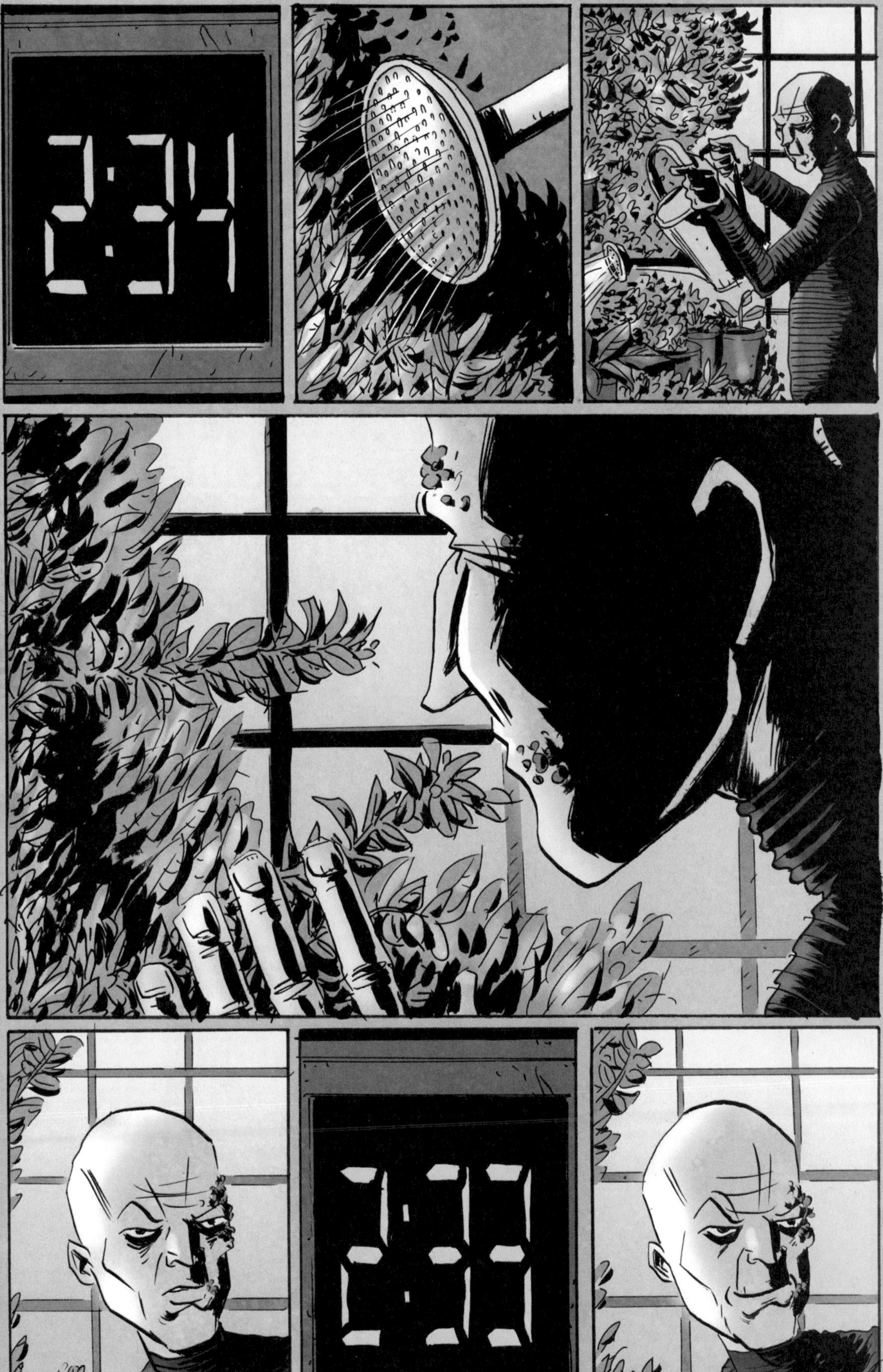

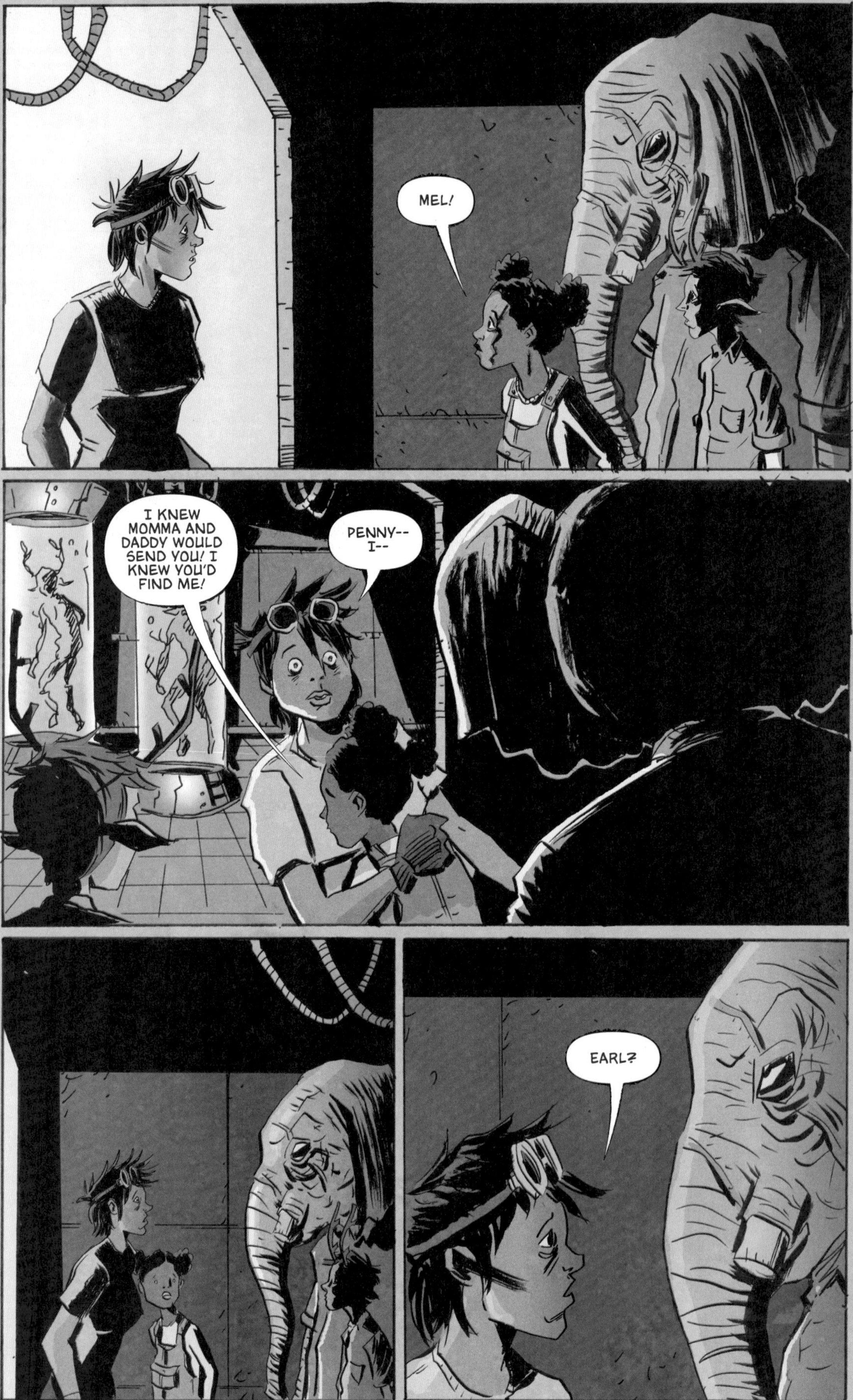
MEL!
I KNEW MOMMA AND DADDY WOULD SEND YOU! I KNEW YOU'D FIND ME!
PENNY-- I--
EARL?

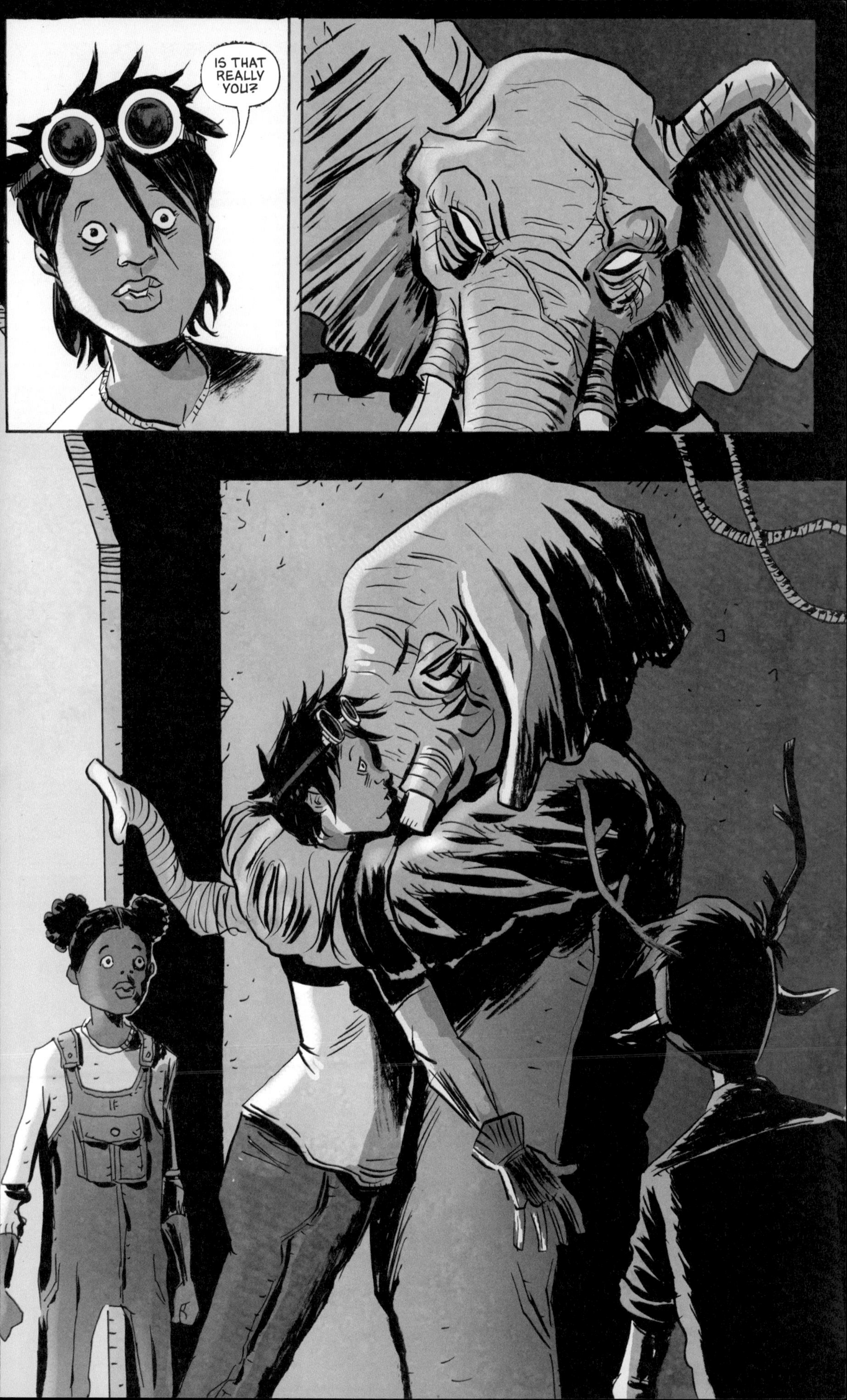
IS THAT REALLY YOU?

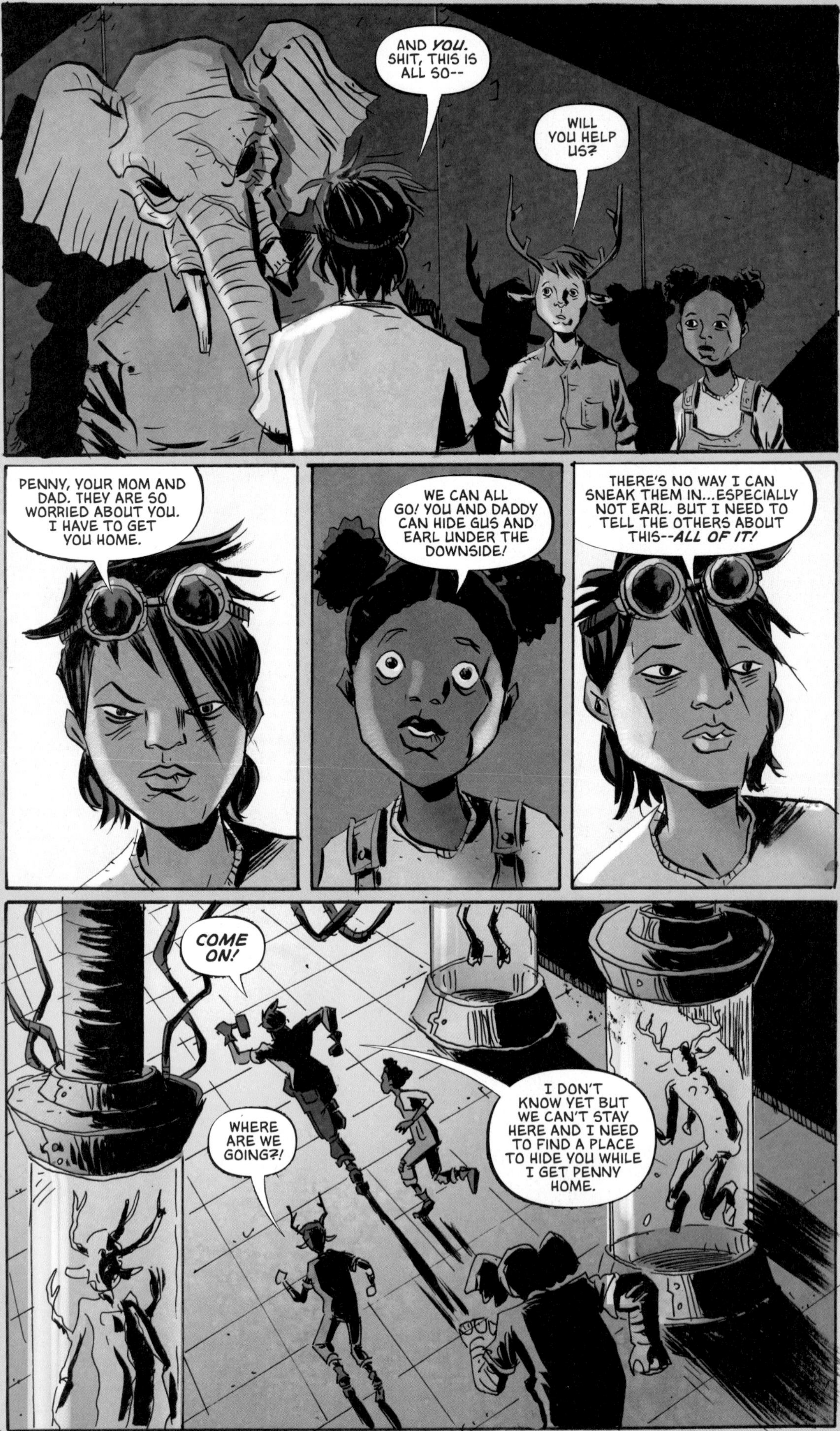
AND *YOU*. SHIT, THIS IS ALL SO--
WILL YOU HELP US?
PENNY, YOUR MOM AND DAD. THEY ARE SO WORRIED ABOUT YOU. I HAVE TO GET YOU HOME.
WE CAN ALL GO! YOU AND DADDY CAN HIDE GUS AND EARL UNDER THE DOWNSIDE!
THERE'S NO WAY I CAN SNEAK THEM IN...ESPECIALLY NOT EARL. BUT I NEED TO TELL THE OTHERS ABOUT THIS--*ALL OF IT!*
COME ON!
WHERE ARE WE GOING?!
I DON'T KNOW YET BUT WE CAN'T STAY HERE AND I NEED TO FIND A PLACE TO HIDE YOU WHILE I GET PENNY HOME.

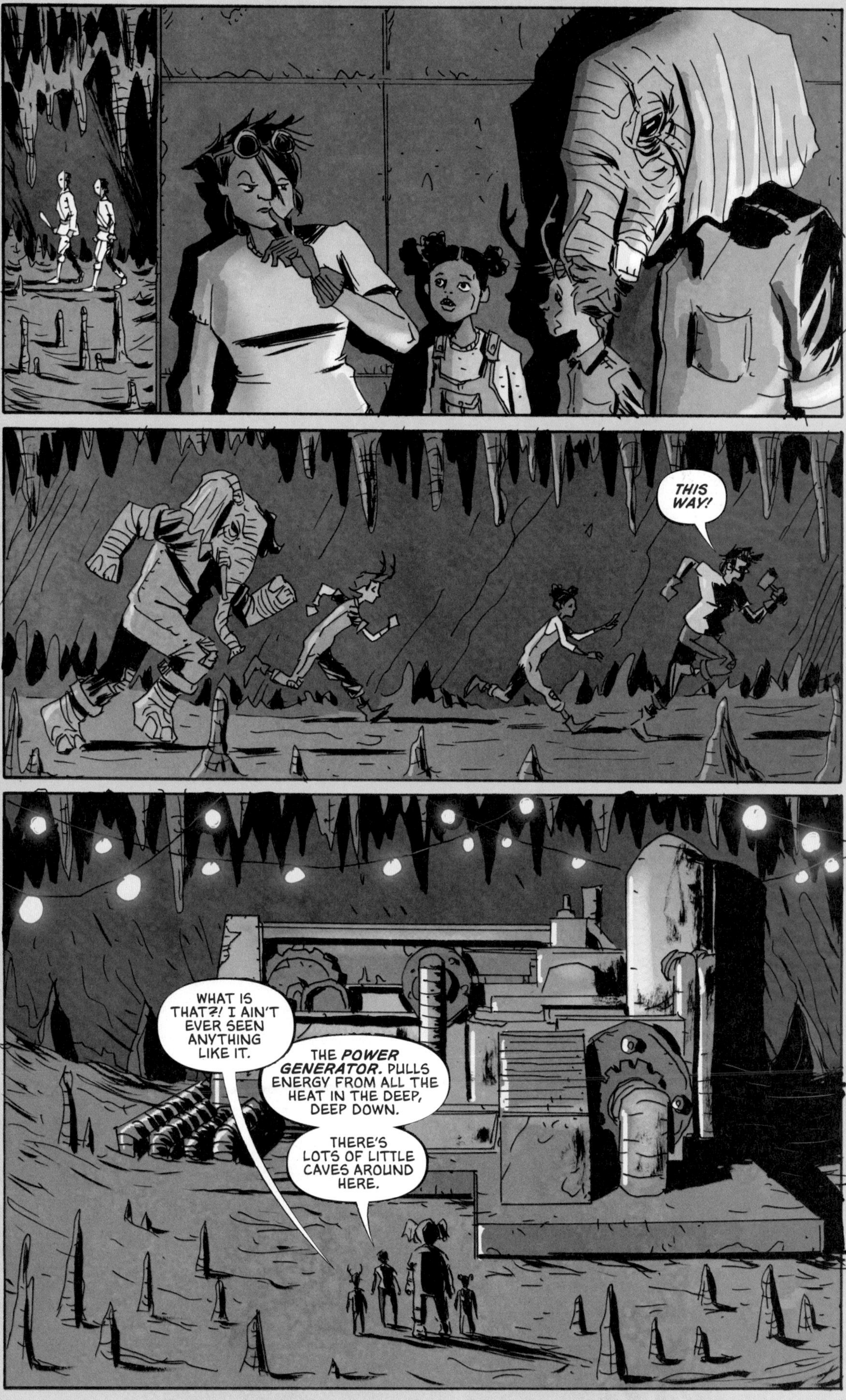

THIS WAY!
WHAT IS THAT?! I AIN'T EVER SEEN ANYTHING LIKE IT.
THE POWER GENERATOR. PULLS ENERGY FROM ALL THE HEAT IN THE DEEP, DEEP DOWN.
THERE'S LOTS OF LITTLE CAVES AROUND HERE.

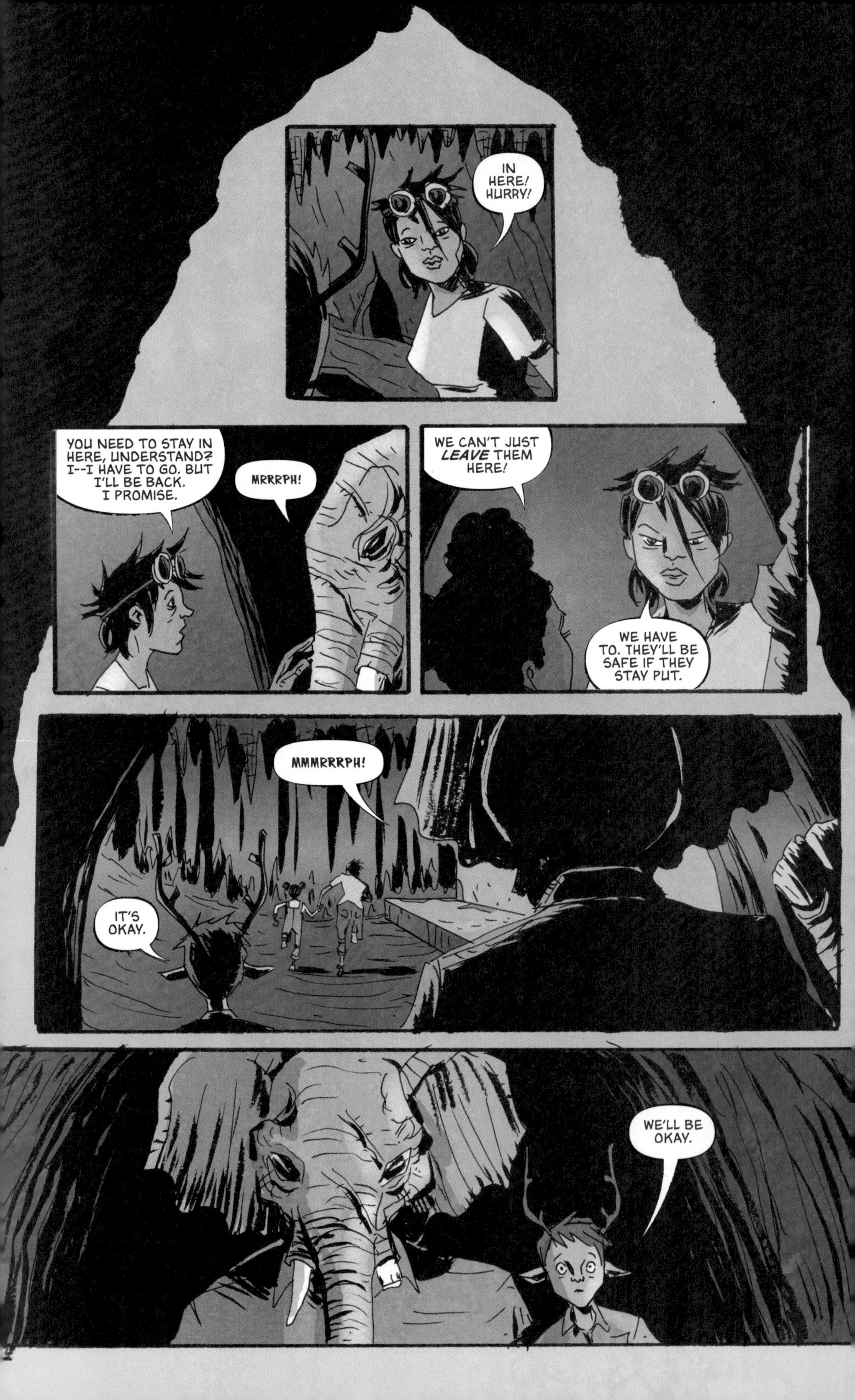
IN HERE! HURRY!
YOU NEED TO STAY IN HERE, UNDERSTAND? I--I HAVE TO GO. BUT I'LL BE BACK. I PROMISE.
MRRRPH!
WE CAN'T JUST *LEAVE* THEM HERE!
WE HAVE TO. THEY'LL BE SAFE IF THEY STAY PUT.
MMMRRRPH!
IT'S OKAY.
WE'LL BE OKAY.

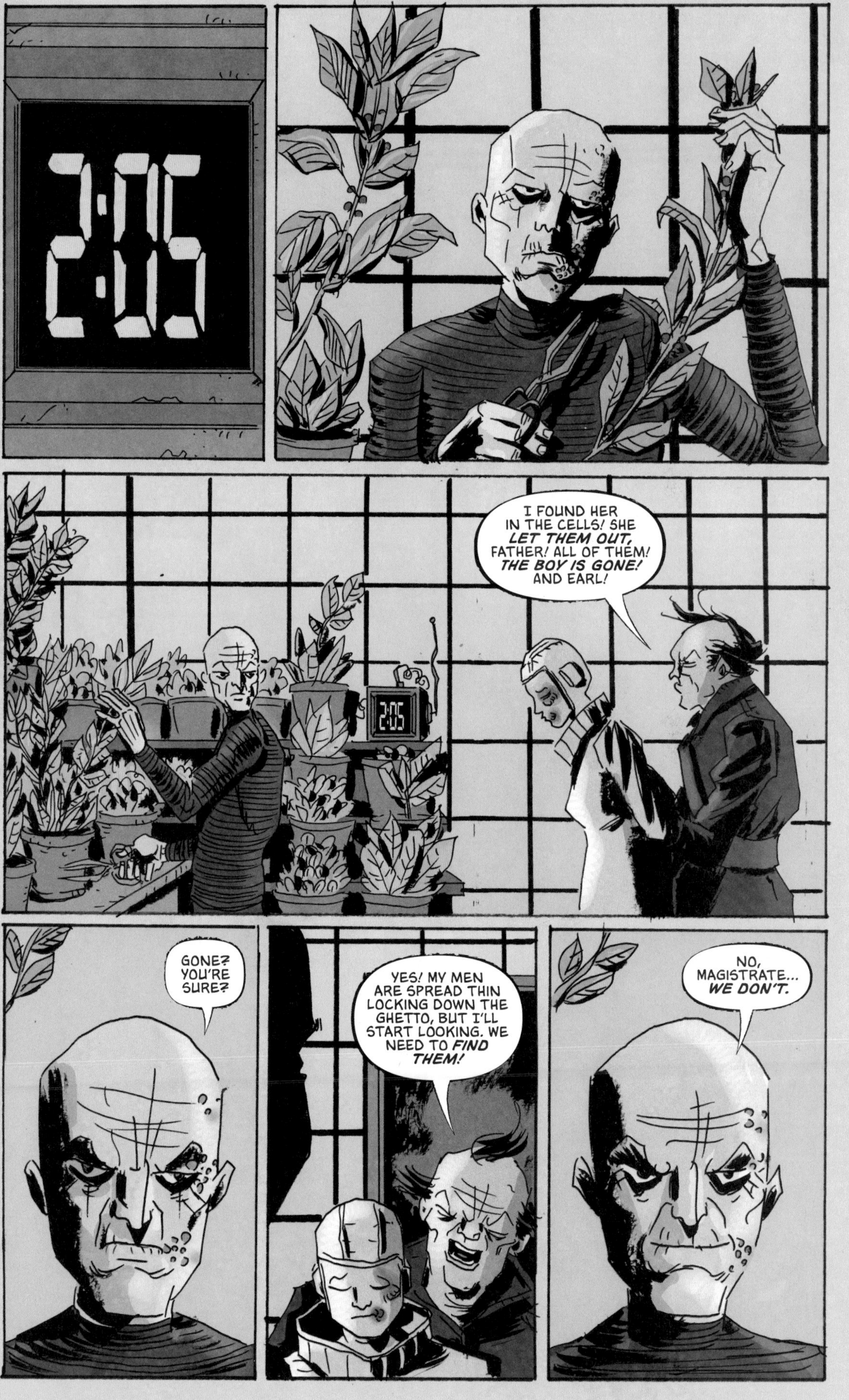
2:05
2:05
I FOUND HER IN THE CELLS! SHE LET THEM OUT, FATHER! ALL OF THEM! THE BOY IS GONE! AND EARL!
GONE? YOU'RE SURE?
YES! MY MEN ARE SPREAD THIN LOCKING DOWN THE GHETTO, BUT I'LL START LOOKING. WE NEED TO FIND THEM!
NO, MAGISTRATE... WE DON'T.

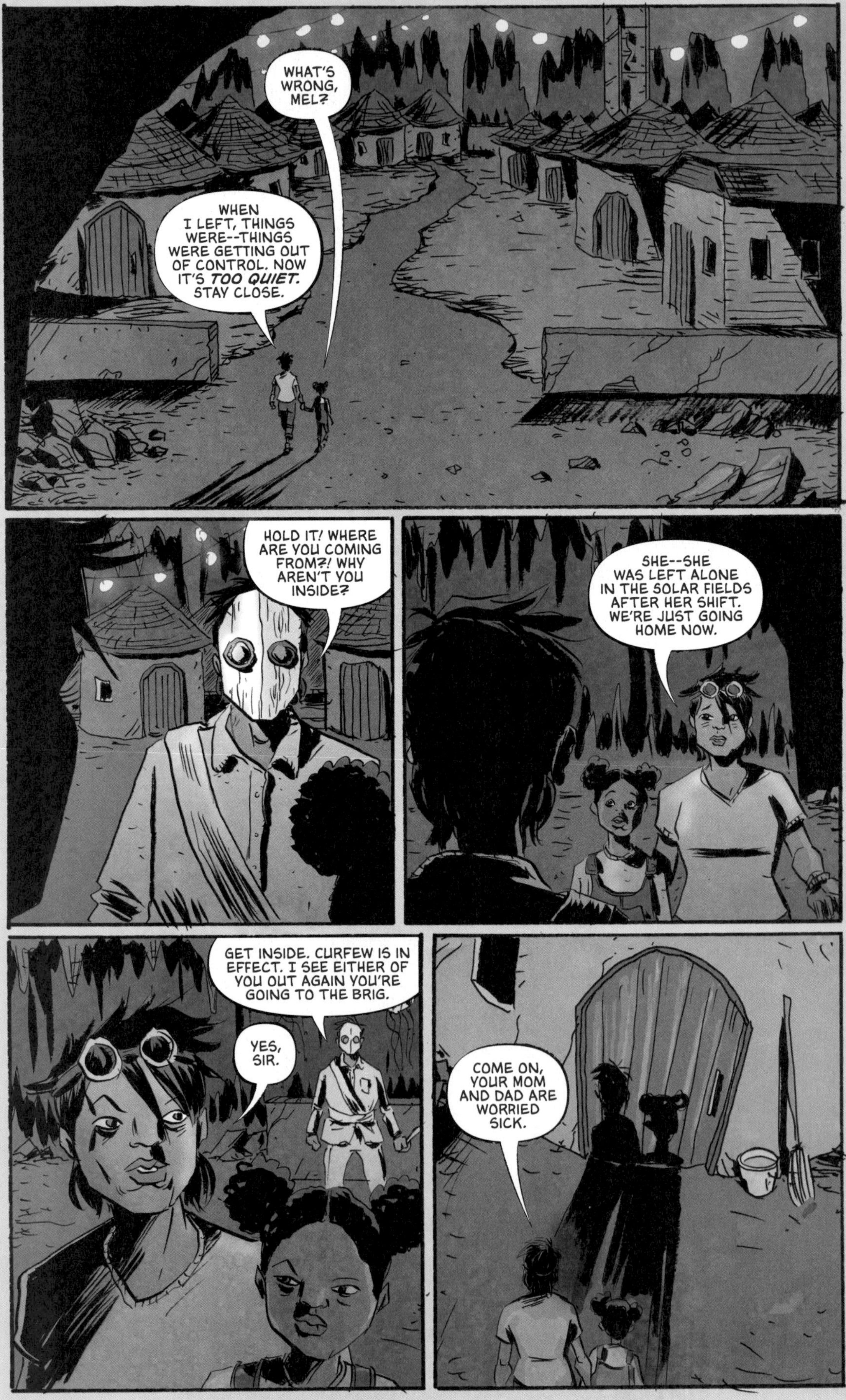
WHAT'S WRONG, MEL?
WHEN I LEFT, THINGS WERE--THINGS WERE GETTING OUT OF CONTROL. NOW IT'S *TOO QUIET.* STAY CLOSE.
HOLD IT! WHERE ARE YOU COMING FROM?! WHY AREN'T YOU INSIDE?
SHE--SHE WAS LEFT ALONE IN THE SOLAR FIELDS AFTER HER SHIFT. WE'RE JUST GOING HOME NOW.
GET INSIDE. CURFEW IS IN EFFECT. I SEE EITHER OF YOU OUT AGAIN YOU'RE GOING TO THE BRIG.
YES, SIR.
COME ON, YOUR MOM AND DAD ARE WORRIED SICK.

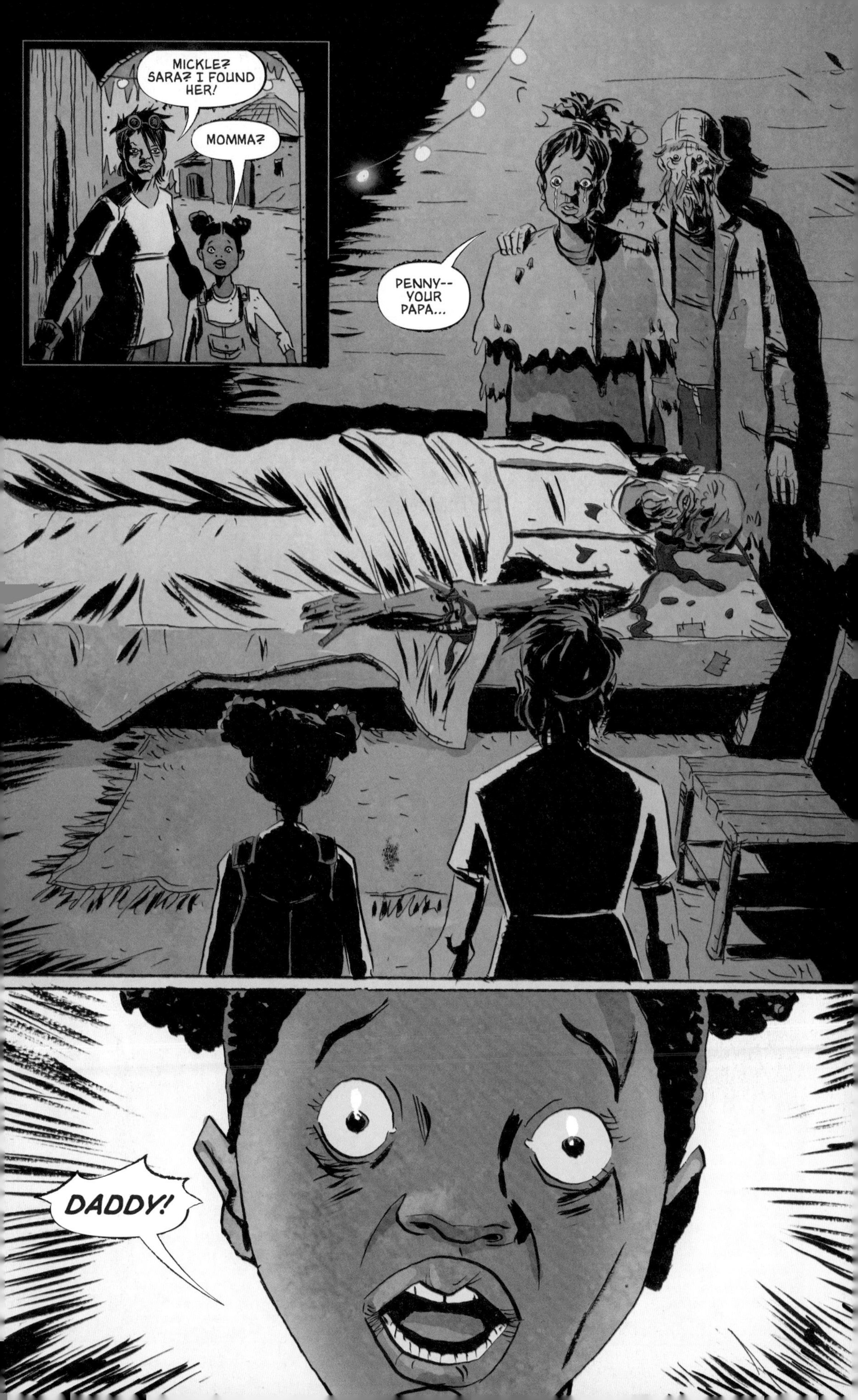
MICKLE? SARA? I FOUND HER!
MOMMA?
PENNY-- YOUR PAPA...
DADDY!

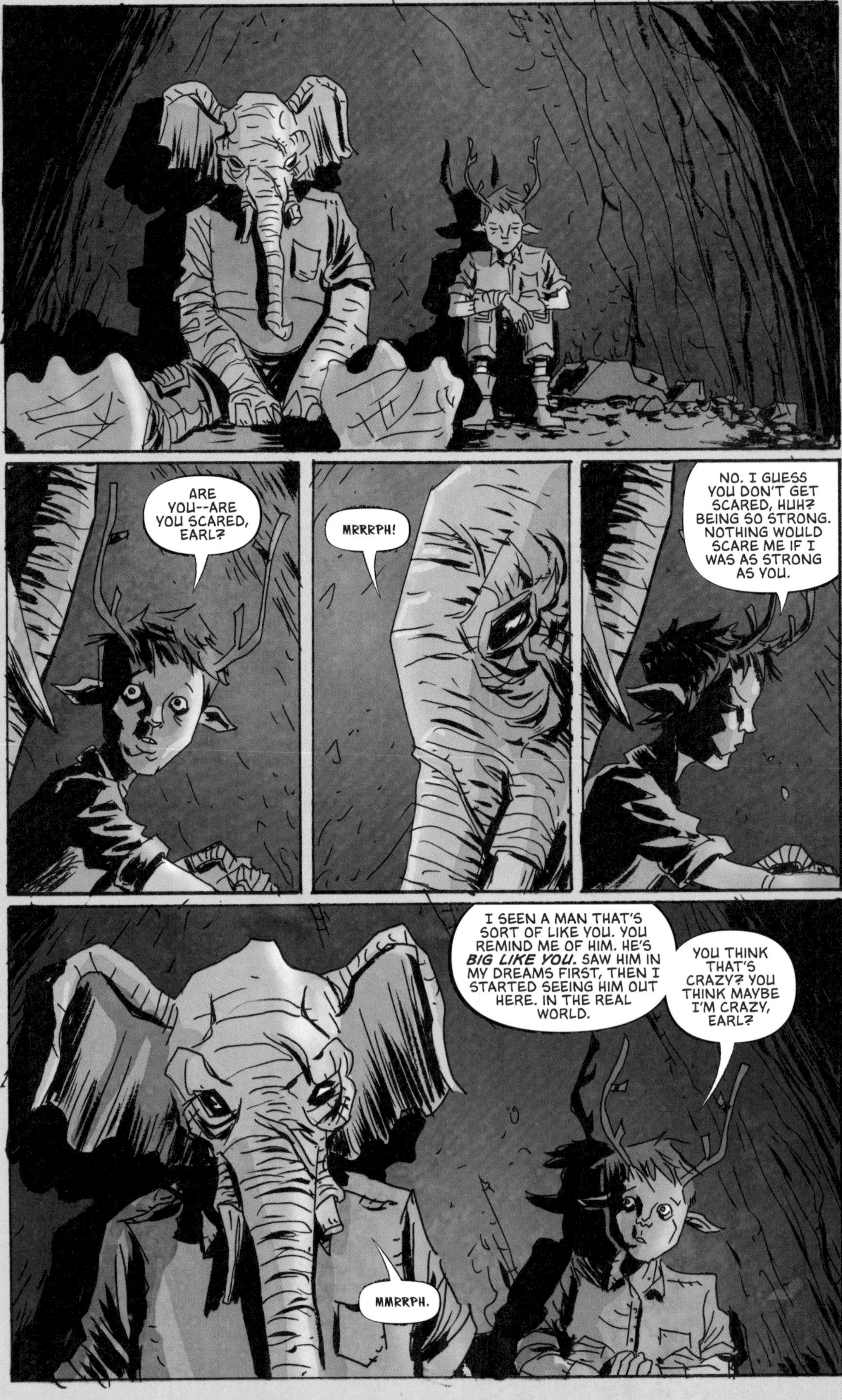
ARE YOU--ARE YOU SCARED, EARL?
MRRRPH!
NO. I GUESS YOU DON'T GET SCARED, HUH? BEING SO STRONG. NOTHING WOULD SCARE ME IF I WAS AS STRONG AS YOU.
I SEEN A MAN THAT'S SORT OF LIKE YOU. YOU REMIND ME OF HIM. HE'S ***BIG LIKE YOU.*** SAW HIM IN MY DREAMS FIRST, THEN I STARTED SEEING HIM OUT HERE. IN THE REAL WORLD.
YOU THINK THAT'S CRAZY? YOU THINK MAYBE I'M CRAZY, EARL?
MMRRPH.

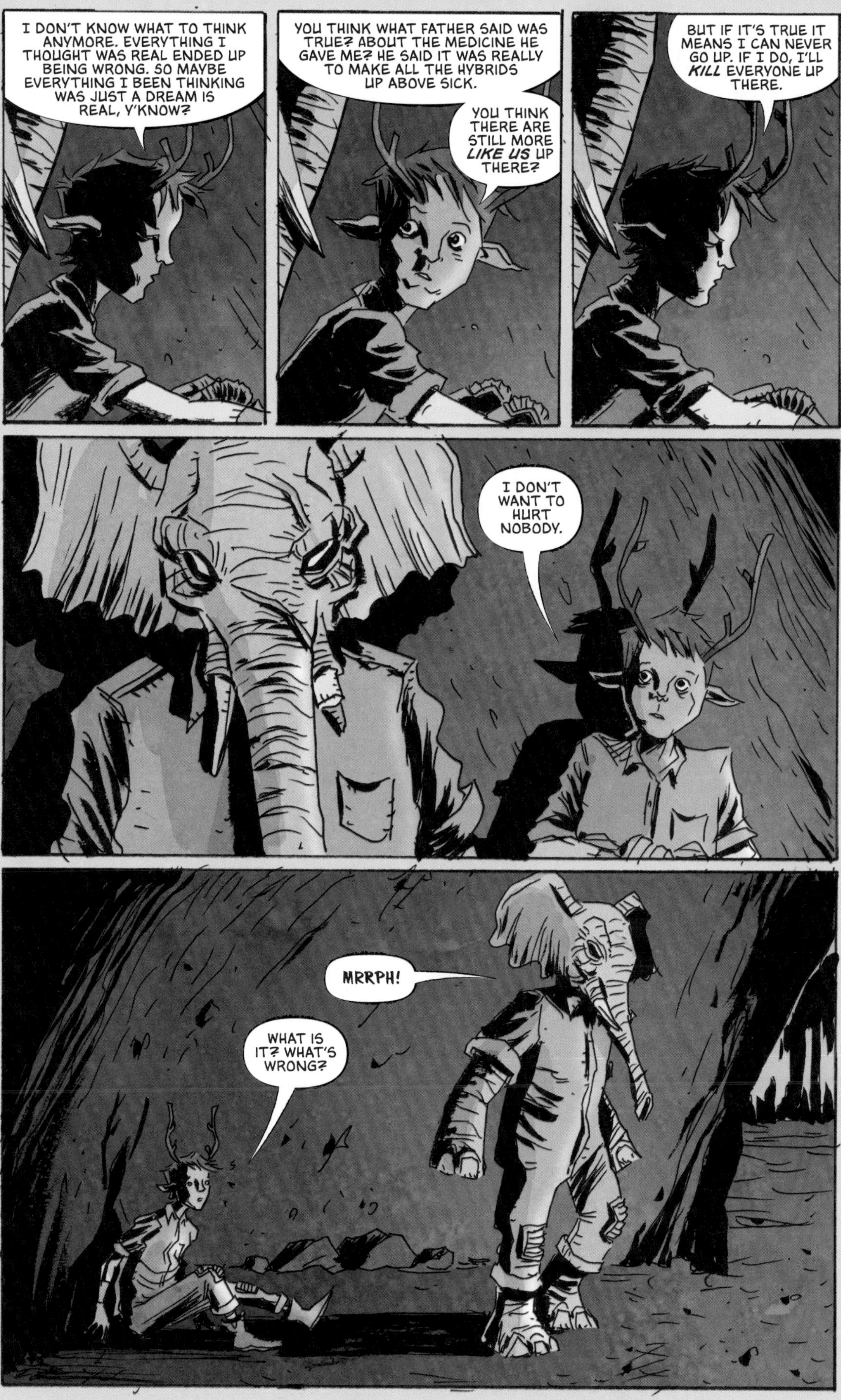
I DON'T KNOW WHAT TO THINK ANYMORE. EVERYTHING I THOUGHT WAS REAL ENDED UP BEING WRONG. SO MAYBE EVERYTHING I BEEN THINKING WAS JUST A DREAM IS REAL, Y'KNOW?
YOU THINK WHAT FATHER SAID WAS TRUE? ABOUT THE MEDICINE HE GAVE ME? HE SAID IT WAS REALLY TO MAKE ALL THE HYBRIDS UP ABOVE SICK.
YOU THINK THERE ARE STILL MORE *LIKE US* UP THERE?
BUT IF IT'S TRUE IT MEANS I CAN NEVER GO UP. IF I DO, I'LL *KILL* EVERYONE UP THERE.
I DON'T WANT TO HURT NOBODY.
MRRPH!
WHAT IS IT? WHAT'S WRONG?

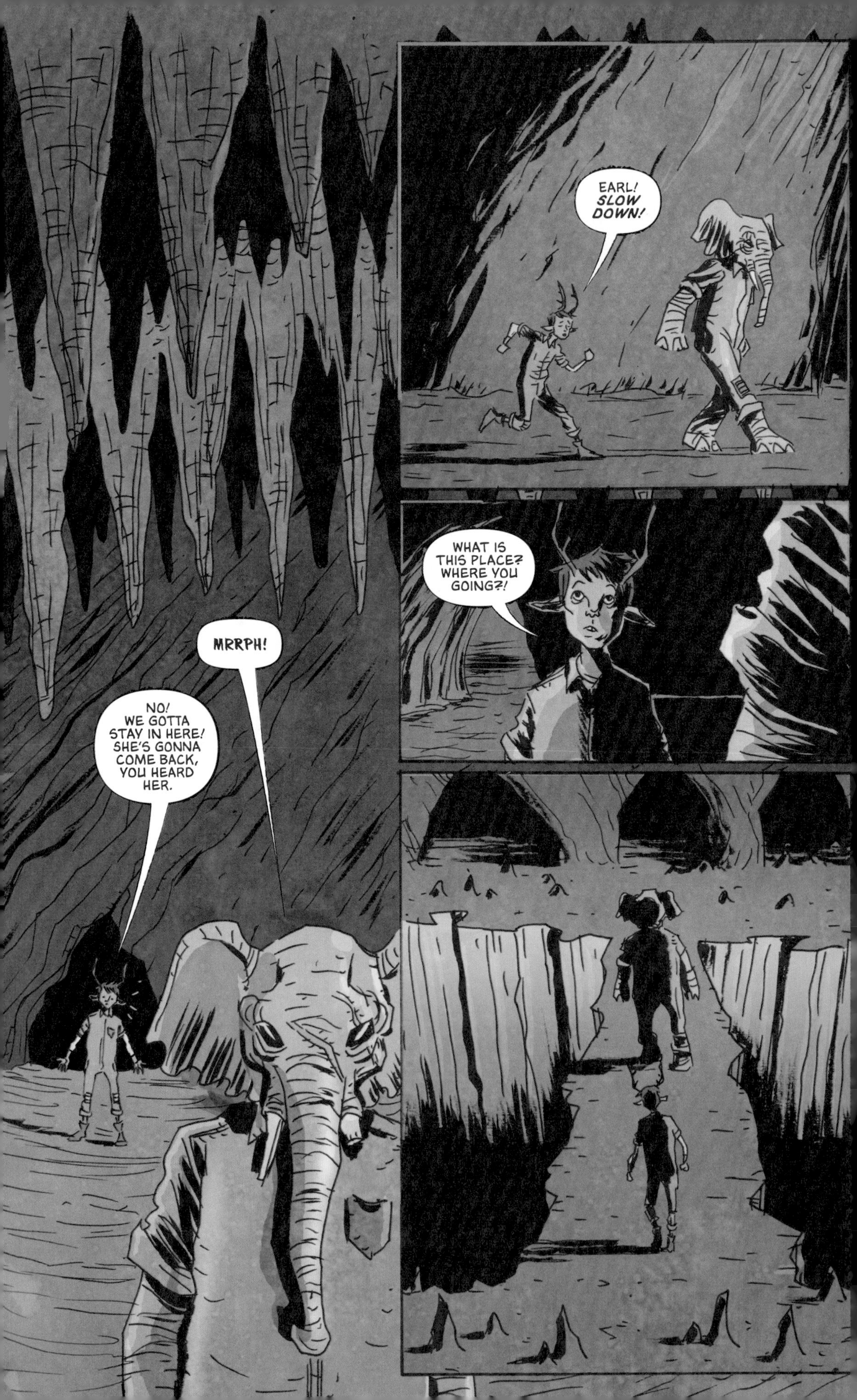
EARL! SLOW DOWN!
WHAT IS THIS PLACE? WHERE YOU GOING?!
MRRPH!
NO! WE GOTTA STAY IN HERE! SHE'S GONNA COME BACK, YOU HEARD HER.

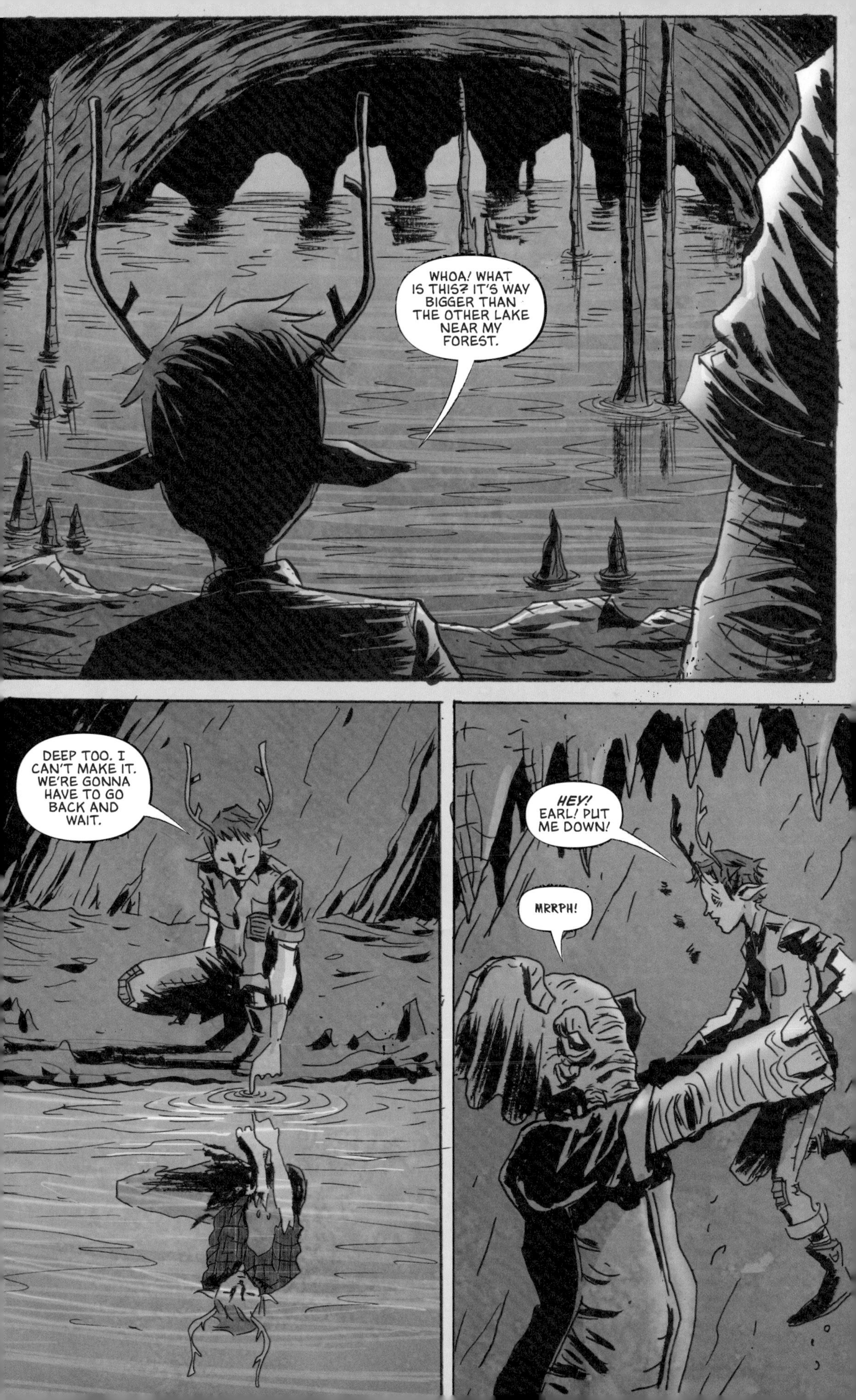
WHOA! WHAT IS THIS? IT'S WAY BIGGER THAN THE OTHER LAKE NEAR MY FOREST.
DEEP TOO. I CAN'T MAKE IT. WE'RE GONNA HAVE TO GO BACK AND WAIT.
HEY! EARL! PUT ME DOWN!
MRRPH!

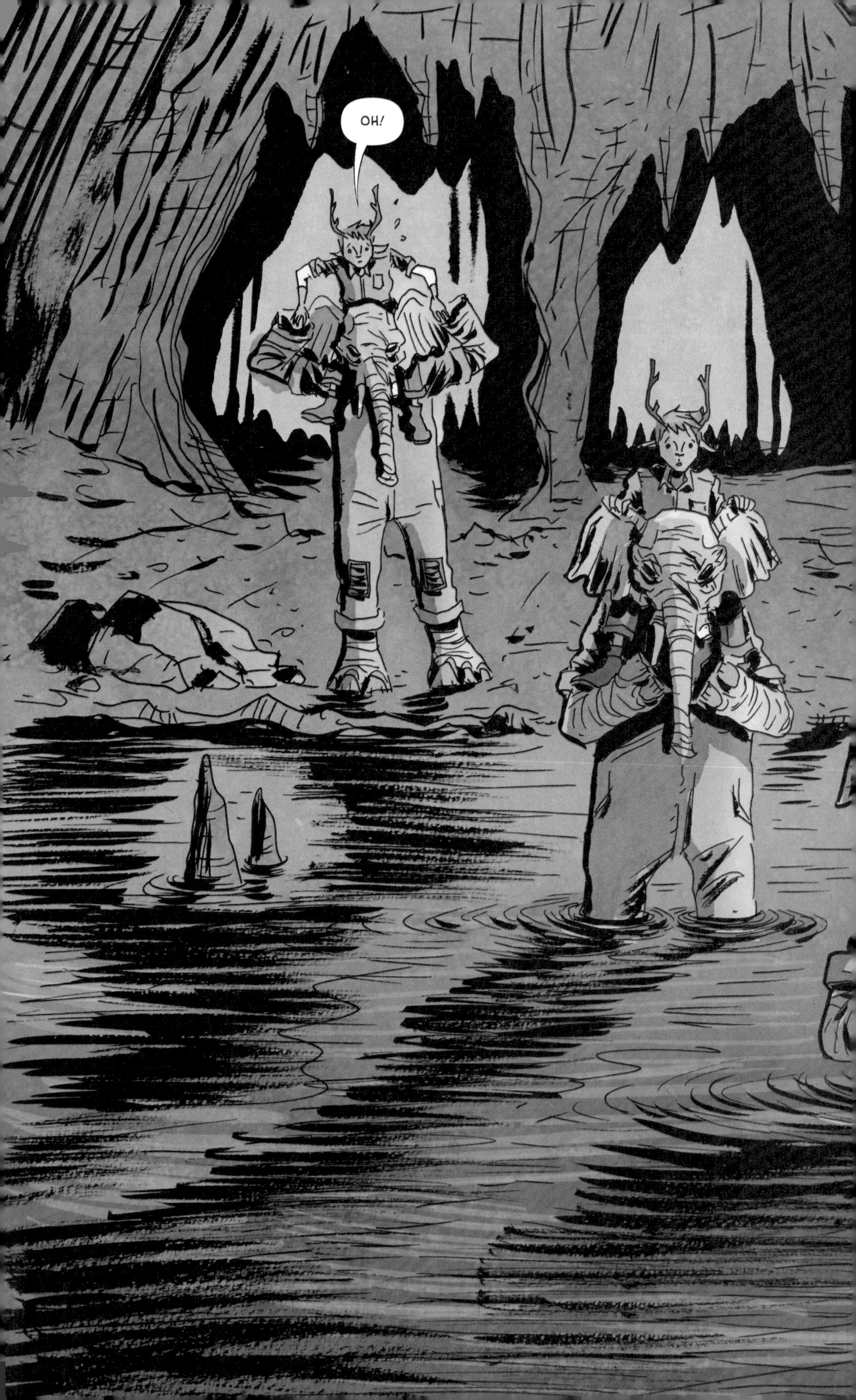
OH!

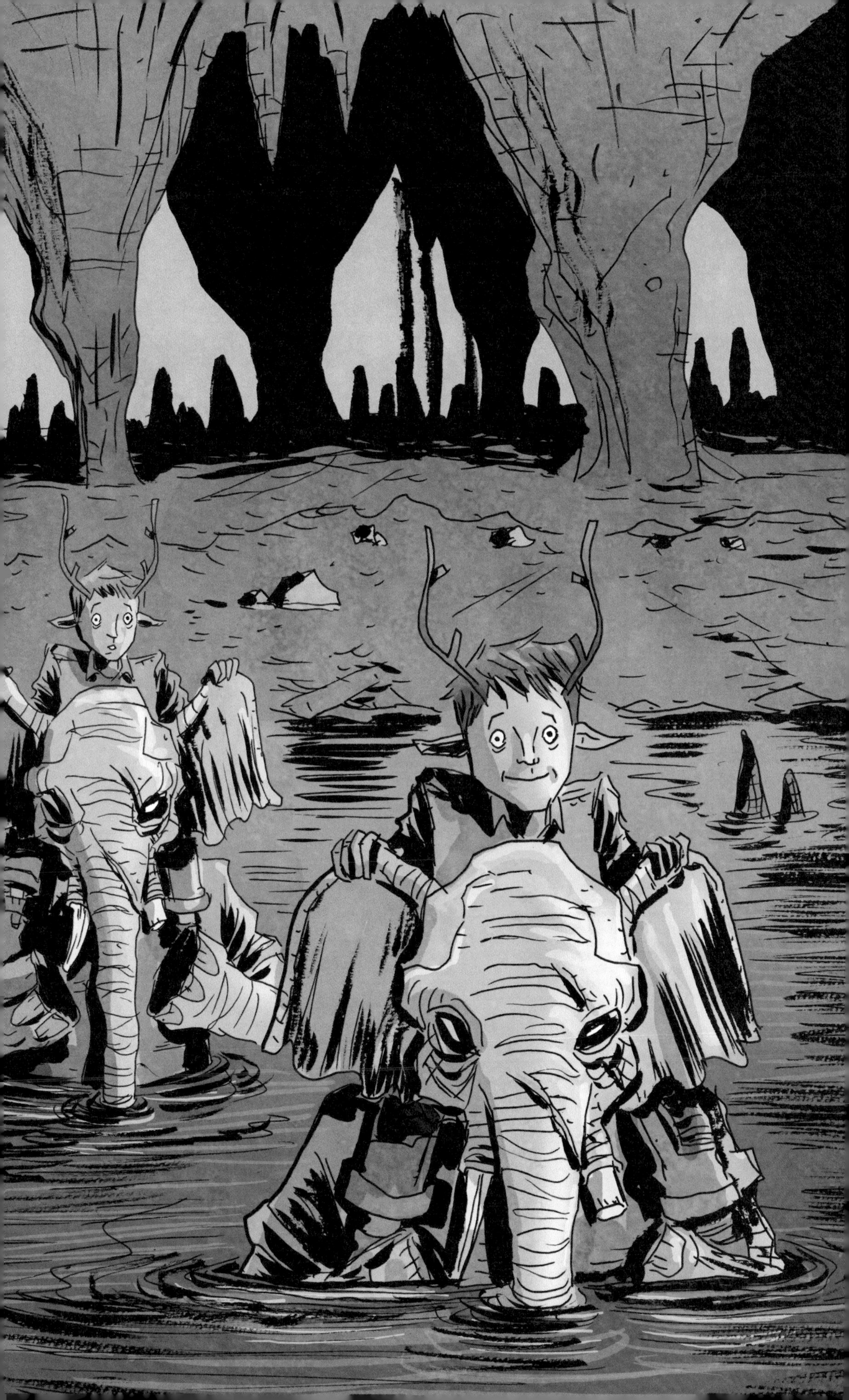

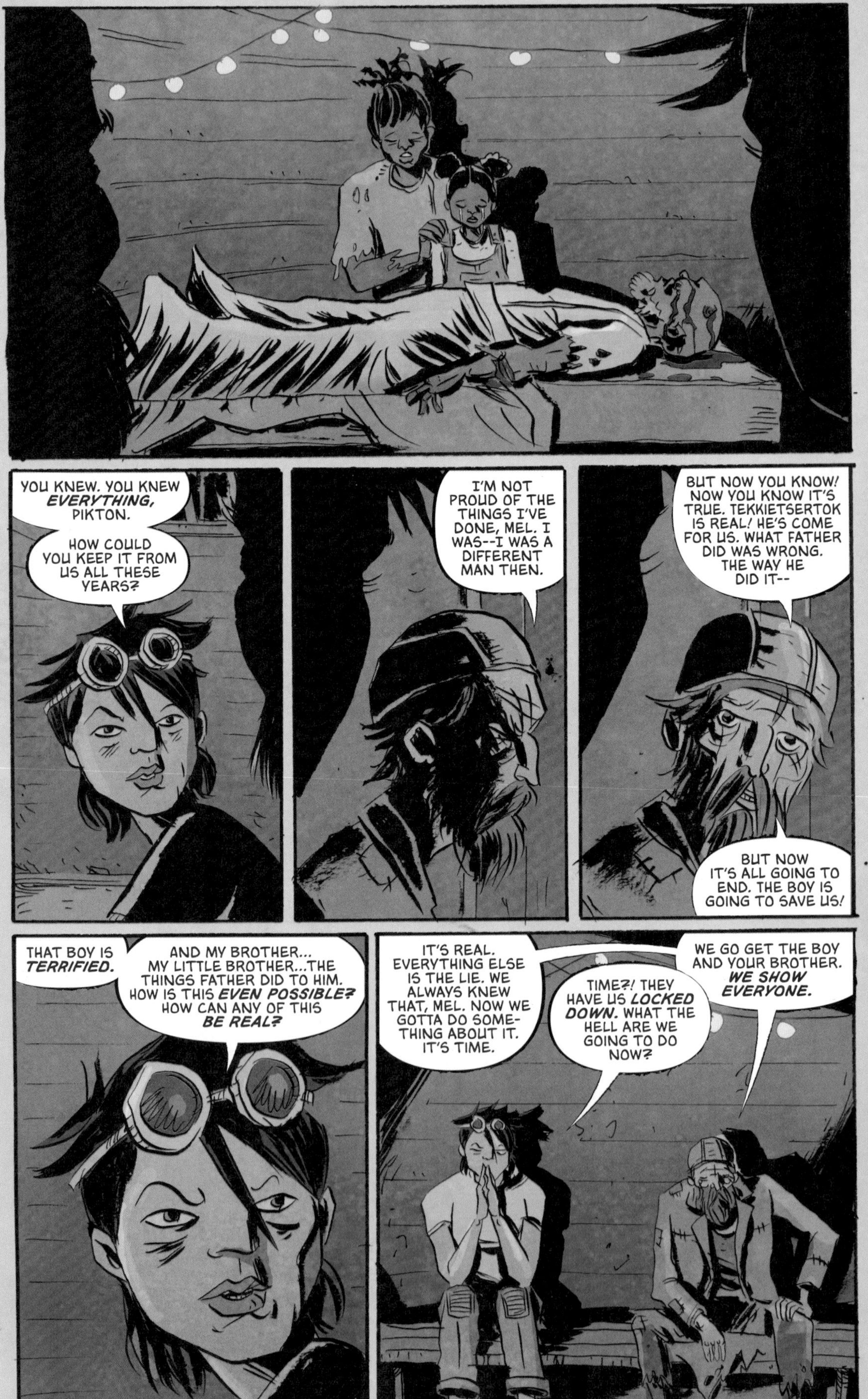
YOU KNEW. YOU KNEW *EVERYTHING,* PIKTON.
HOW COULD YOU KEEP IT FROM US ALL THESE YEARS?
I'M NOT PROUD OF THE THINGS I'VE DONE, MEL. I WAS--I WAS A DIFFERENT MAN THEN.
BUT NOW YOU KNOW! NOW YOU KNOW IT'S TRUE. TEKKIETSERTOK IS REAL! HE'S COME FOR US. WHAT FATHER DID WAS WRONG. THE WAY HE DID IT--
BUT NOW IT'S ALL GOING TO END. THE BOY IS GOING TO SAVE US!
THAT BOY IS *TERRIFIED.*
AND MY BROTHER... MY LITTLE BROTHER...THE THINGS FATHER DID TO HIM. HOW IS THIS *EVEN POSSIBLE?* HOW CAN ANY OF THIS *BE REAL?*
IT'S REAL. EVERYTHING ELSE IS THE LIE. WE ALWAYS KNEW THAT, MEL. NOW WE GOTTA DO SOME-THING ABOUT IT. IT'S TIME.
TIME?! THEY HAVE US *LOCKED DOWN.* WHAT THE HELL ARE WE GOING TO DO NOW?
WE GO GET THE BOY AND YOUR BROTHER. ***WE SHOW EVERYONE.***

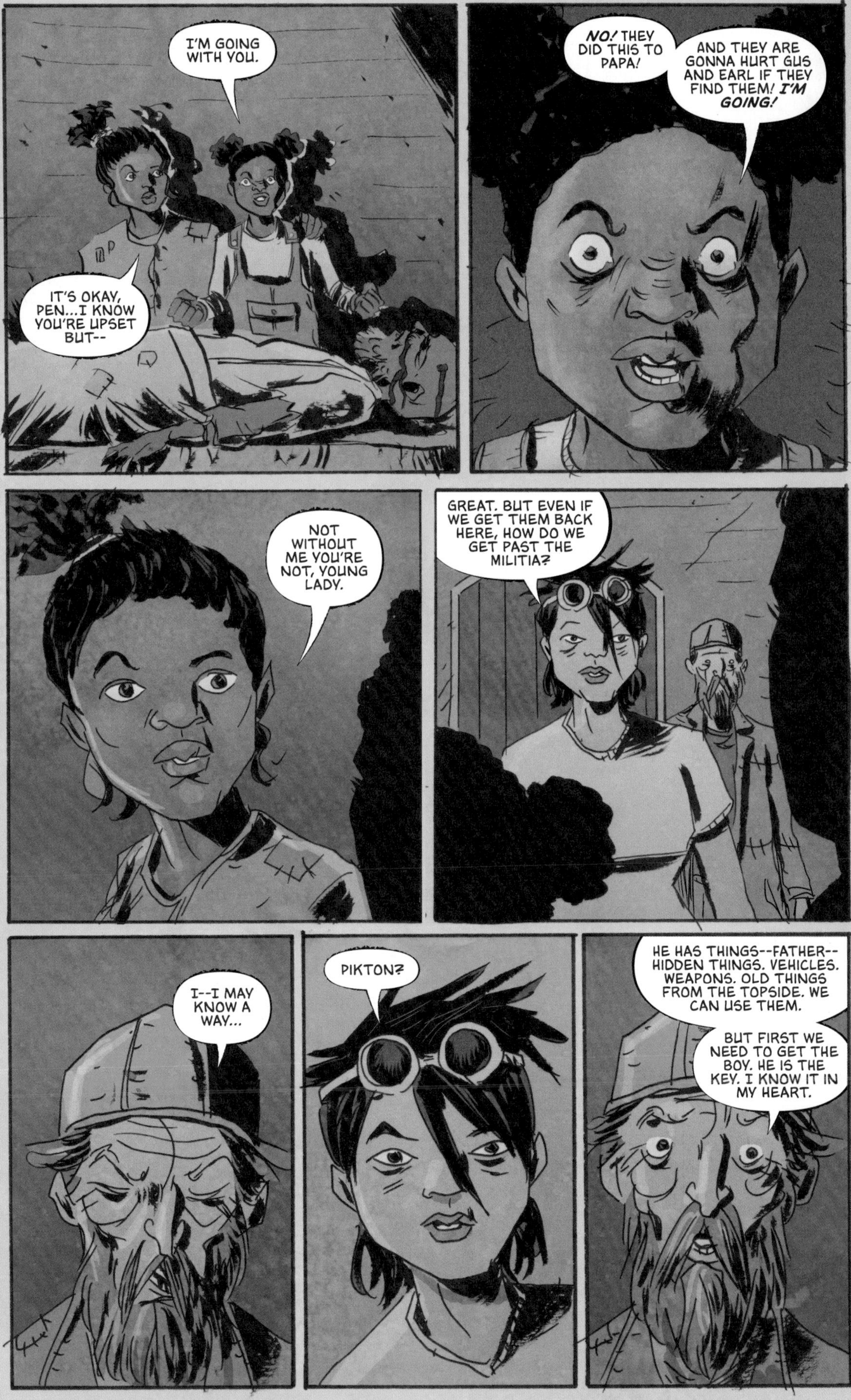
I'M GOING WITH YOU.
IT'S OKAY, PEN...I KNOW YOU'RE UPSET BUT--
NO! THEY DID THIS TO PAPA!
AND THEY ARE GONNA HURT GUS AND EARL IF THEY FIND THEM! I'M GOING!
NOT WITHOUT ME YOU'RE NOT, YOUNG LADY.
GREAT. BUT EVEN IF WE GET THEM BACK HERE, HOW DO WE GET PAST THE MILITIA?
I--I MAY KNOW A WAY...
PIKTON?
HE HAS THINGS--FATHER--HIDDEN THINGS. VEHICLES. WEAPONS. OLD THINGS FROM THE TOPSIDE. WE CAN USE THEM.
BUT FIRST WE NEED TO GET THE BOY. HE IS THE KEY. I KNOW IT IN MY HEART.

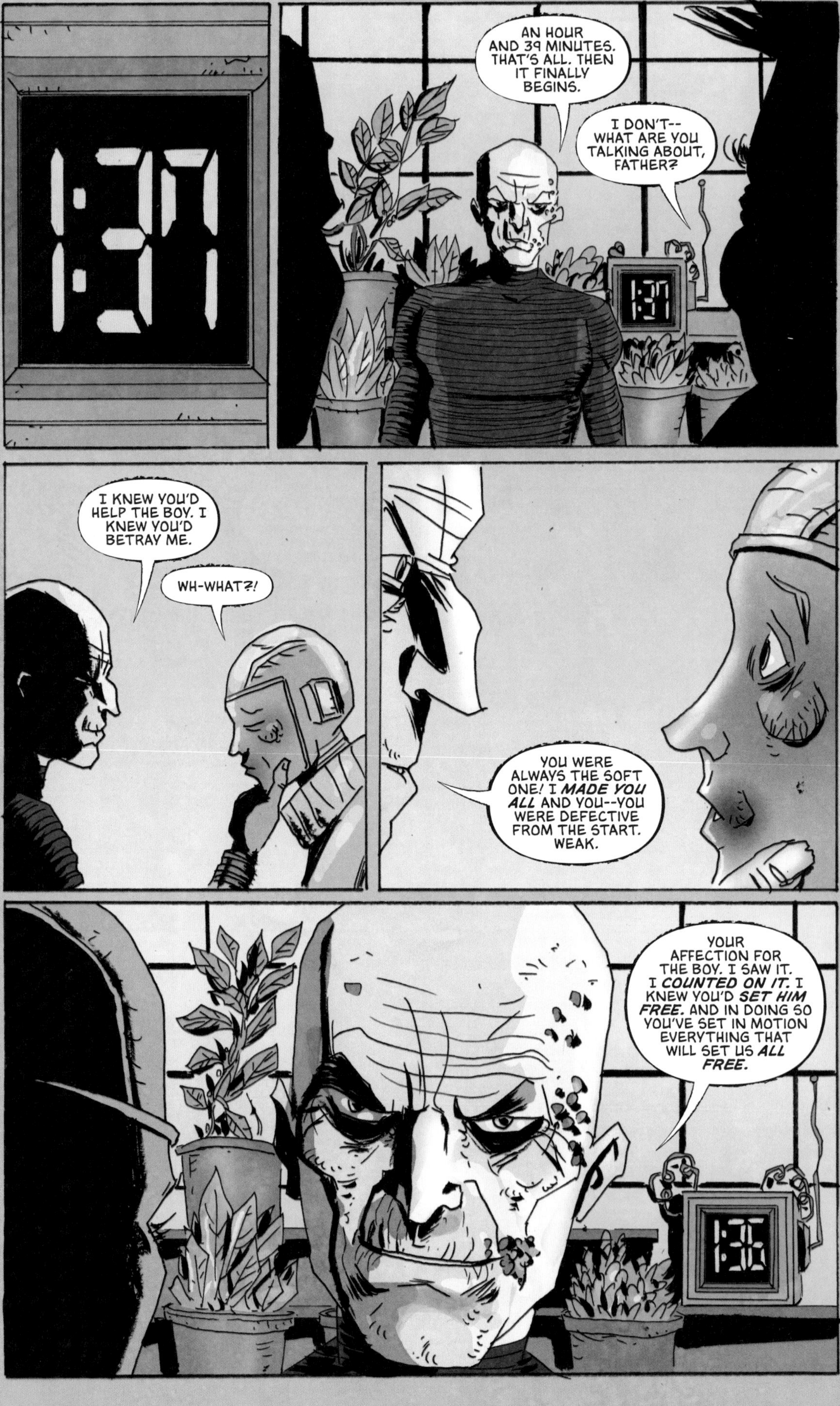

1:37
AN HOUR AND 39 MINUTES. THAT'S ALL. THEN IT FINALLY BEGINS.
I DON'T-- WHAT ARE YOU TALKING ABOUT, FATHER?
I KNEW YOU'D HELP THE BOY. I KNEW YOU'D BETRAY ME.
WH-WHAT?!
YOU WERE ALWAYS THE SOFT ONE! I *MADE YOU ALL* AND YOU--YOU WERE DEFECTIVE FROM THE START. WEAK.
YOUR AFFECTION FOR THE BOY. I SAW IT. I *COUNTED ON IT.* I KNEW YOU'D *SET HIM FREE.* AND IN DOING SO YOU'VE SET IN MOTION EVERYTHING THAT WILL SET US *ALL FREE.*

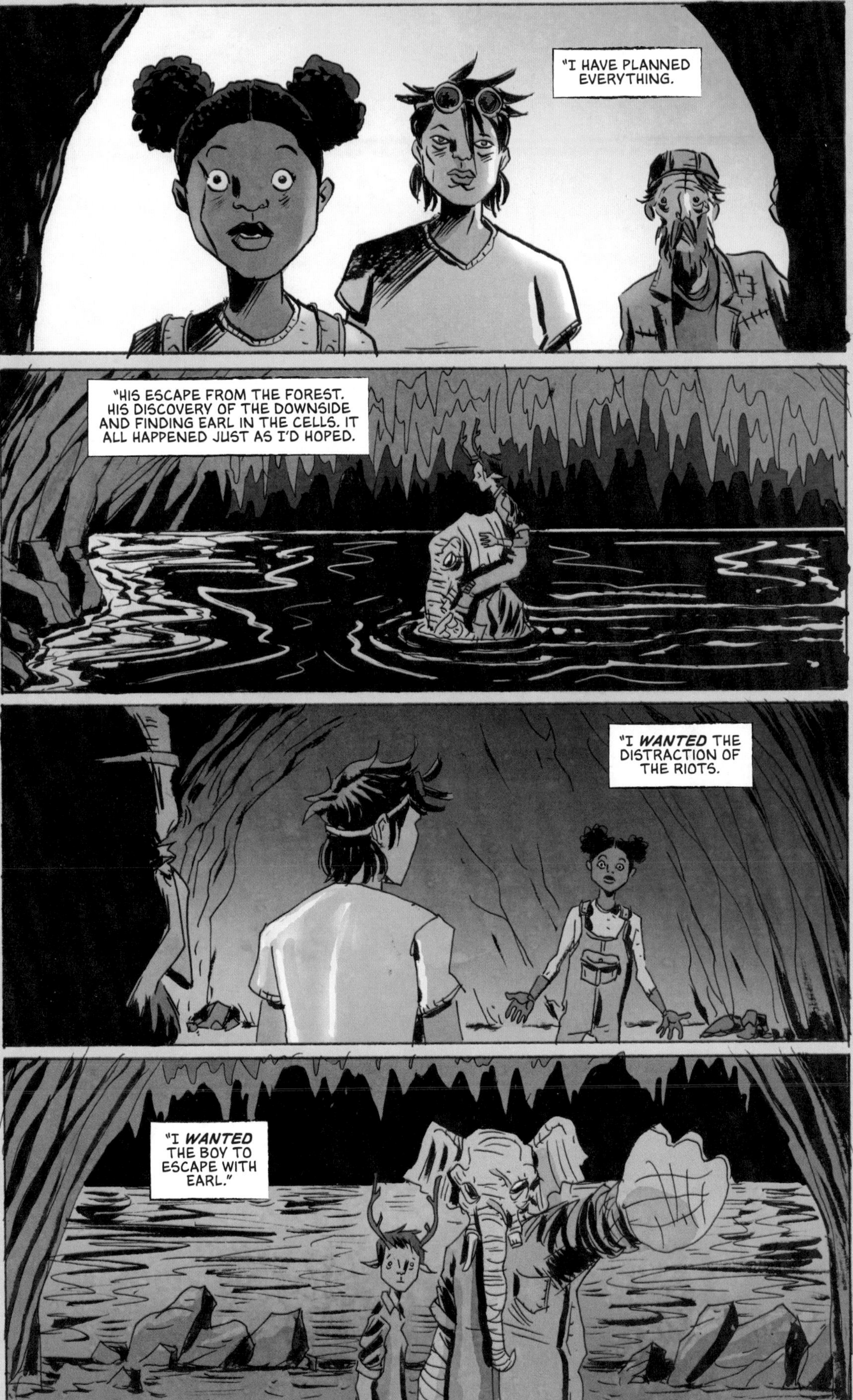
"I HAVE PLANNED EVERYTHING.
"HIS ESCAPE FROM THE FOREST. HIS DISCOVERY OF THE DOWNSIDE AND FINDING EARL IN THE CELLS. IT ALL HAPPENED JUST AS I'D HOPED.
"I WANTED THE DISTRACTION OF THE RIOTS.
"I WANTED THE BOY TO ESCAPE WITH EARL."

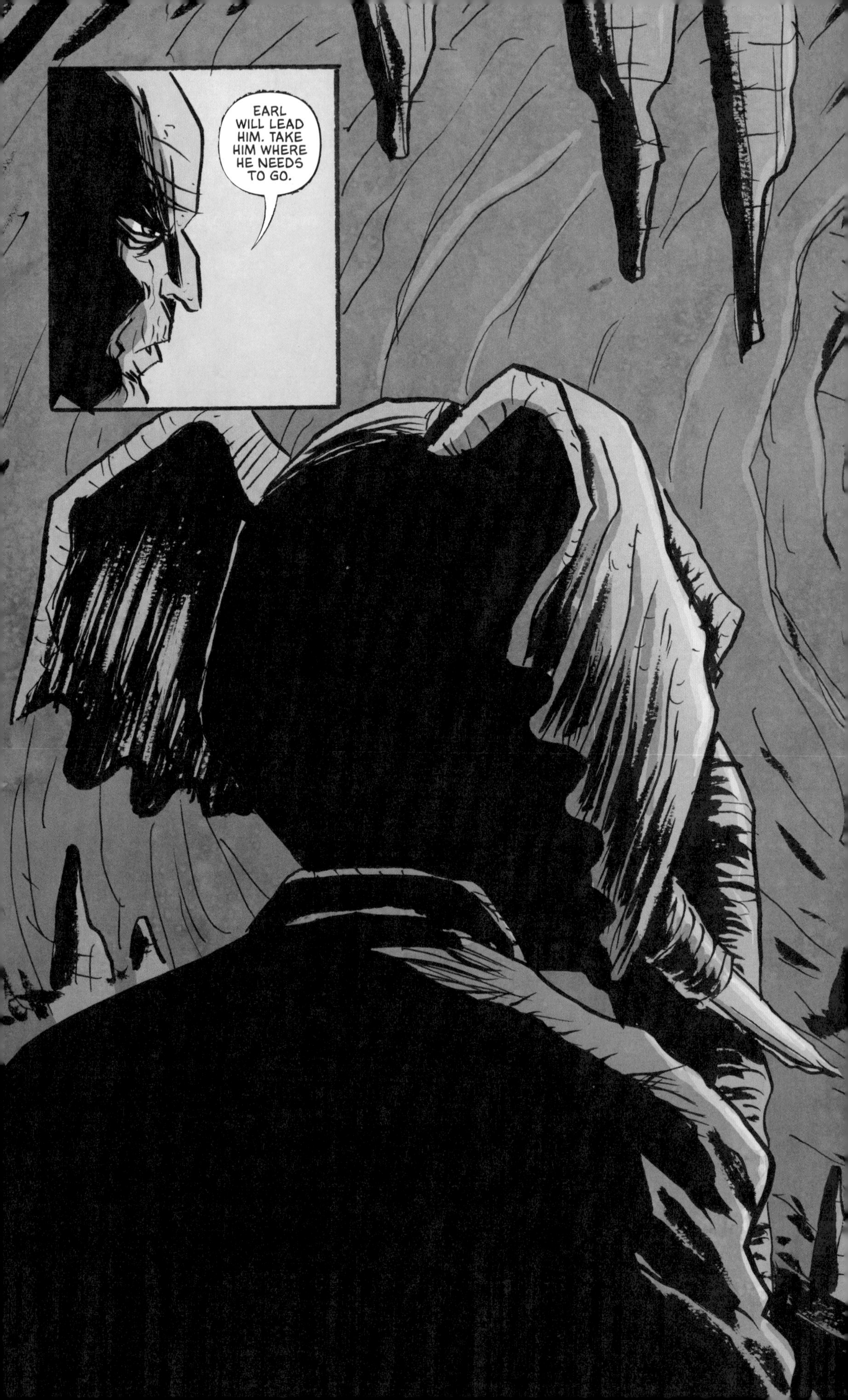
EARL WILL LEAD HIM. TAKE HIM WHERE HE NEEDS TO GO.

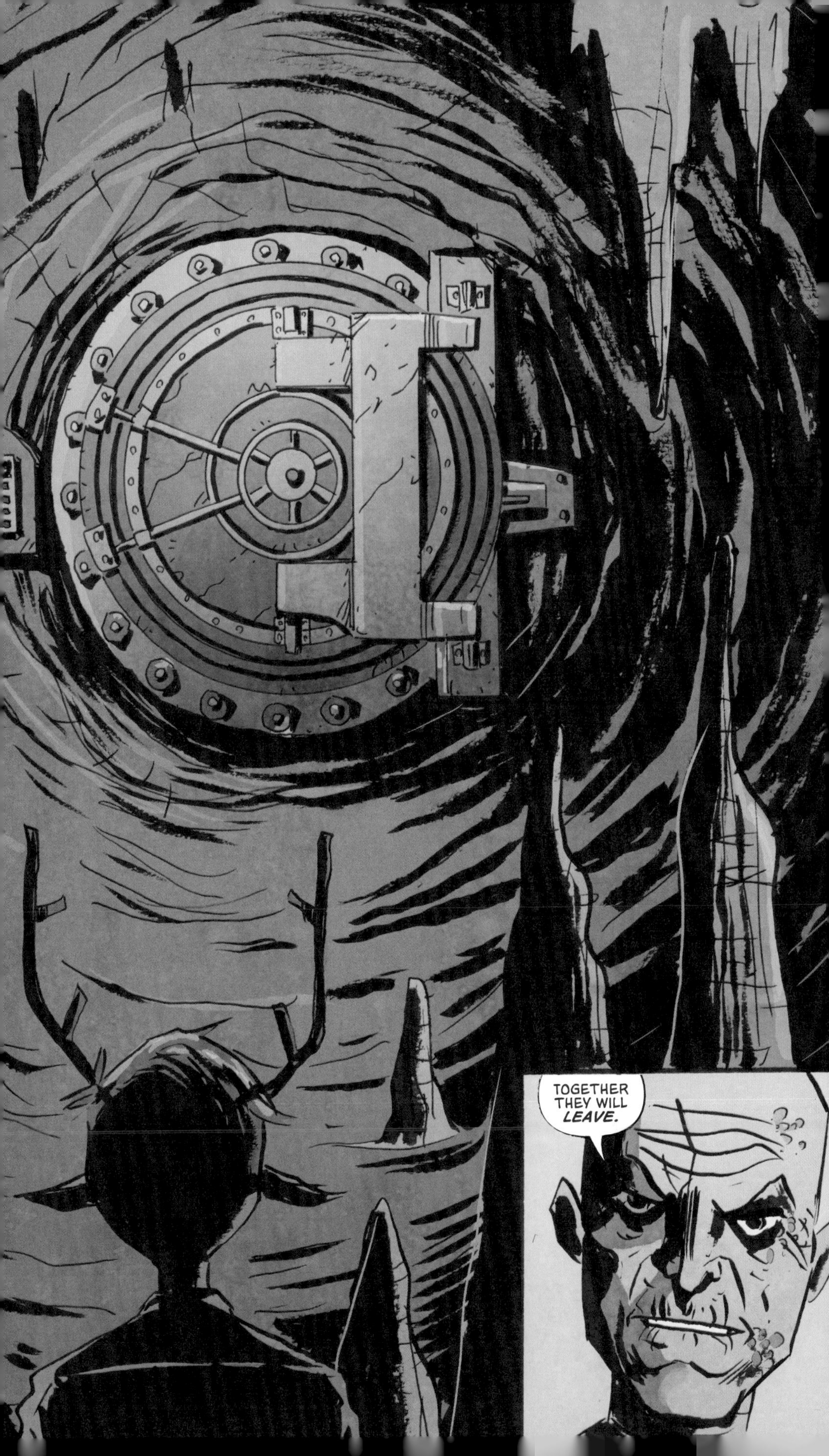
TOGETHER THEY WILL *LEAVE.*

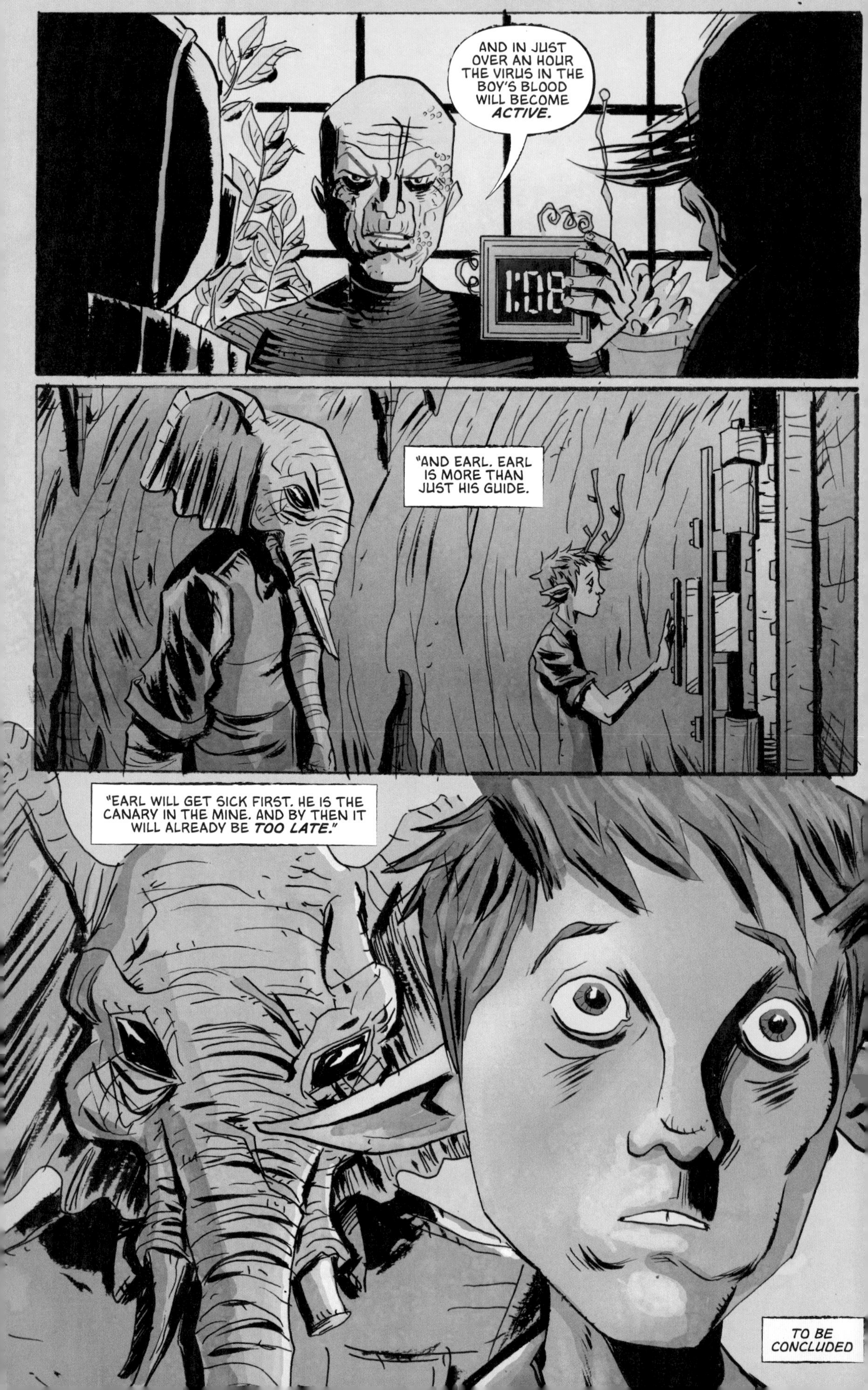
AND IN JUST OVER AN HOUR THE VIRUS IN THE BOY'S BLOOD WILL BECOME ACTIVE.
1:08
"AND EARL. EARL IS MORE THAN JUST HIS GUIDE.
"EARL WILL GET SICK FIRST. HE IS THE CANARY IN THE MINE. AND BY THEN IT WILL ALREADY BE TOO LATE."
TO BE CONCLUDED

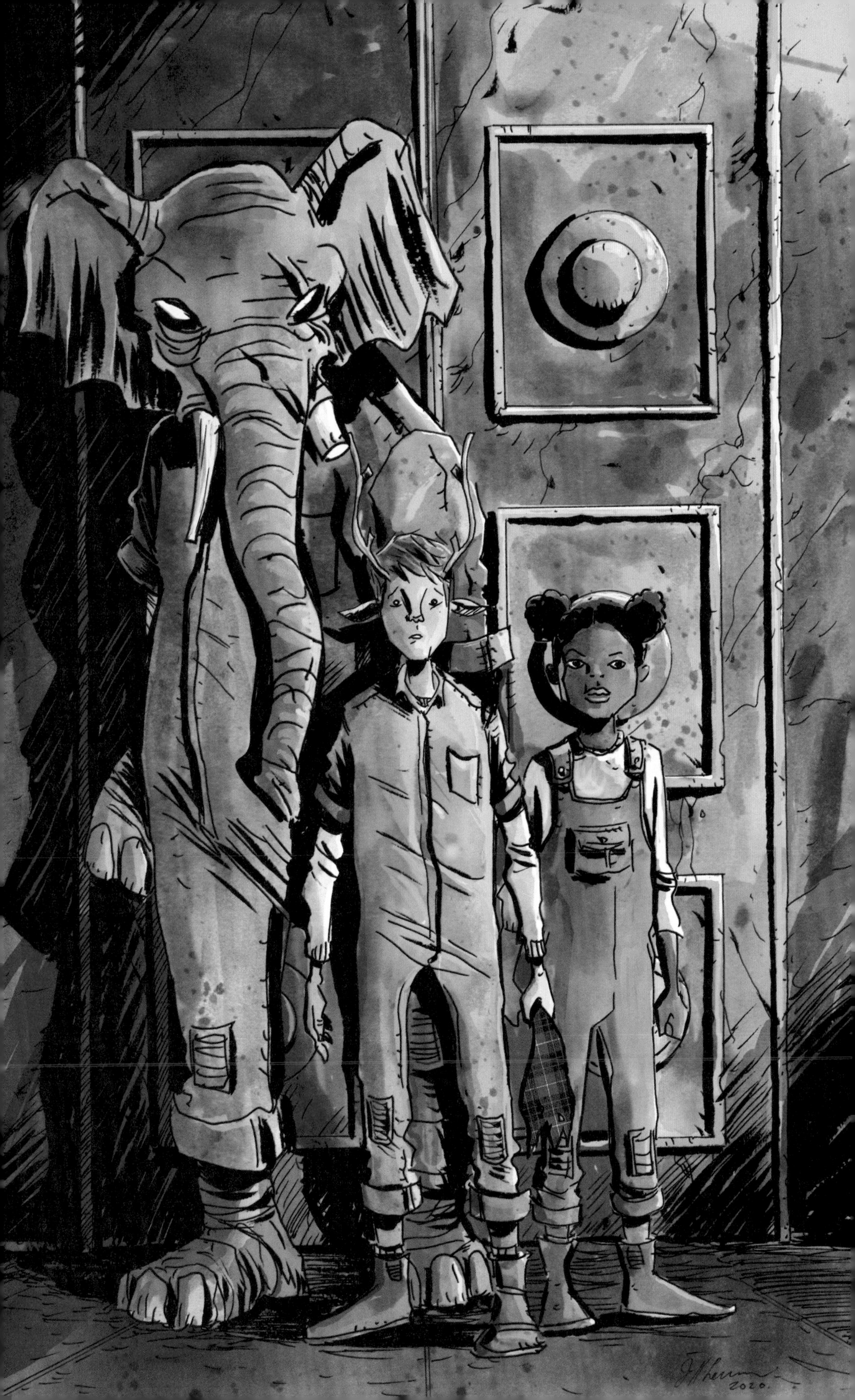

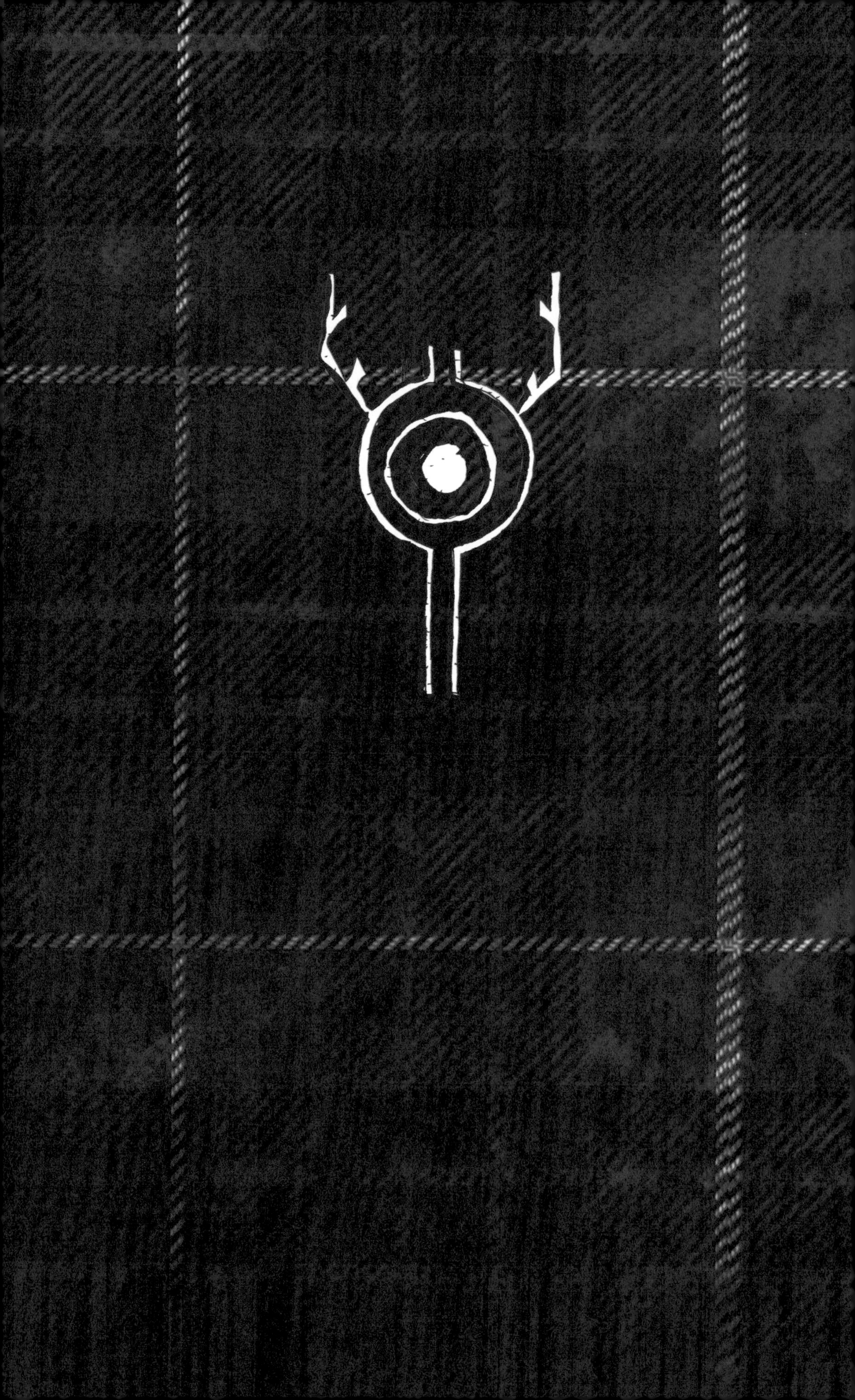

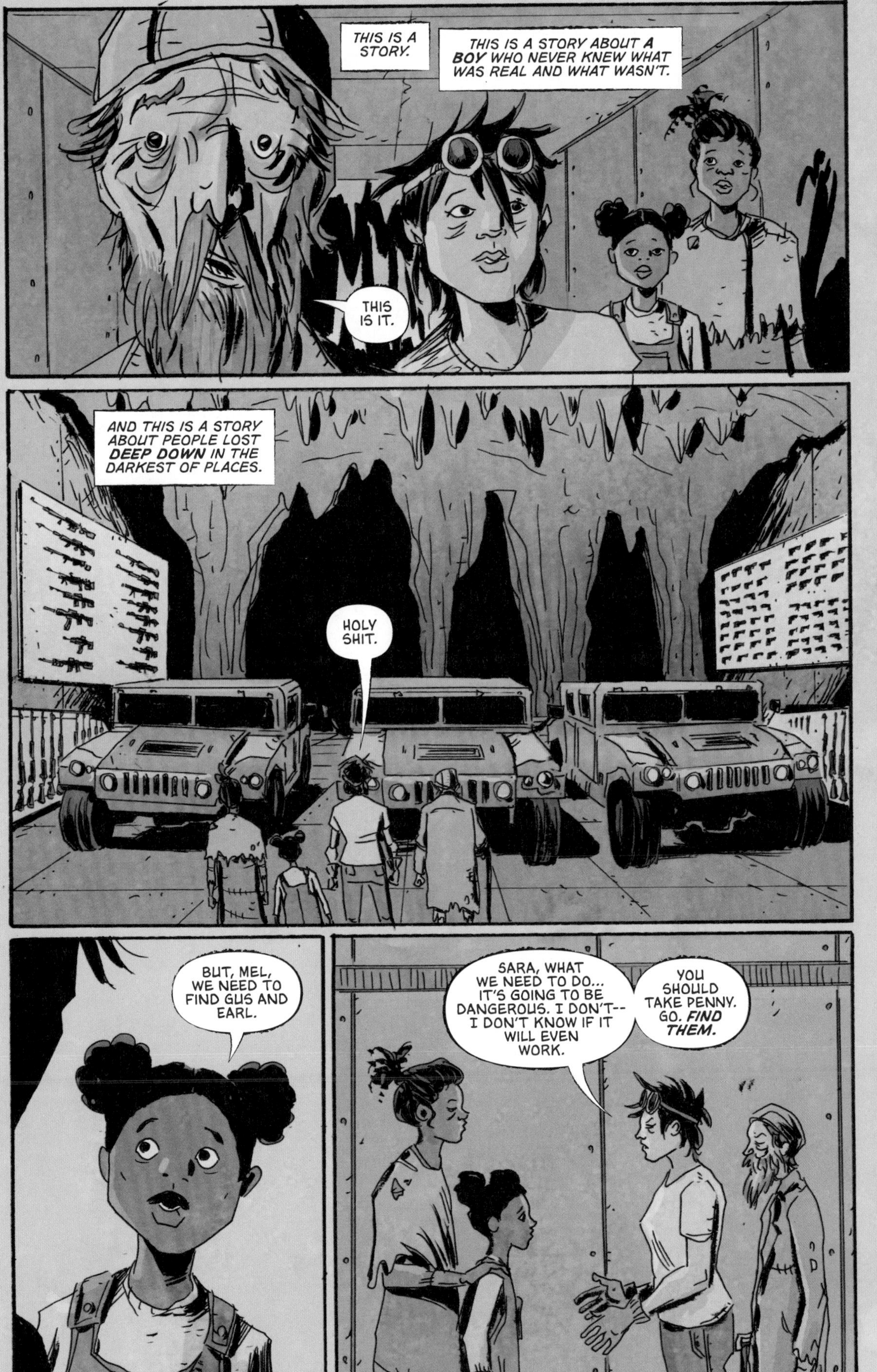
THIS IS A STORY.
THIS IS A STORY ABOUT A BOY WHO NEVER KNEW WHAT WAS REAL AND WHAT WASN'T.
THIS IS IT.
AND THIS IS A STORY ABOUT PEOPLE LOST DEEP DOWN IN THE DARKEST OF PLACES.
HOLY SHIT.
BUT, MEL, WE NEED TO FIND GUS AND EARL.
SARA, WHAT WE NEED TO DO... IT'S GOING TO BE DANGEROUS. I DON'T-- I DON'T KNOW IF IT WILL EVEN WORK.
YOU SHOULD TAKE PENNY. GO. FIND THEM.

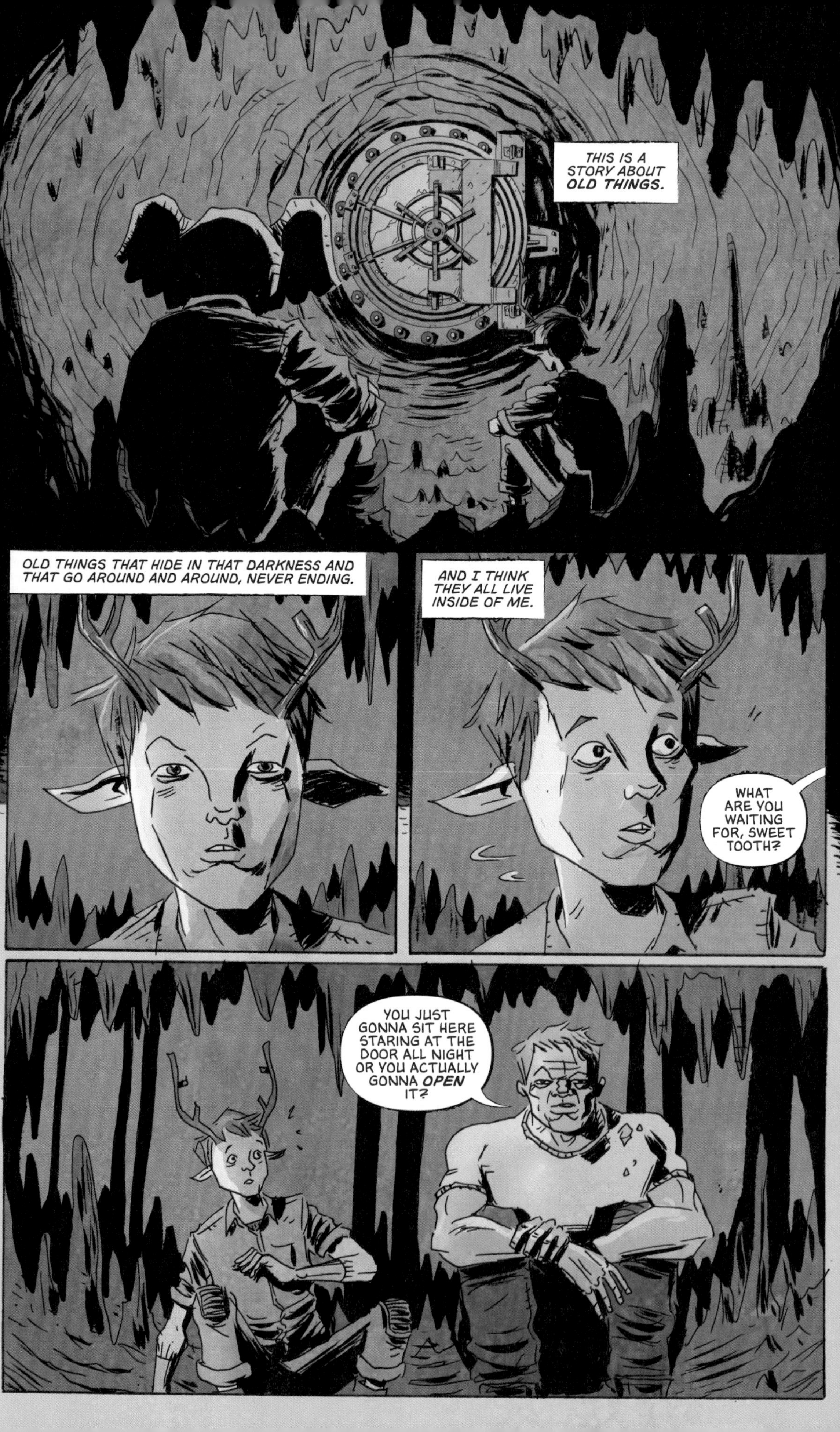
THIS IS A STORY ABOUT OLD THINGS.
OLD THINGS THAT HIDE IN THAT DARKNESS AND THAT GO AROUND AND AROUND, NEVER ENDING.
AND I THINK THEY ALL LIVE INSIDE OF ME.
WHAT ARE YOU WAITING FOR, SWEET TOOTH?
YOU JUST GONNA SIT HERE STARING AT THE DOOR ALL NIGHT OR YOU ACTUALLY GONNA OPEN IT?

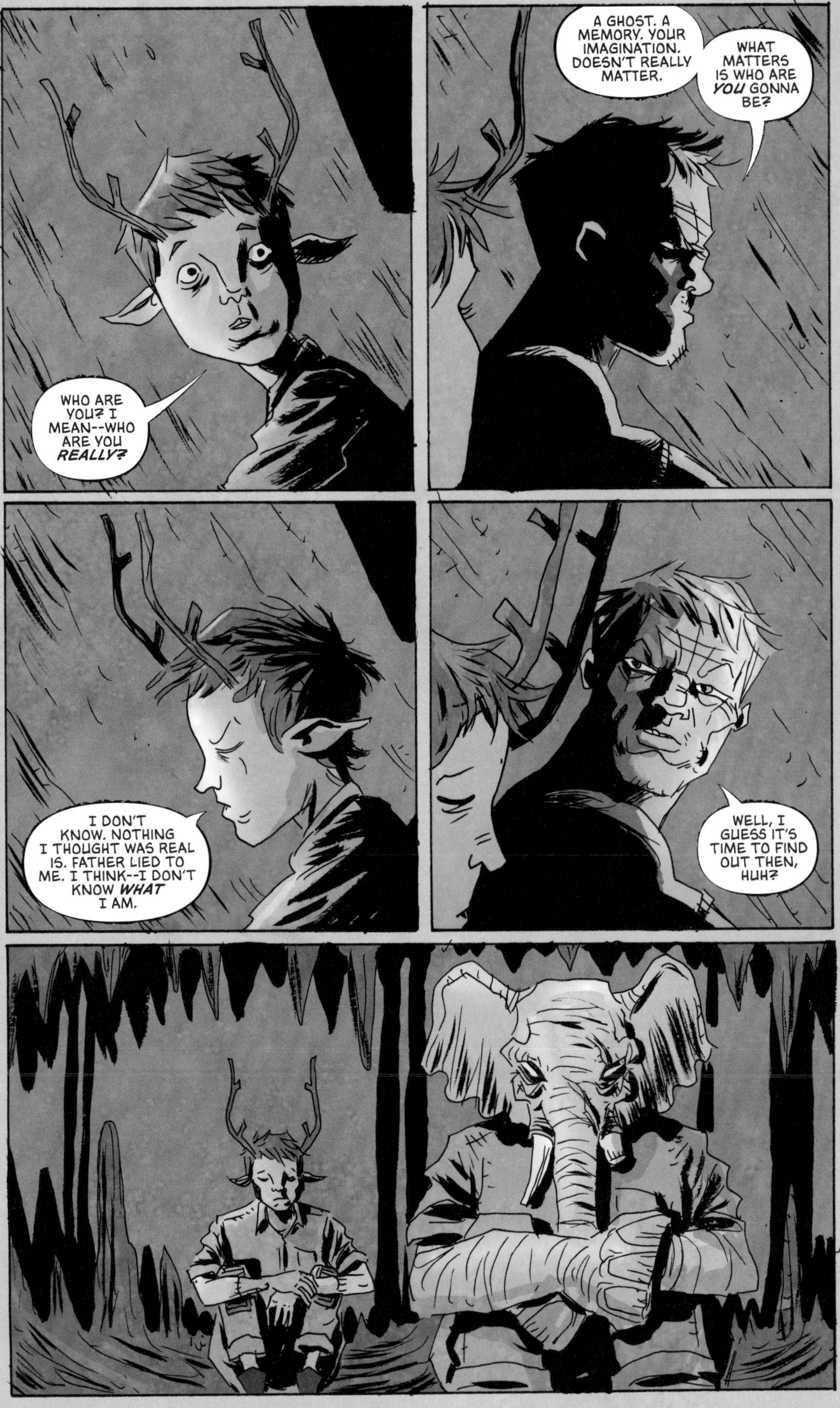
WHO ARE YOU? I MEAN--WHO ARE YOU *REALLY?*
A GHOST. A MEMORY. YOUR IMAGINATION. DOESN'T REALLY MATTER.
WHAT MATTERS IS WHO ARE *YOU* GONNA BE?
I DON'T KNOW. NOTHING I THOUGHT WAS REAL IS. FATHER LIED TO ME. I THINK--I DON'T KNOW *WHAT* I AM.
WELL, I GUESS IT'S TIME TO FIND OUT THEN, HUH?

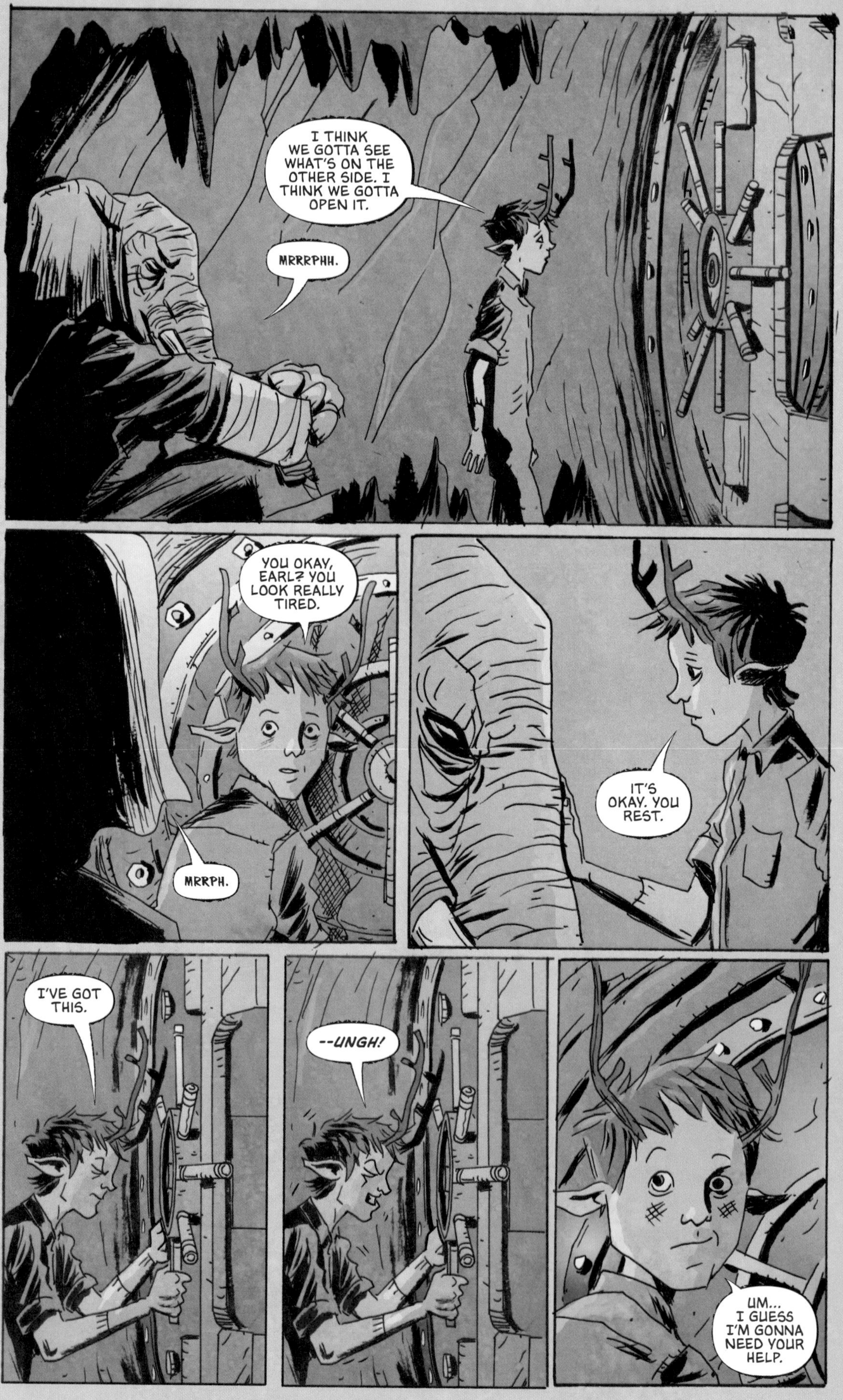
I THINK WE GOTTA SEE WHAT'S ON THE OTHER SIDE. I THINK WE GOTTA OPEN IT.
MRRRPHH.
YOU OKAY, EARL? YOU LOOK REALLY TIRED.
MRRPH.
IT'S OKAY. YOU REST.
I'VE GOT THIS.
--UNGH!
UM... I GUESS I'M GONNA NEED YOUR HELP.

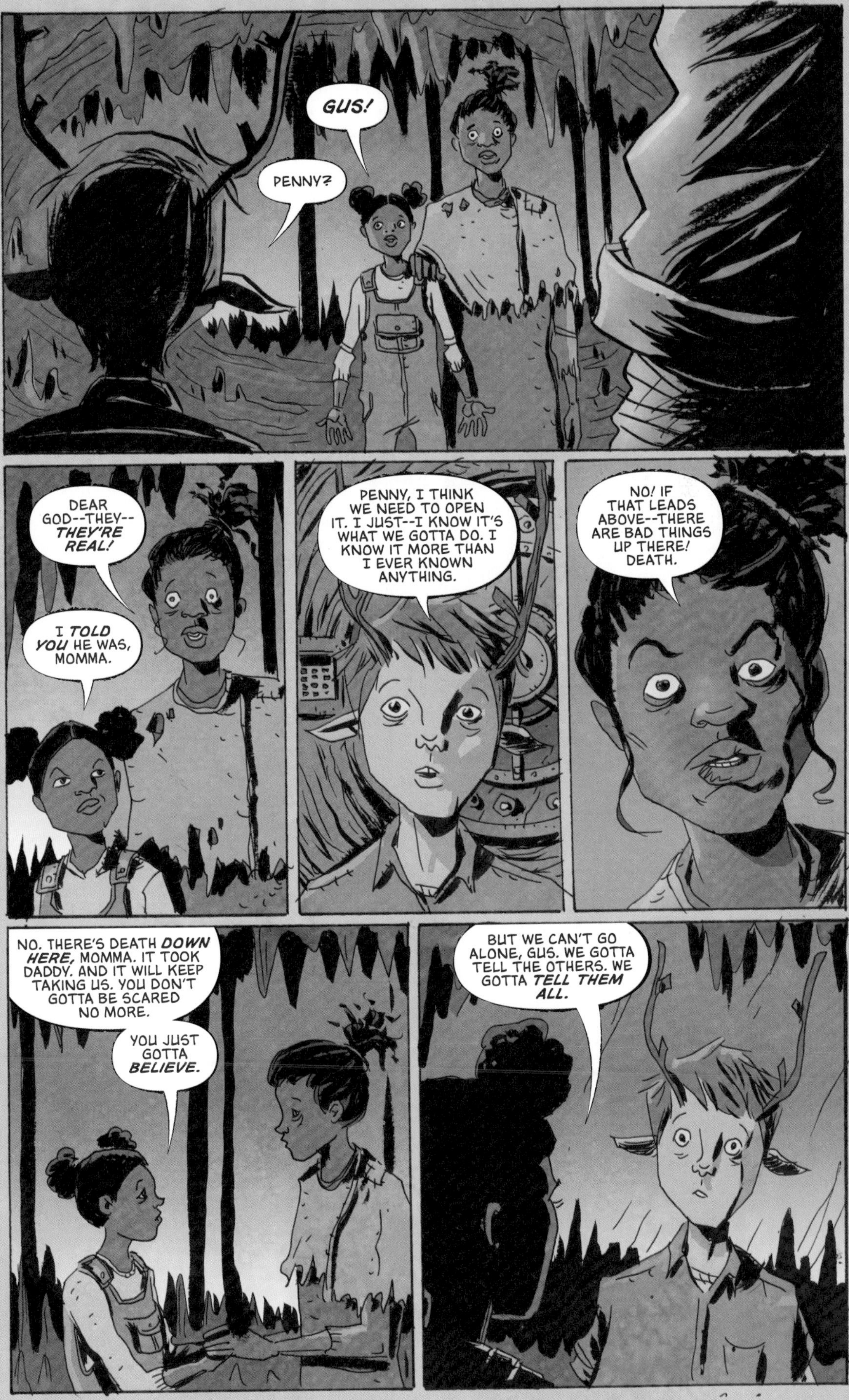
GUS!
PENNY?
DEAR GOD--THEY--THEY'RE REAL!
I TOLD YOU HE WAS, MOMMA.
PENNY, I THINK WE NEED TO OPEN IT. I JUST--I KNOW IT'S WHAT WE GOTTA DO. I KNOW IT MORE THAN I EVER KNOWN ANYTHING.
NO! IF THAT LEADS ABOVE--THERE ARE BAD THINGS UP THERE! DEATH.
NO. THERE'S DEATH DOWN HERE, MOMMA. IT TOOK DADDY. AND IT WILL KEEP TAKING US. YOU DON'T GOTTA BE SCARED NO MORE.
YOU JUST GOTTA BELIEVE.
BUT WE CAN'T GO ALONE, GUS. WE GOTTA TELL THE OTHERS. WE GOTTA TELL THEM ALL.

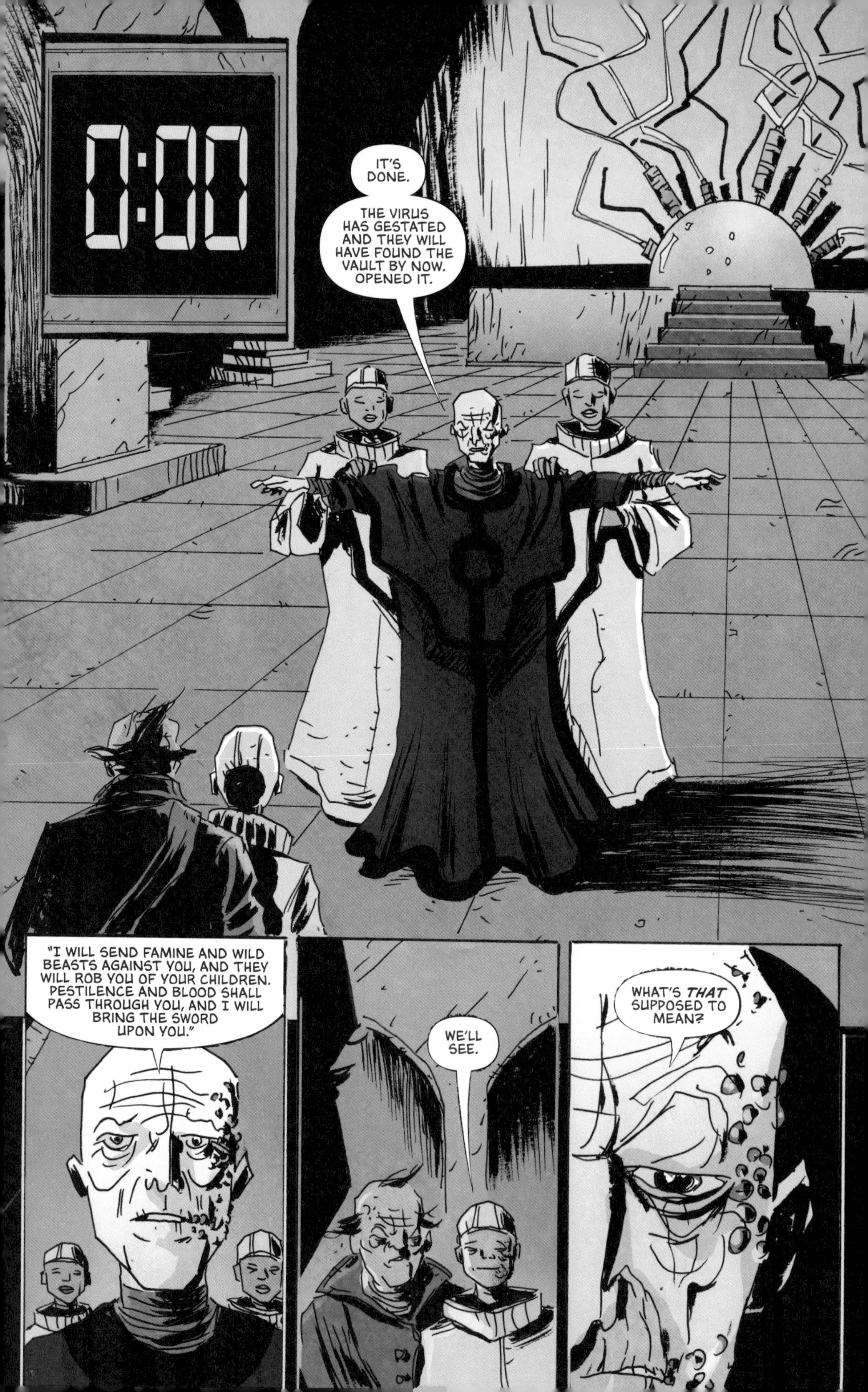
0:00
IT'S DONE.
THE VIRUS HAS GESTATED AND THEY WILL HAVE FOUND THE VAULT BY NOW. OPENED IT.
"I WILL SEND FAMINE AND WILD BEASTS AGAINST YOU, AND THEY WILL ROB YOU OF YOUR CHILDREN. PESTILENCE AND BLOOD SHALL PASS THROUGH YOU, AND I WILL BRING THE SWORD UPON YOU."
WE'LL SEE.
WHAT'S *THAT* SUPPOSED TO MEAN?

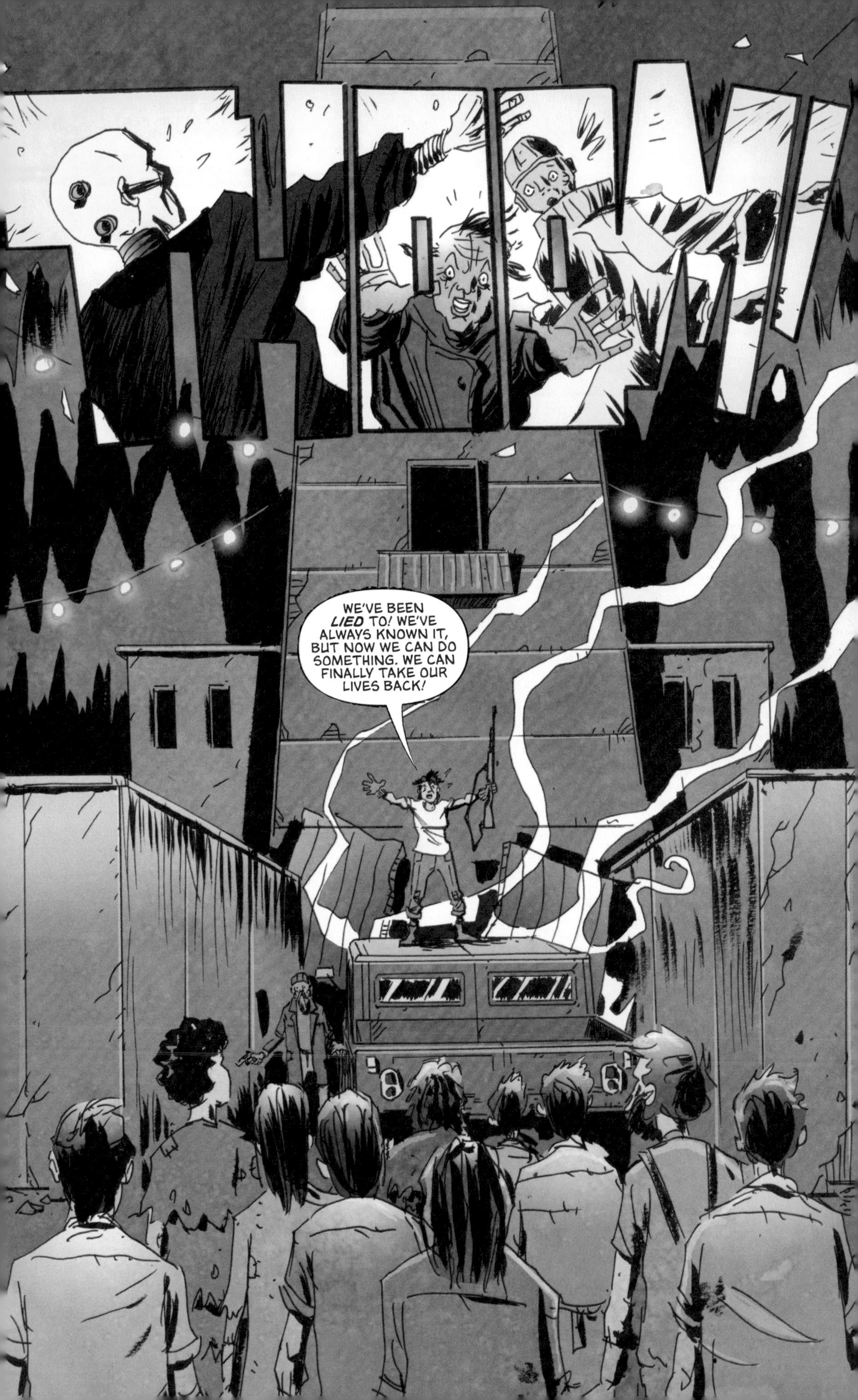
WE'VE BEEN *LIED* TO! WE'VE ALWAYS KNOWN IT, BUT NOW WE CAN DO SOMETHING. WE CAN FINALLY TAKE OUR LIVES BACK!

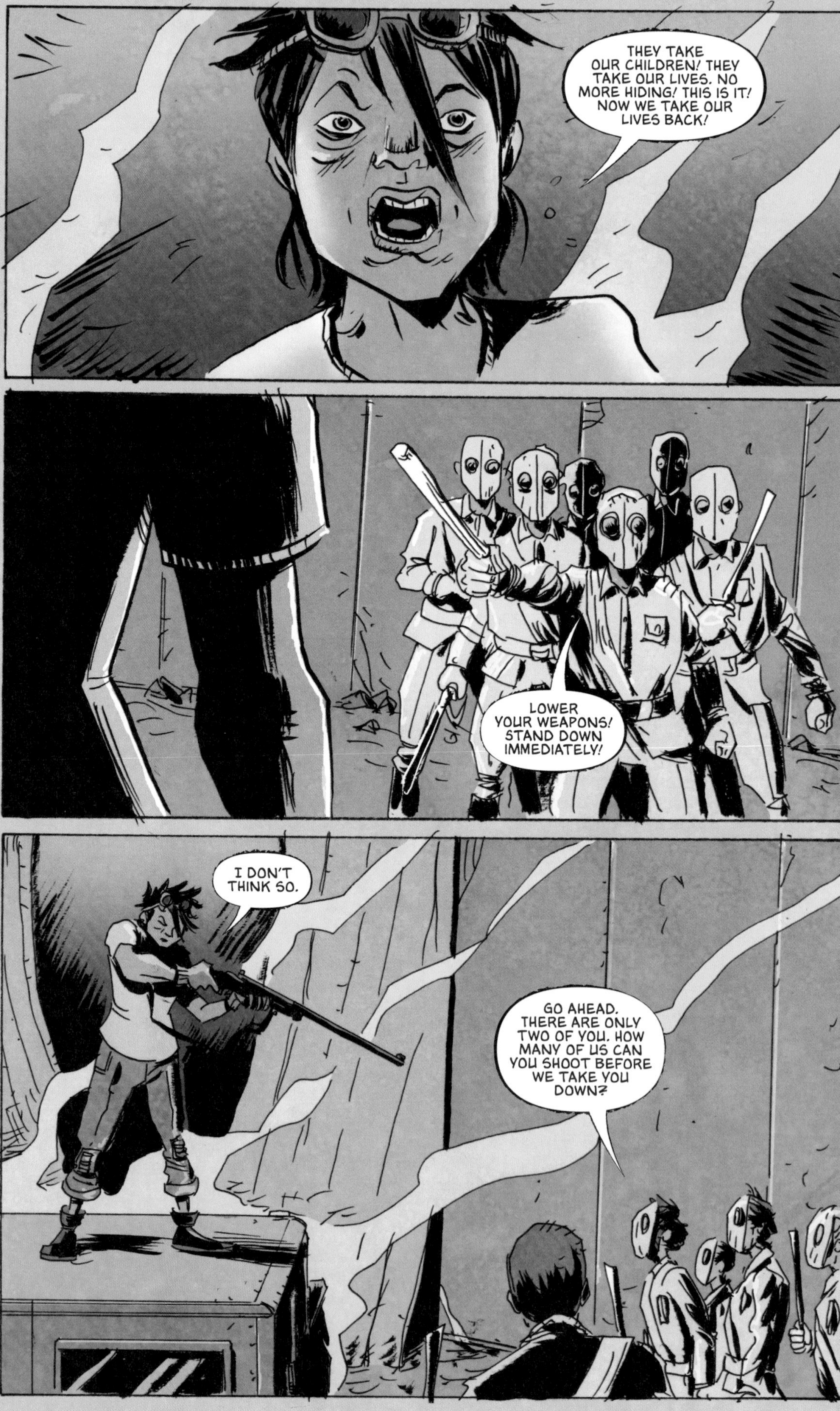
THEY TAKE OUR CHILDREN! THEY TAKE OUR LIVES. NO MORE HIDING! THIS IS IT! NOW WE TAKE OUR LIVES BACK!
LOWER YOUR WEAPONS! STAND DOWN IMMEDIATELY!
I DON'T THINK SO.
GO AHEAD. THERE ARE ONLY TWO OF YOU. HOW MANY OF US CAN YOU SHOOT BEFORE WE TAKE YOU DOWN?

COME ON! IT'S TIME! WE STAND TOGETHER AND THEY CAN'T STOP US ALL!

PHILISTINES! THESE TWO ARE PHILISTINES, MY CHILDREN! BLINDED TO THE TRUTH! THEIR WORDS ARE POISON!

EVEN NOW, MY PROMISES TO YOU ARE BEING DELIVERED! THERE IS NO LONGER ANY NEED TO FIGHT. NO NEED TO STRUGGLE.

I HAVE SENT A SPECIAL SERVANT ABOVE! A BLESSED CHILD. AND THAT CHILD OF GOD DELIVERS US FROM HIS SHADOW!

DON'T LISTEN TO HIM! IT'S ALL LIES!

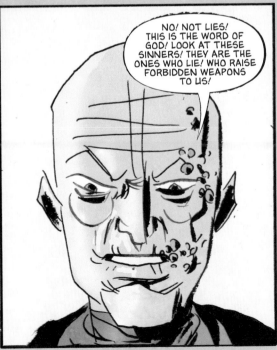

NO! NOT LIES! THIS IS THE WORD OF GOD! LOOK AT THESE SINNERS! THEY ARE THE ONES WHO LIE! WHO RAISE FORBIDDEN WEAPONS TO US!

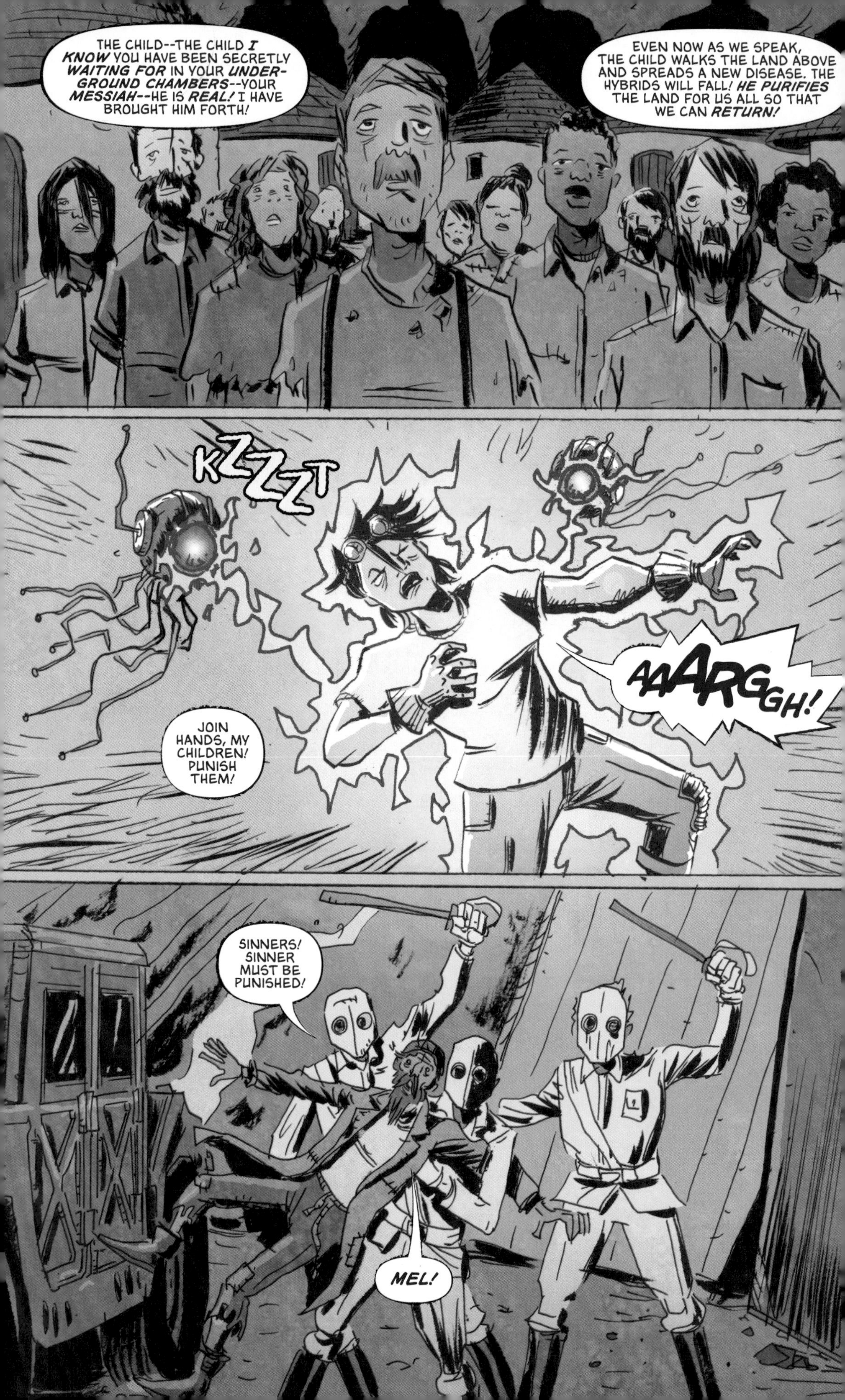

THE CHILD--THE CHILD I KNOW YOU HAVE BEEN SECRETLY WAITING FOR IN YOUR UNDER-GROUND CHAMBERS--YOUR MESSIAH--HE IS REAL! I HAVE BROUGHT HIM FORTH!
EVEN NOW AS WE SPEAK, THE CHILD WALKS THE LAND ABOVE AND SPREADS A NEW DISEASE. THE HYBRIDS WILL FALL! HE PURIFIES THE LAND FOR US ALL SO THAT WE CAN RETURN!
KZZZT
AAARGGH!
JOIN HANDS, MY CHILDREN! PUNISH THEM!
SINNERS! SINNER MUST BE PUNISHED!
MEL!

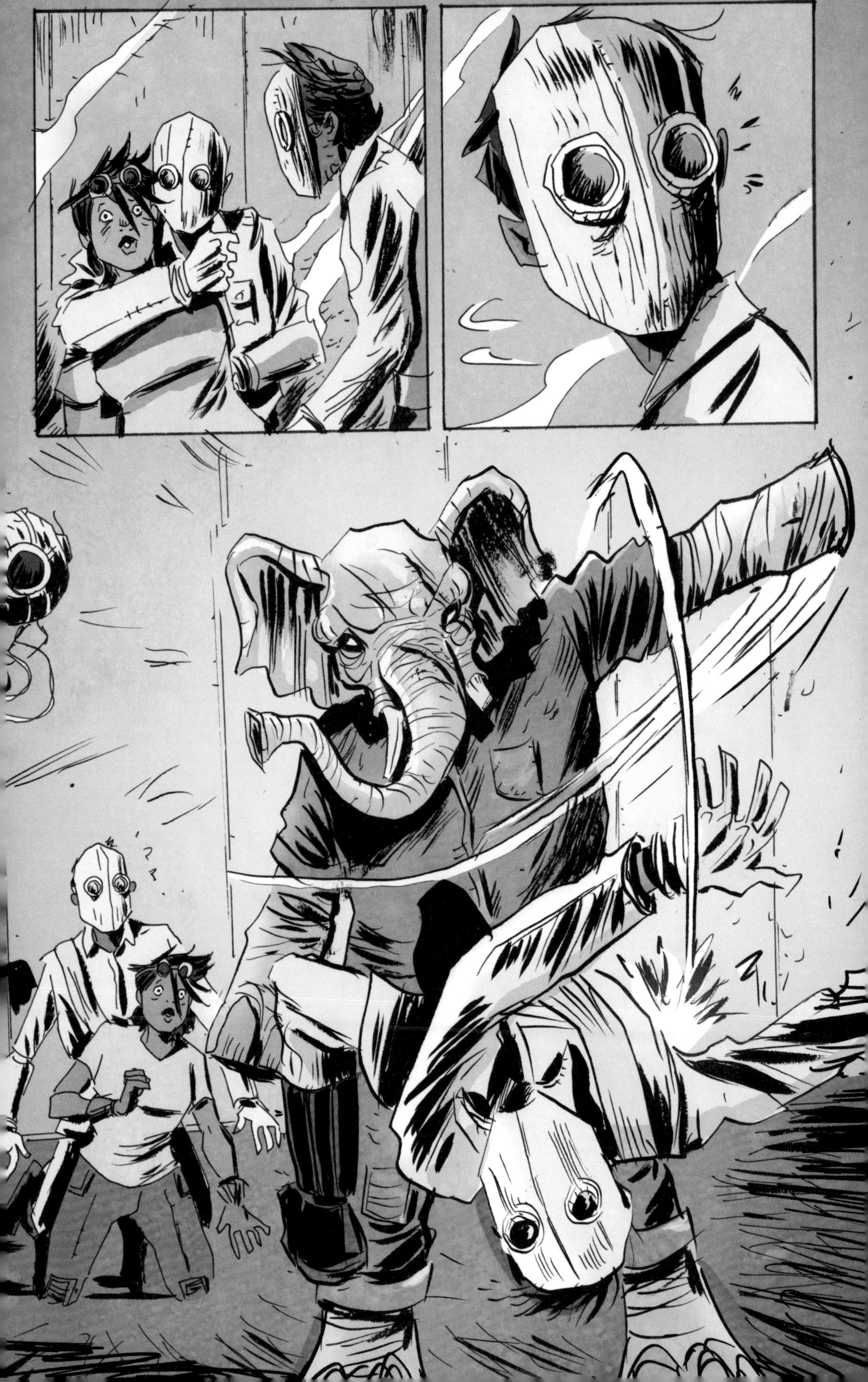

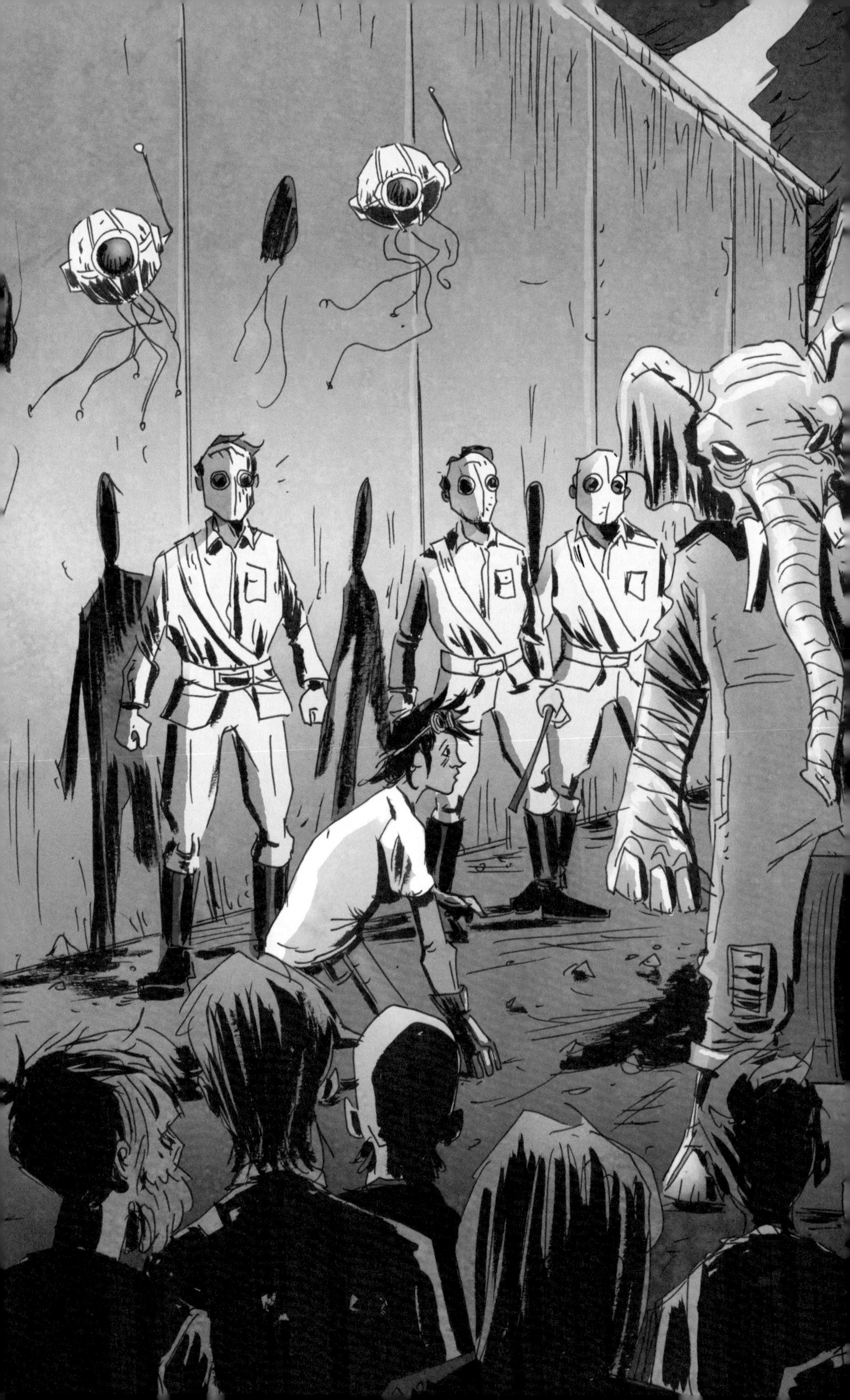

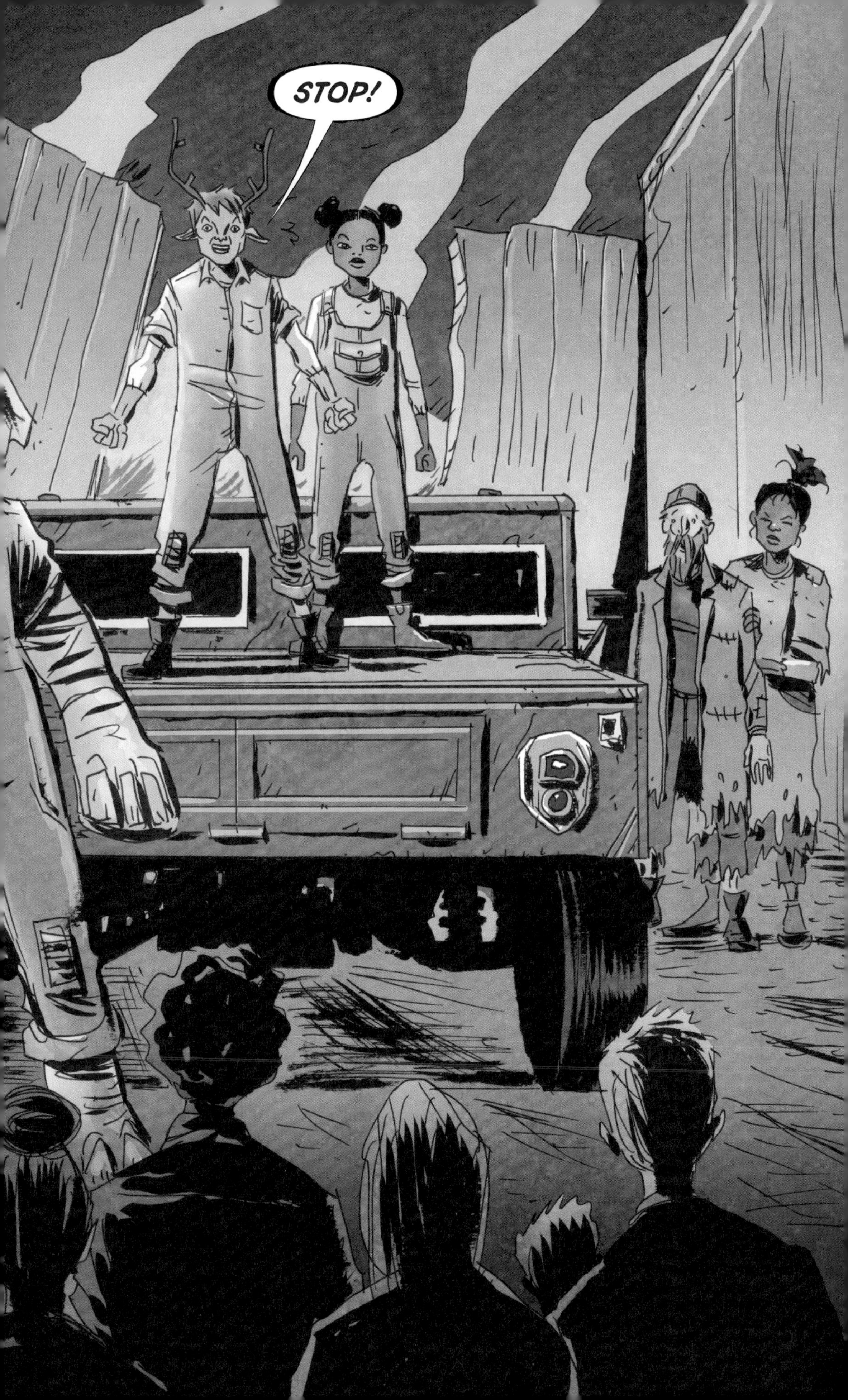
STOP!

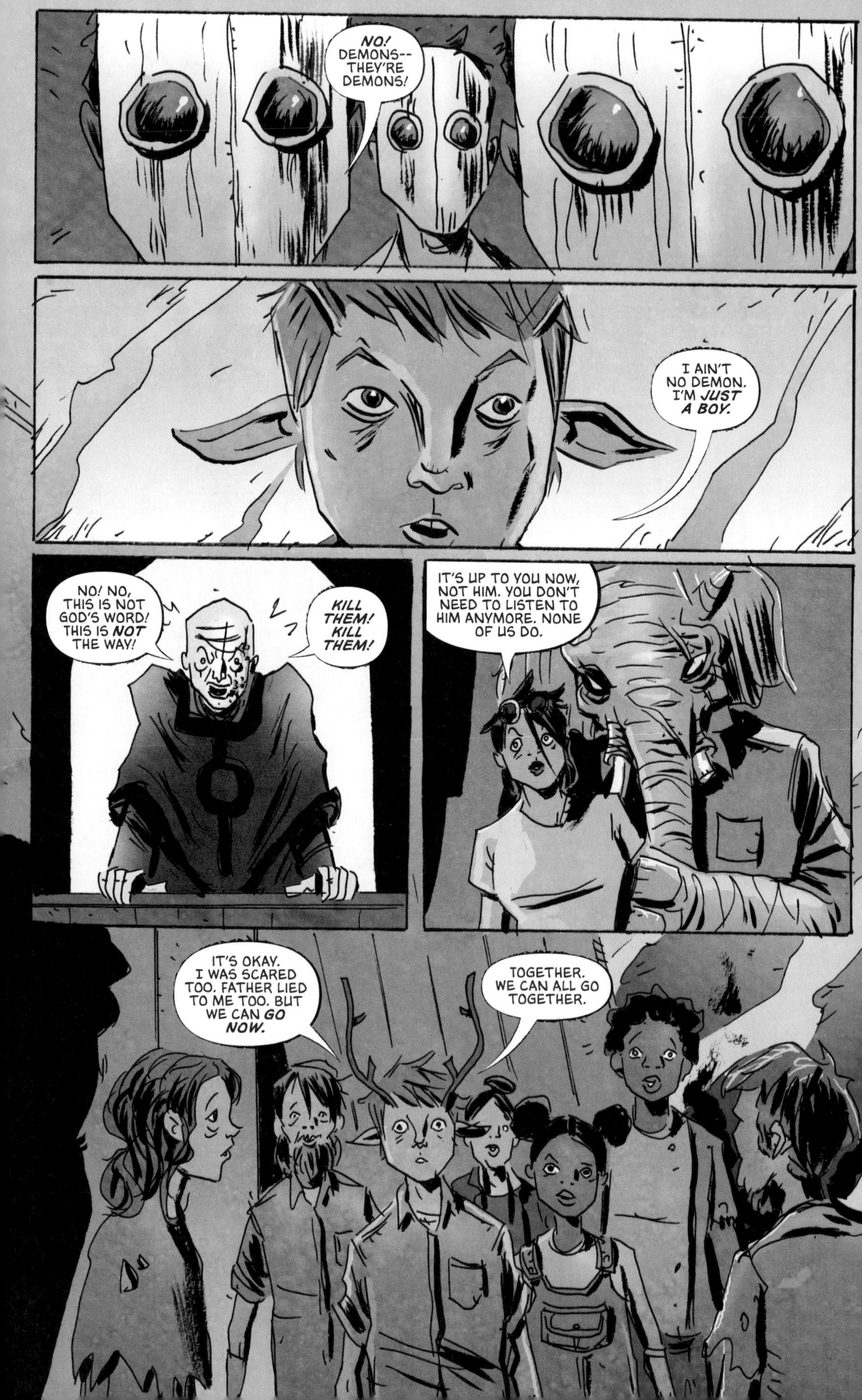
NO! DEMONS-- THEY'RE DEMONS!
I AIN'T NO DEMON. I'M JUST A BOY.
NO! NO, THIS IS NOT GOD'S WORD! THIS IS NOT THE WAY!
KILL THEM! KILL THEM!
IT'S UP TO YOU NOW, NOT HIM. YOU DON'T NEED TO LISTEN TO HIM ANYMORE. NONE OF US DO.
IT'S OKAY. I WAS SCARED TOO. FATHER LIED TO ME TOO. BUT WE CAN GO NOW.
TOGETHER. WE CAN ALL GO TOGETHER.

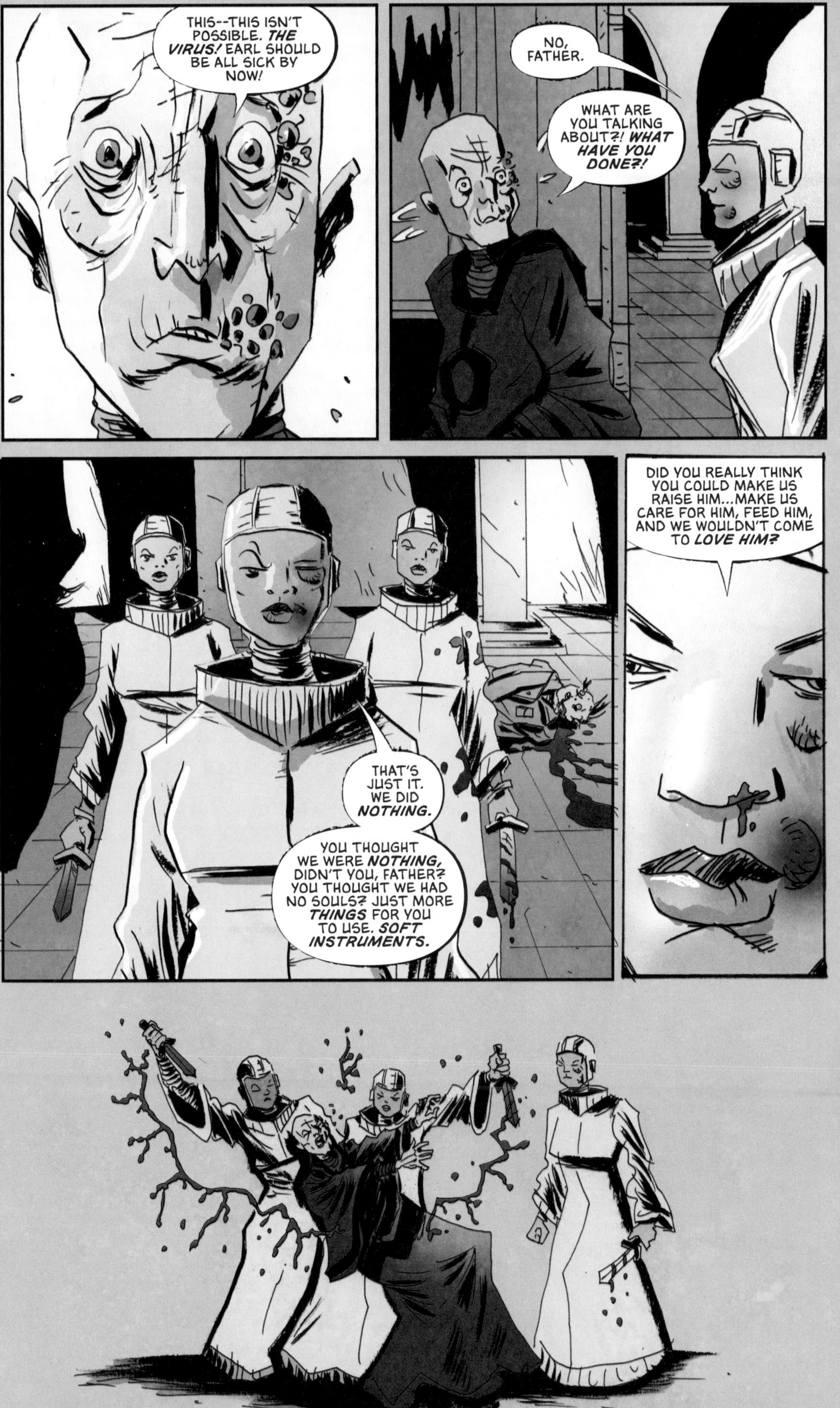
THIS--THIS ISN'T POSSIBLE. THE VIRUS! EARL SHOULD BE ALL SICK BY NOW!
NO, FATHER.
WHAT ARE YOU TALKING ABOUT?! WHAT HAVE YOU DONE?!
THAT'S JUST IT. WE DID NOTHING.
YOU THOUGHT WE WERE NOTHING, DIDN'T YOU, FATHER? YOU THOUGHT WE HAD NO SOULS? JUST MORE THINGS FOR YOU TO USE. SOFT INSTRUMENTS.
DID YOU REALLY THINK YOU COULD MAKE US RAISE HIM...MAKE US CARE FOR HIM, FEED HIM, AND WE WOULDN'T COME TO LOVE HIM?

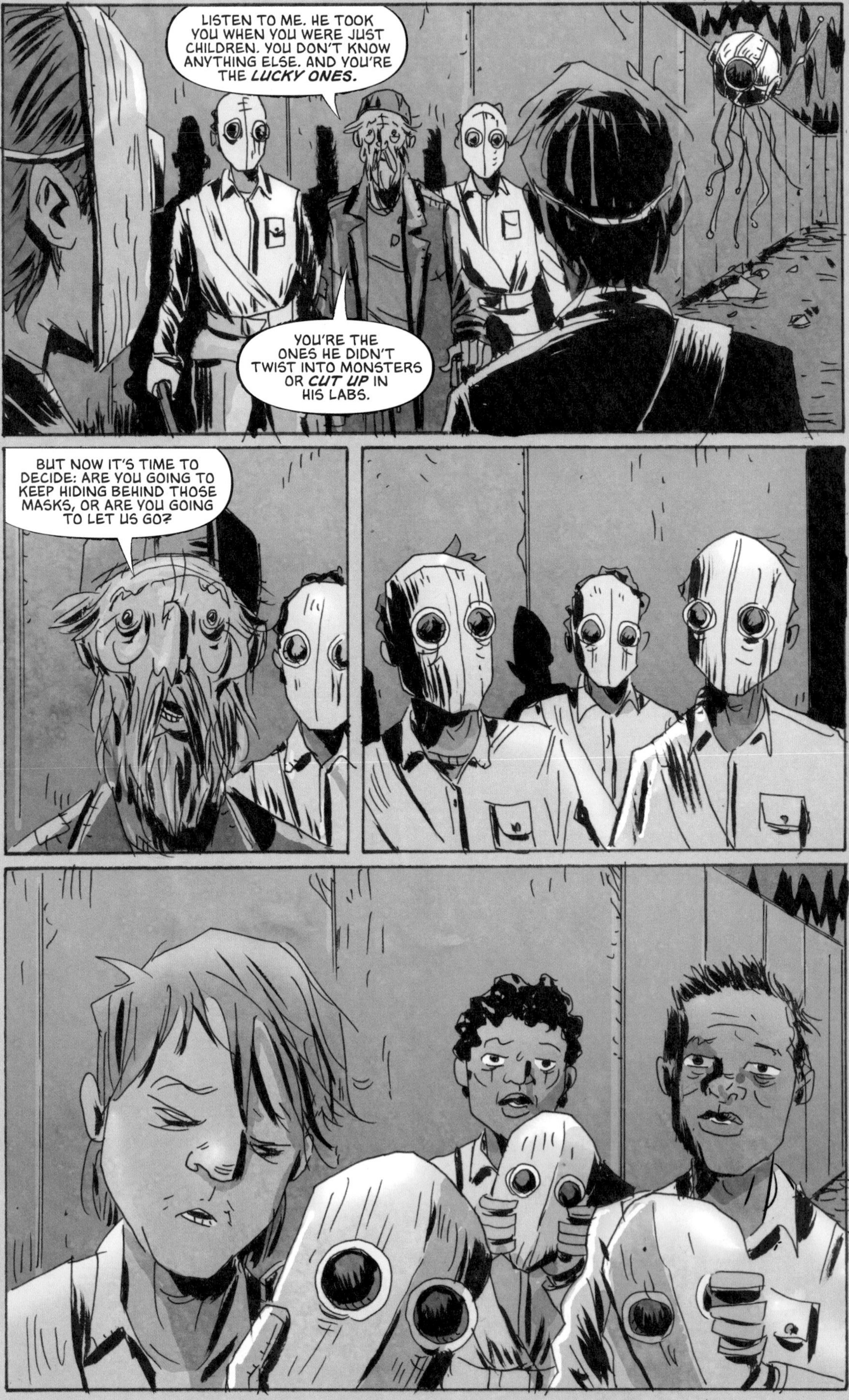
LISTEN TO ME. HE TOOK YOU WHEN YOU WERE JUST CHILDREN. YOU DON'T KNOW ANYTHING ELSE. AND YOU'RE THE LUCKY ONES.
YOU'RE THE ONES HE DIDN'T TWIST INTO MONSTERS OR CUT UP IN HIS LABS.
BUT NOW IT'S TIME TO DECIDE: ARE YOU GOING TO KEEP HIDING BEHIND THOSE MASKS, OR ARE YOU GOING TO LET US GO?

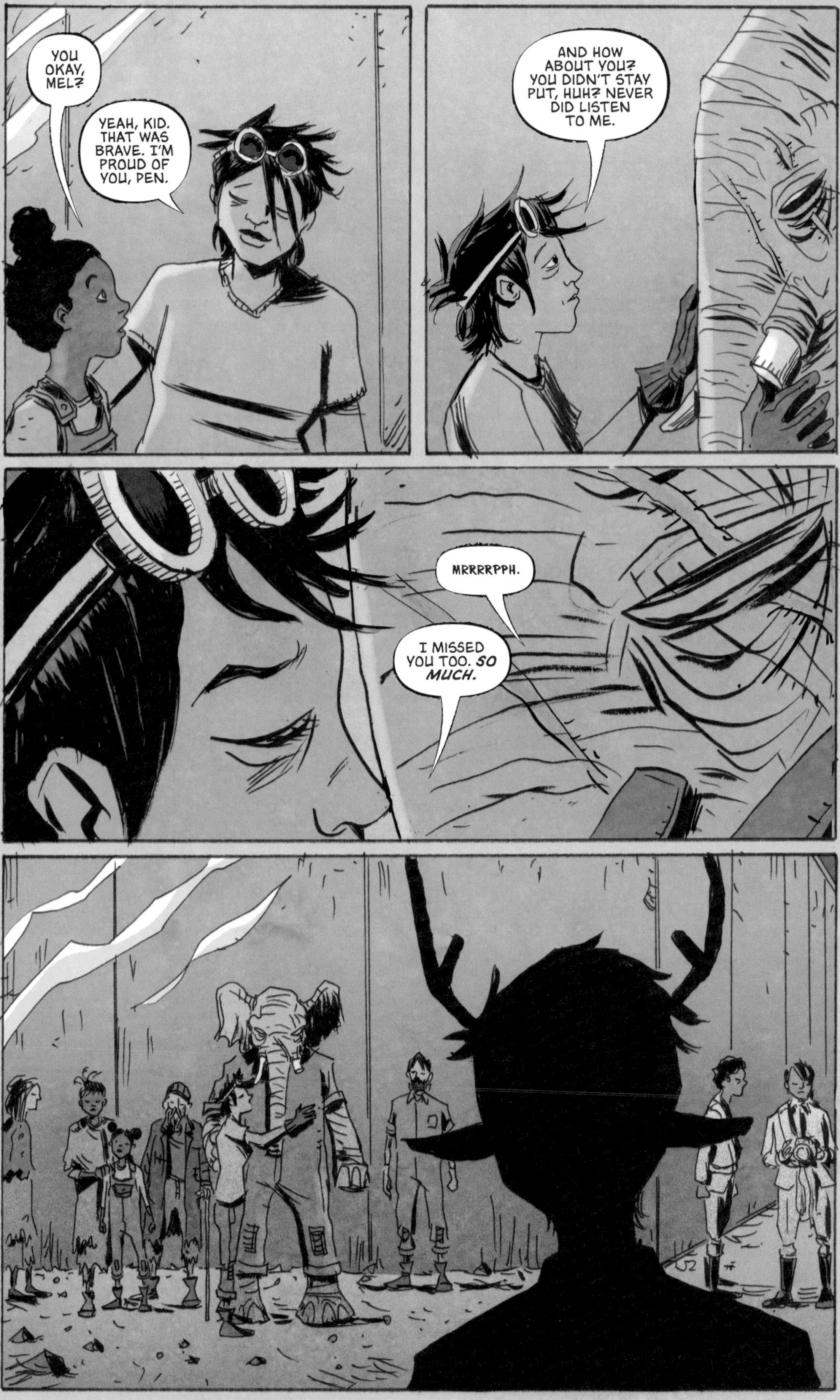
YOU OKAY, MEL?
YEAH, KID. THAT WAS BRAVE. I'M PROUD OF YOU, PEN.
AND HOW ABOUT YOU? YOU DIDN'T STAY PUT, HUH? NEVER DID LISTEN TO ME.
MRRRRPPH.
I MISSED YOU TOO. *SO MUCH.*

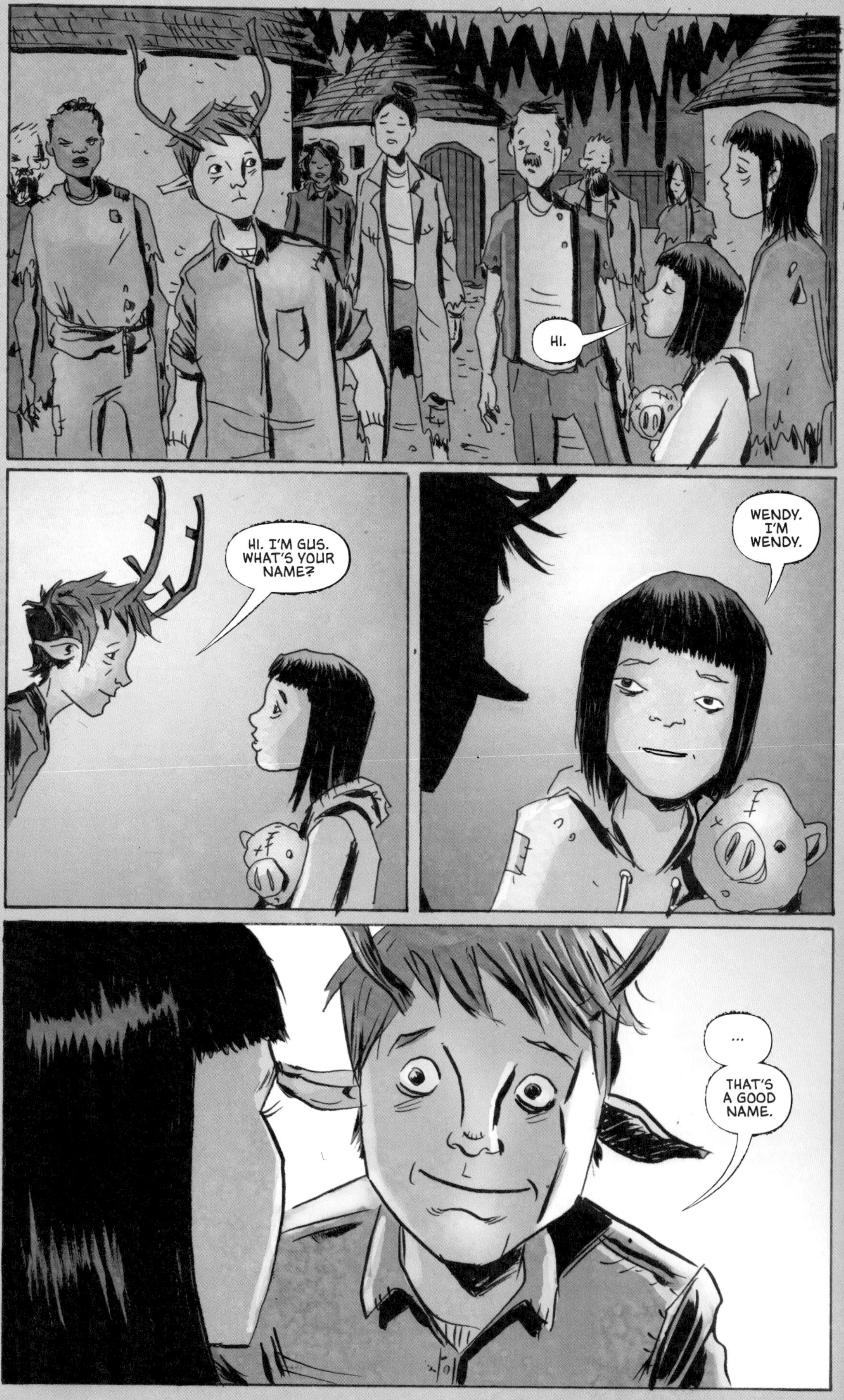
HI.
HI. I'M GUS. WHAT'S YOUR NAME?
WENDY. I'M WENDY.
...
THAT'S A GOOD NAME.

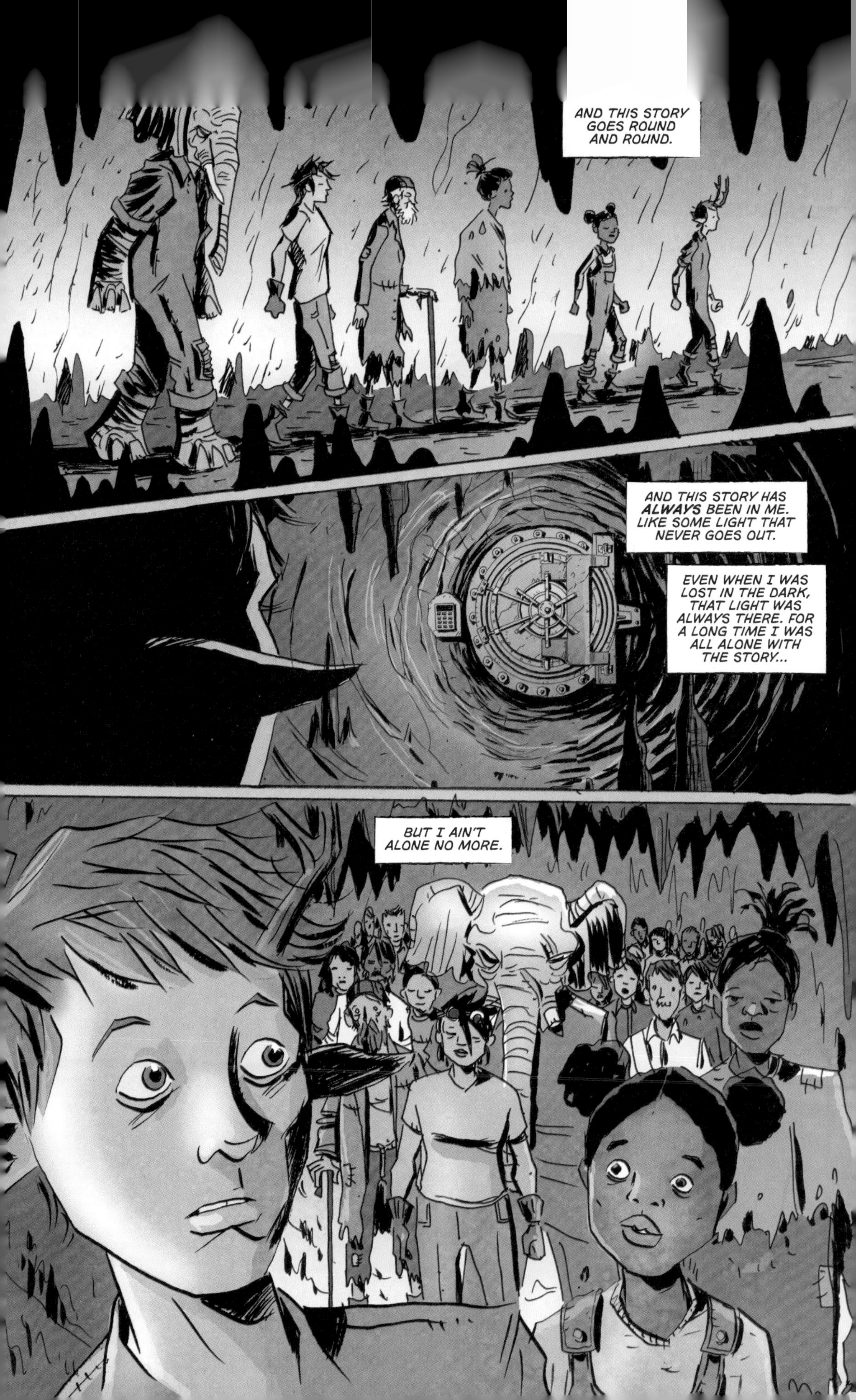
AND THIS STORY GOES ROUND AND ROUND.
AND THIS STORY HAS ALWAYS BEEN IN ME. LIKE SOME LIGHT THAT NEVER GOES OUT.
EVEN WHEN I WAS LOST IN THE DARK, THAT LIGHT WAS ALWAYS THERE. FOR A LONG TIME I WAS ALL ALONE WITH THE STORY...
BUT I AIN'T ALONE NO MORE.

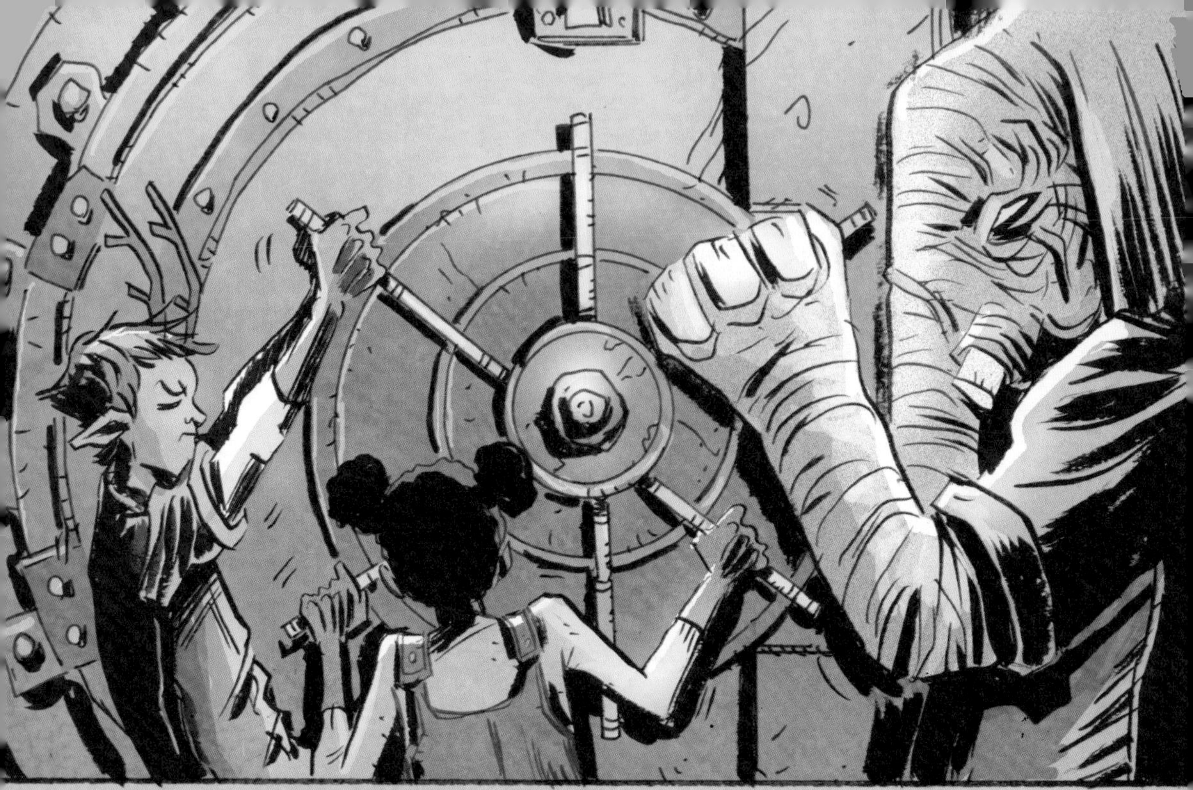
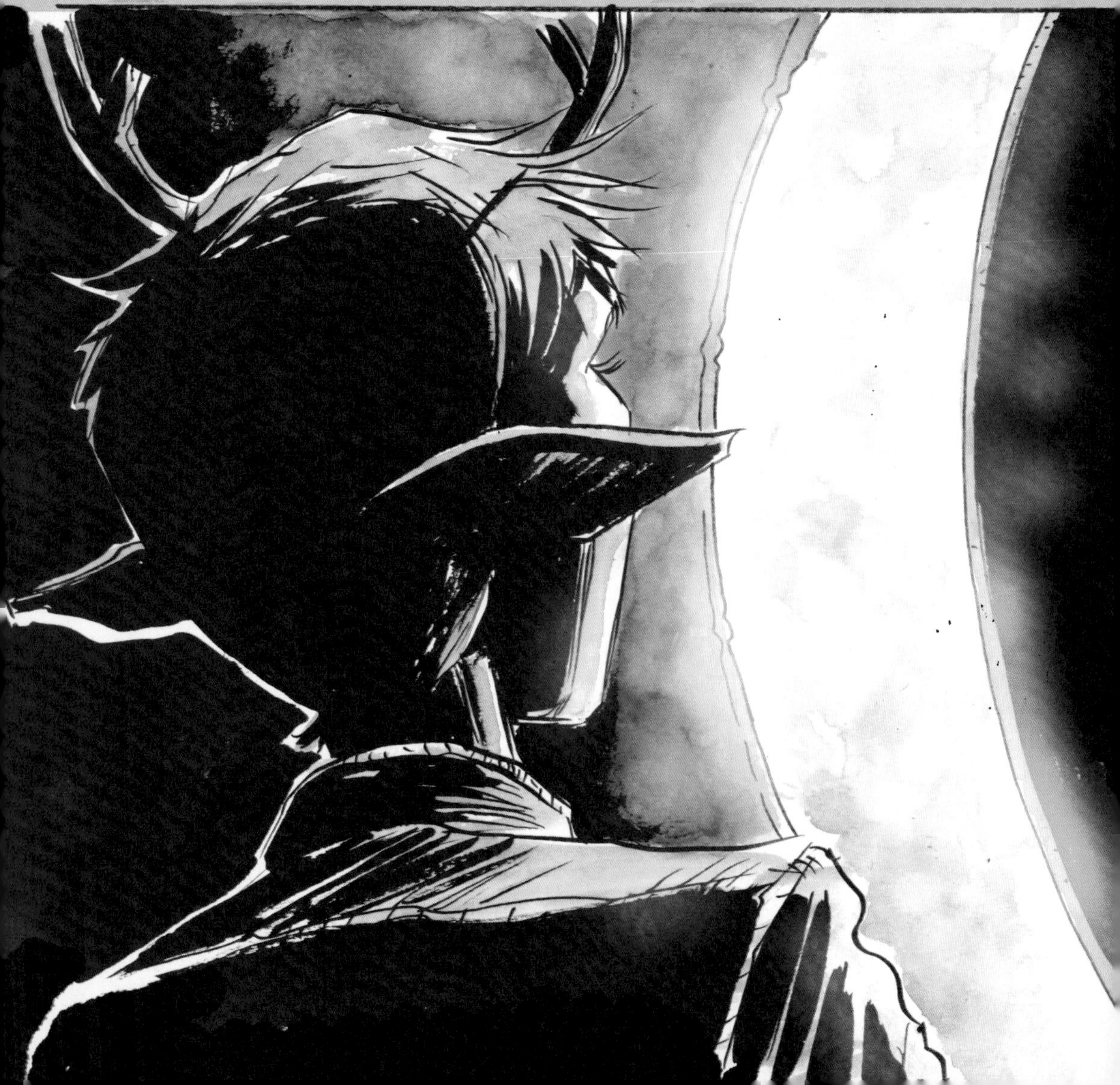

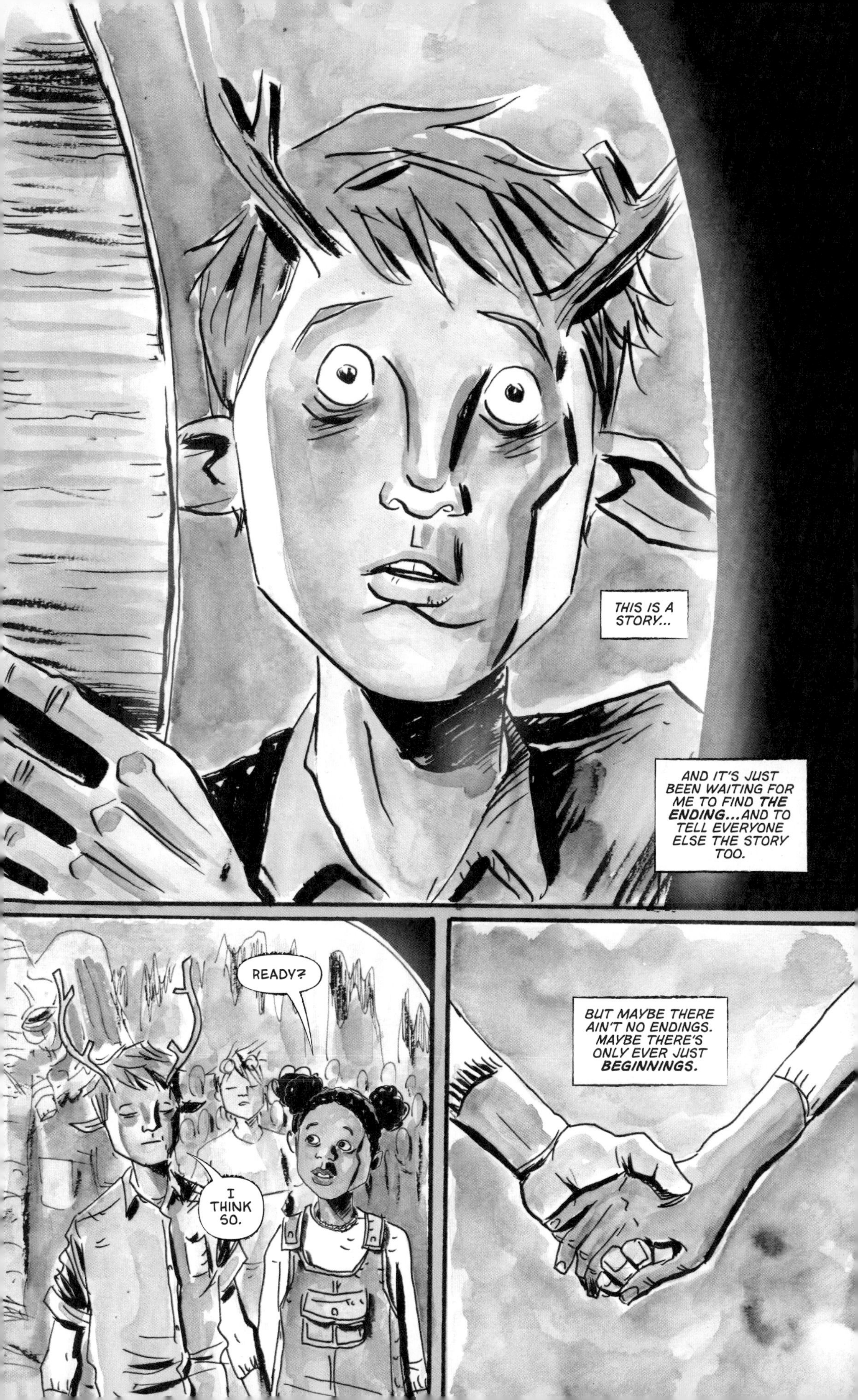
THIS IS A STORY...
AND IT'S JUST BEEN WAITING FOR ME TO FIND **THE ENDING...** AND TO TELL EVERYONE ELSE THE STORY TOO.
READY?
I THINK SO.
BUT MAYBE THERE AIN'T NO ENDINGS. MAYBE THERE'S ONLY EVER JUST **BEGINNINGS.**

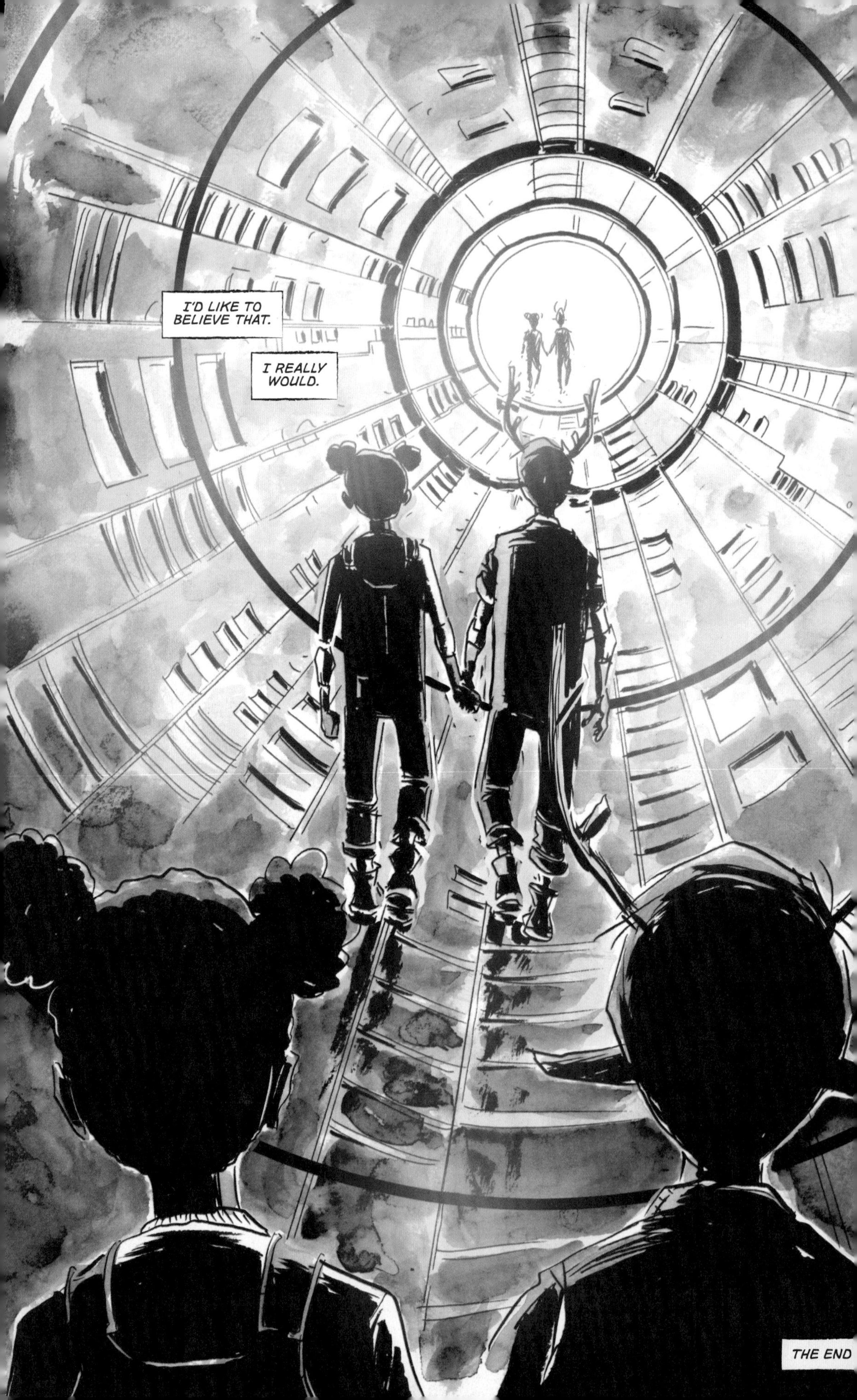
I'D LIKE TO BELIEVE THAT.
I REALLY WOULD.
THE END